BANGALORE
Tiger

*How Indian Tech Upstart Wipro Is Rewriting
the Rules of Global Competition*

STEVE HAMM

McGraw-Hill

New York   Chicago   San Francisco   Lisbon   London   Madrid   Mexico City
Milan   New Delhi   San Juan   Seoul   Singapore   Sydney   Toronto

The *McGraw-Hill* Companies

1 2 3 4 5 6 7 8 9 0   DOC/DOC   0 9 8 7 6

ISBN-13: 978-0-07-147478-8
ISBN-10: 0-07-147478-1

McGraw-Hill books are available at special quantity discounts to use as premiums and sales promotions, or for use in corporate training programs. For more information, please write to the Director of Special Sales, Professional Publishing, McGraw-Hill, Two Penn Plaza, New York, NY 10121-2298. Or contact your local bookstore.

This book is printed on acid-free paper.

Library of Congress Cataloging-in-Publication Data
Hamm, Steve.
    Bangalore tiger : how Indian tech upstart Wipro is rewriting the rules of global competition / by Steve Hamm.
        p. cm.
    ISBN 0-07-147478-1 (hardcover : alk. paper)
1. Wipro Corp. (India)   2. High technology services industries—India.   3. Information technology—India.   4. Customer services—India.   5. Business logistics—India.   I. Title.
    HD2900.12.W56H35 2006
    338.7'610040954—dc22

                                                      2006015472

CONTENTS

ACKNOWLEDGMENTS

I would like to thank Azim Premji for inviting me into his company; Jessie Paul and Aravind Madhavan of Wipro for setting up interviews and getting me all the information I needed; my friend Maureen Rolla for her thoughtful suggestions; *BusinessWeek* for sending me to India; and my editor, Jeffrey Krames.

Steve Hamm

Introduction

India's New Breed of Tech Company

It was 4 p.m. on February 8, 2006, and Azim Premji, chairman of Wipro Ltd., one of the largest Indian information technology outsourcing companies, stood proudly on the marble balcony overlooking the 103-year-old main floor of the New York Stock Exchange (NYSE). He was dressed elegantly in a charcoal gray suit with a Nehru collar, with his shock of white hair in sharp contrast. Crowded around him were John Thaine, the chief executive of the stock exchange, and a half-dozen Wipro lieutenants. This was the fifth-year anniversary celebration of the Wipro listing on the NYSE, and Premji was back to ring the closing bell.

Wipro had come a long way in those five years. On October 18, 2000, when it debuted on the NYSE, Premji's company had annual revenues just over $500 million and was barely known outside of India. Now it was a $2.4 billion company and a symbol of India's rise. When Premji rang the bell, Wipro's stock price stood at $14.15 and its market capitalization was just over $20 billion. In contrast, Electronic Data Systems, the American company that had essentially invented outsourcing and dominated it for many years, had a market cap of just $13 billion. If ever there was a sign of the changing of the guard, this was it.

The Rise of India

India. The name summons up all sorts of powerful images, from the Taj Mahal, to Mahatma Gandhi sitting cross-legged at his spindle, to the latest swami to catch on with American spiritual seekers, to, most indelibly, the faces of thousands of poor people poisoned at Bhopal. But since the beginning of the twenty-first century, a new image for India is emerging.

Seemingly out of nowhere, it has become the world's new high-tech powerhouse. More than 800,000 engineers are busy there today, writing the software that keeps Wall Street, the Motor City, and Hollywood running. They are designing computer chips, circuit boards, and sophisticated machinery for the world's consumer electronics, aerospace, and health-care industries. At the same time, another 400,000 young Indians work in the booming business process outsourcing (BPO) segment, an offshoot of the tech industry, handling accounting, medical claims processing, customer service, and other basic business functions for Western clients.

The bright-eyed, hopeful, 25-year-old Indian working in a modern office complex in Bangalore—India's Silicon Valley—is elbowing aside those old images of illness and privation. "I see India as a big player," says Jack Welch, former chairman of General Electric Company. "It's a billion people with great intellect. It will get bigger and bigger, and it will be a significant player in the global economy."

How did this economic miracle happen? Liberalization of the Indian economy has a lot to do with it. But one can trace another crucial ingredient back to 1993. That's when Marc Andreessen, an undergraduate at the University of Illinois at Urbana–Champaign, designed (with help from colleagues) the first Internet browser. The Internet, a network linking computer networks, had been in existence for years, but it was used primarily by academics and scientists for sharing scholarly papers and technical data. Andreessen's browser, called Mosaic, democratized the Internet. It was an easy-to-use doorway to the Net that made it possible, ultimately, for anybody in the world with a computer and Internet access to connect with anybody else.

Andreessen's invention gave rise to Netscape, Yahoo!, Amazon .com, eBay, and Google. It underpinned the dot-com boom of the late 1990s. And it made it possible for the world's brainwork to be done just as easily in Bangalore as in Boston. That put young Sanjay on an equal footing with Steven, Shawn, and Sven in the global competitive marketplace.

The computer industry's executives love to talk about killer applications, or killer apps, for short. Those are the uses of technology that prove to be so compelling that they accelerate the adoption of a new technology to the point where it becomes mainstream. The spreadsheet and word processor were the killer apps for the personal computer. Browsers, Web sites, and e-mail were the killer apps in the early stage of the Internet. But when the history of our era is written, it may turn out that one of the most important uses of the Internet is that it made the minds of India available to Western businesses.

Using the Internet as the digital equivalent of America's interstate highway system, more than 700 Indian tech services companies are delivering vital, high-quality brainwork for hundreds of large American, European, and Japanese corporations. These Indian tigers are a new breed of tech company. They harness a seemingly inexhaustible supply of raw talent. India produces 120,000 college graduates with information technology degrees each year, and 3 million people with other undergraduate degrees, according to NASSCOM (National Association of Software and Service Companies), the Indian software and tech services trade association. And since Indian knowledge workers are paid about 20 percent of the level of their counterparts in the West, the Indian companies start off with a large cost advantage over their clients' traditional ways of getting work done and a big pricing advantage over the tech services industry's traditional powers, such as EDS, IBM, and Accenture.

This shifting of work to low-cost countries is called labor arbitrage. The practice of dividing the labor for a particular client between people at the client's office, nearby, and in India or other low-cost countries is called "global service delivery." A typical ratio is 30 percent near the customer to 70 percent offshore. So the basic Indian tech formula is simple:

Internet + Brains − High Costs = Huge Business Opportunity

But supplying low-cost brains via the Internet is just the beginning of what the Indian tech services outfits do for their clients. They are expert at managing people and business processes. They typically can do everything from writing computer programs to processing mortgages and insurance claims more efficiently than their clients can. Think of how the Japanese auto manufacturers took on and are besting General Motors and Ford, based primarily on superior engineering, quality, and efficiency. That's what the Indian tech services outfits are doing to the old ways of processing data and running basic business functions in the West. They have turned these things into factorylike activities.

This approach takes not only much of the cost out of the equation, but the uncertainty as well. In a tech world where much of the success had traditionally been achieved through unpredictable art, the Indian companies have turned the management of technology and business processes into a highly productive craft.

While the United States, Western Europe, and Japan still possess the lion's share of the world's *financial* capital, the Indians have a wealth in *intellectual* capital—and they know how to use it. In fact, India's tech industry is well on its way to building the most efficient intellectual capital supply in the world. While most of these companies' employees are in India, they deploy highly trained specialists in or near clients' offices. And they operate around the clock, around the year, 24/7/365.

The Indians deliver sophisticated services globally with the right people, in the right place, and at the right time. "We're pioneers in establishing the global delivery model, which the whole services world is adopting today," says Wipro's Premji. "This model gives customers more value for their money. It will make the world more competitive, to the advantage of the customer. And it will generate a lot of employment in developing countries where there's a strong knowledge infrastructure and a strong education system."

Bursts of economic growth and employment in places that meet those criteria—in India, China, and elsewhere worldwide—translate into more demand for the goods and services produced by the

West. Wrap it all together and you have the potential for a much more vibrant and equitable global economy, with India's tech industry as one of its cornerstones.

Wipro Stands Out from the Pack

There are plenty of tech tigers in India. Tata Consultancy Services, or TCS, the largest of them, with nearly $3 billion in fiscal 2006 sales, was the pioneer of the so-called body shop business model: It assembled masses of bright, young Indian programmers and put them to work doing the routine software updating and patching jobs for Western corporations. It got started way back in 1968. Infosys Technologies, the second largest, was born from scratch as a tech services outfit in the Silicon Valley mold. It's the most efficient of the larger Indian players, with an operating profit margin of 31 percent. Infosys is now pushing hard to add a strong high-end consulting practice to its global delivery portfolio.

Yet it's Wipro, the number 3 player, that stands out as an icon of this new way of doing business. This book is an attempt to tell the amazing tale of the rise of the Indian tech industry through a single participant, and I have chosen Wipro (pronounced *whip-row*) to tell the story of India's tigers. Among them, Wipro has the broadest array of services, including software programming, tech systems integration, systems management, business process outsourcing, consulting, and hardware product engineering. In 2006, the International Association of Outsourcing Professionals ranked Wipro number 7 on its list of the top 100 global outsourcing companies of all types, ahead of the other Indian companies. Among the Indian outfits, it pioneered the strategy of developing expertise in a wide range of different industries, from banking to retail, which is proving to be hugely successful. While all of the top Indian tech companies are expert at managing people and processes, Wipro has brought these activities to the level of science through a combination of careful structuring, close management, and constant improvements. Lastly, Wipro is an amazingly open company. Internally, it has a "zero-politics" policy. That means business decisions and personnel promotions are based on merits and facts; everything is transparent. Externally, it communicates forthrightly with investors, customers, and the press. It reveals itself, issues and all.

Then there's Premji himself, a colorful protagonist. He's the Bill Gates of India. He built Wipro from a small, failing vegetable oil company in Bombay into one of the top three tech companies in India and a fearsome global competitor. The company's revenues skyrocketed from $400 million in 1999 to $2.4 billion in the fiscal year ended in March 2006. Premji's roughly 81 percent share of Wipro stock makes him the second-richest person in India, worth between $10 billion and $15 billion, depending on shifts in the stock price. But, like Microsoft's Gates, he's also a thought leader. Premji, now 61, saw the opportunity to create a home-grown Indian computer business in 1977, when restrictive governmental policies forced Western tech giants such as IBM to leave the country. When the Western tech giants made their reentry in the early 1990s, he shifted to offering an electronics R&D lab for hire and software programming services. And thanks to that move, when the Year 2000 (Y2K) computer glitch made necessary a mammoth overhaul of the world's existing software programs, Wipro was standing ready to help out with a small army of programmers.

Though Premji never got an MBA, he's an avid student of management theory and practice. Early on, he realized that for Wipro to grow and thrive, he would have to create or adopt world-class business processes and management techniques. He took a stand and decreed that his company would pay no bribes—a risky move in a country where corruption was a routine part of business life. Rules of behavior now permeate the company, which goes through an earnest self-examination of its values every few years to make sure they're up to date.

Wipro pays the same keen attention to long-term strategy. Not only does the company establish a three-year strategic plan every January, but every five years or so it puts itself through an elaborate "visioning" exercise, starting with a clean sheet of paper to rethink what it should strive to become and decide what it needs to do to get there.

Wipro is slavishly dedicated to customer satisfaction. While all tech services arrangements are based on detailed contracts laying out exactly what is expected from the service provider, Wipro has gained a reputation for being willing to set aside the contract and do more than is formally required of it—if that's what it takes to keep a customer happy.

Ralph Szygenda, the powerful and not-easily-pleased chief information officer at General Motors Corporation, recalls a 2002 meeting with Vivek Paul, Wipro's former vice chairman. Wipro had been doing software programming projects for GM for several years, but Paul wanted a bigger chunk of Szygenda's business. While Szygenda had been impressed with Wipro's programming work, he told Paul that if he wanted a deeper relationship, Wipro would have to learn the auto business so it could help GM improve its competitiveness. And to do that, Szygenda said, Paul would have to put people in Detroit. "Until I can see you from my office window, I won't know if you're committed," Szygenda told him. At the time, in the wake of the 9/11 attacks, Wipro couldn't get enough U.S. visas to station people in Detroit itself, so Paul set up an office in Canada, right across the Detroit River from GM's headquarters. "Damned if they didn't put an office so I could see it. They impressed me," Szygenda says.

Ultimately, Szygenda handed Wipro a crucial job: writing the so-called middleware that ties GM's software applications together. And in February 2006, Szygenda lifted the profile of Indian tech by naming Wipro a "tier one" services supplier alongside IBM, EDS, and Hewlett-Packard, and gave it a multimillion-dollar piece of GM's tech business over a five-year period. Girish Paranjpe, president of one of Wipro's business units, said the company was delighted to be selected. "It's a huge morale booster for us to be able to play with the big boys," he says. "Also, because we're the only tier-one player GM picked from India, it's a big kick for us."

All of this attention at Wipro to process, discipline, ethics, and customer satisfaction has resulted in a smooth running machine tuned to take on the challenges of global competition in the twenty-first century. For India, Wipro has become a symbol of what the country can achieve on the global stage. "Wipro isn't just a company. It's a concept," says Subroto Bagchi, chief operating officer of MindTree Consulting Company and a former Wipro executive during the 1990s. "Wipro proved that this business model could be done. It proved to the world that India could build something world class."

Premji is mindful of what Wipro means for India. He has a dream for the country that includes better public education, improved health care, more opportunities for rural people, and an economy so strong and vibrant that its brightest young people don't have to leave the country to find opportunities. Wipro is helping to fulfill his dream. "We create wealth that trickles down. We create social consciousness in our employees that spreads throughout society. We teach them values, which makes them better parents," Premji says.

Wipro isn't just a shaper of young Indians. It's an important model for other Indian enterprises. If they successfully adopt its ways, values, and ambitions, there soon may be hundreds of Indian companies that are capable of being global players.

Changing the Rules of the Game

Already, Wipro and other Indian tech companies have changed the rules of the game for the world's $600 billion tech services industry. They're the tail that's wagging the dog. Western tech services companies grew fat and happy by collecting huge fees for advising corporations on technical matters, writing complex custom software applications, and running data centers. Now they're finding that the way they operate is out of date. The new winning formula is to have large numbers of employees working in India or other low-cost countries, a thinner layer of highly compensated employees close to their clients, and factorylike business processes. "We don't consider the Big Six outsourcers to be our main threat," says Larry Longseth, a vice president in IBM's strategic outsourcing business. "Our competition is Wipro and Infosys."

The Western giants are trying to adapt. Most of them now have large software programming and business process outsourcing operations in India. IBM, for instance, had 43,000 employees there by the middle of 2006 and, at the same time, was rapidly developing technologies to replace human labor in services. Capgemini, the Paris-based services giant, which grew its Indian workforce by 80 percent to 4,000 in 2005, flew its 12-person executive board to India for a meeting in March 2006. Group CEO Paul Hermelin has tremendous respect for the top Indian tech firms. "Nobody can beat the Indians in projects that are well defined because they're high quality and cost competitive," he says. "For us to win, we have to take advantage of being close to the customers and deliver high-value-added services." Yet for most of the Western firms, this is an add-on to their normal ways of doing business rather than a wholesale makeover. They'll likely have to do much more. "The U.S. and European companies don't understand," says Paul, who is now a partner with San Francisco private equity firm Texas Pacific Group. "This isn't about adding a subcompact to an auto company's product line. It's about changing every car. They don't get it."

The superiority of the new business model is clear when you compare the profit margins of the combatants. The average net profit margin for the top six Indian tech services firms was 21.7 percent in 2005, compared to just 4.3 percent for the top six Western competitors, according to Bernstein Research. "We're looking at a fundamental change in the way companies use IT services. It's a realignment of the marketplace," says Ian Marriott, analyst at tech industry market researcher Gartner Inc.

Once limited to routine software programming tasks, the Indian tech companies now can do practically everything the Western tech services giants can do. They're expert at quickly developing new electronics products from a combination of standard off-the-shelf technologies and their own patented inventions. They build complex software applications from scratch. And they advise clients how best to design and deploy their new technologies. As a result, contracts that used to come in dollops and last only as long as it took to complete a project have turned into multiyear and multimillion-dollar deals. TCS, for example, in late 2005 won an $850 million, 12-year BPO contract with Britain's insurance giant Pearl Group. And this isn't about low-cost Indian labor. The work is being done in the United Kingdom. It signals that the Indians are becoming so accomplished that they don't need to rely on cheap labor anymore.

As the tech world shifts from its early formative phase into maturity, the Indian companies gain advantages over their Western counterparts. During the 1990s, corporations were hungry for the latest and greatest technologies, fearful that if they didn't catch the Internet wave, they might be left behind. Now they're more concerned with managing their computers efficiently and with integrating technologies more effectively with their business goals and processes. "When technology is at a stage where the need in the market is greater than the technology can deliver, the product innovator has the advantage," Nandan Nilekani, CEO of Infosys, told me during an outdoor dinner last summer in Bangalore. "But now, the tech industry has overshot corporations' ability to absorb technology, so the balance of power shifts from product innovation to those who distribute, like Dell and Google, and those, like the Indian companies, that integrate technologies and make them work in companies."

So it's no wonder India's tech industry is growing like a bamboo forest. Indian software and services exports reached $23.6 billion in fiscal 2006, up 33 percent over the previous year. And it's still an immature industry. So far, only about 3 percent of more than $750 billion in global IT services spending (including in-house staffing by corporations) is handled through offshoring, most of it in India. Gartner analyst Marriott expects that number to go as high as 10 percent by 2008. Over the past half decade, the top Indian firms established their reputations with a few hundred corporations that are among the most aggressive users of technology, the so-called early adopters. Now, they're selling an ever-broadening array of services to those companies and at the same time reaching out to a second tier of slower adopters, plus an army of smaller firms. Mainstream European and Japanese corporations are only now accepting the Indians as their tech service providers.

The outsourcing of business process management to India is still in its infancy, as well. So far, it has mostly been about accounting, medical claims processing, customer service, and handling travel and entertainment expenses. But Indian firms are starting to provide a host of new offerings including legal, financial, and market research; medical services such as reading X-rays; and online education and training services. "Anything that can be done remotely, will be done remotely," predicts Raj Reddy, a computer science professor at Carnegie Mellon University.

If these trends continue to pick up momentum, analysts expect the value of Indian tech services to soar. The total—including business process outsourcing—is expected to top $60 billion by 2010 and could top $80 billion, according to a NASSCOM–McKinsey report in 2005. That would require a high-tech workforce of nearly 2.3 million. While that number seems like a drop in the bucket compared to the country's 1.2 billion population, the growth of the tech industry workforce is bolstering the fast-growing middle class and helping to boost the country's annual GDP growth rate to 6 to 8 percent per year. If these trends keep up, India could have the third largest economy in the world by 2050, behind only China and the United States, according to Goldman Sachs & Company.

A Boon—and Challenge—for the West

These are heady thoughts, and they have come on quite suddenly. As recently as early 2001, when I traveled to Mumbai for NASSCOM's annual trade conference, India's tech industry was beset with angst. The country's dot-com bubble had just burst, taking with it the hopes of thousands of entrepreneurs and the investors who had bet on it. The economic recession in the United States had put a damper on demand for Indian tech services. My new Indian friends told me that their tech industry seemed to perpetually be on the verge of making it big—but never quite pulled it off. It was a gloomy time.

Well, India has finally made it. The rekindling of Western economies combined with relentless drive by corporations to improve their efficiencies means India is in the right place at the right time with the right portfolio of services.

My second trip to India, in 2005, revealed a country in the midst of a transformation. Bangalore, in the country's south-central region, has the feel of Silicon Valley in the late 1990s. The roads are overflowing with cars, and everywhere you look there's a new office building sprouting up. In Bangalore, it can take two hours to travel 10 miles during the morning or evening commute. A Wipro employee told me an emblematic story: One evening, she was stuck in a traffic jam within sight of her own apartment for two hours. She used her cell phone to call her husband, who worked at home for a software company, and he walked down to her car and sat with her to keep her company during her wait.

In Silicon Valley, office buildings normally go up one at a time. In Bangalore, they rise up in bunches. Wipro's global tech business added 14,000 people in the fiscal year ended in March 2006, bringing the total to 53,742 and the Wipro Ltd. total to more than 60,000, which is nearly as large as Microsoft. To handle the flood of new employees, it recently completed a brand-new campus that consists of nine buildings in Bangalore's Electronics City technology office park. To take the pressure off Bangalore, Wipro and other Indian tech companies are rapidly opening new offices in Delhi, Hyderabad, Chennai, and smaller cities.

All of this activity has changed the psychology of India. For decades, the country had a serious inferiority complex. "We had a view of ourselves as also-rans, in business, in sports, everything. The success of Indian technology globally has transformed the idea of India about itself. We now see we can be the best and we can compete with the best in the world," says Anurag Behar, managing director for Wipro's Infrastructure Engineering Division.

Now there's a new attitude on the rise: Hope. It's personified by Priya P.V., a 28-year-old woman with a master's degree in commerce from Bangalore University who manages a small team at Wipro's BPO unit. She was the first woman in her family to go to college. Now she's hoping to climb the corporate ladder. "When I was in college, I was told, 'You have to go out of India to have a good career,'" she says. "Now that's not true. You can see everything happening in India."

Indeed, now the world is coming to India in search of its talented young people. And companies like Wipro are shaping the talent of India and delivering it up to the West. The people possess the brains and enthusiasm for the job. But Wipro is taking that raw material and applying the organizational discipline to fashion a new kind of company—designed for the era of globalization—that one day may come to be admired alongside the likes of GE, IBM, and Microsoft.

It's not just the psychology of India that has changed. The world's view of India has shifted dramatically, too. There's no better illustration of that shift than the scene at the World Economic Forum in Davos, Switzerland, in January 2006. India went on a charm offensive, and the world's A-list government officials, business moguls, intellectuals, and socially minded entertainers allowed themselves to be charmed. Picture the last night of the weeklong gathering: India brought in 20 of its top chefs and a troupe of Bollywood musicians and dancers and held a gala for 600 people that lasted from 11 p.m. to 5 a.m. "We had a room of Europeans and North Americans dancing all night at our party," says a beaming Premji. India was officially "hot."

Yet successes of India and its tech industry could have a decidedly cooling effect on employment in the United States. Market researcher Forrester Research estimates that by 2015, 3.4 million U.S. service jobs will have moved offshore. That's a threat to both the American economy and the job prospects of millions of Americans. It's possible that the U.S. government will try to put up barriers to stem the tide of job losses. But the globalization genie is out of the bottle. It's likely that, in the long haul, nothing can stop it. So it's up to Americans themselves to see this huge change coming and react to it. They have to reinvent themselves.

Think of Wipro as a wake-up call for complacent Americans. With its intensity to win and its hard work ethic, it's a reminder of the America of 100 years ago. "Are we hungry enough?" asks Nicholas M. Donofrio, executive vice president for innovation and technology at IBM. Donofrio's father was an Italian immigrant who worked three jobs to support his family in the gritty factory town of Beacon, New York. Now the IBM executive questions whether Americans still possess that kind of drive. "Or are we going to amble along and take our time? If so, the Indians and Chinese will close the gap and perhaps even surpass us. You can see the passion in their eyes. They're people on a mission."

Like American workers, American companies need to learn to compete with the vigorous Asian upstarts. But at the same time, they must tap into India for services and partnerships. It's no longer a go-it-alone world. "I don't see India as a threat. I see it as an opportunity," says Welch, the former GE chairman.

The challenge is the same for companies and individuals: If they mean to succeed in a world turned upside down, they will learn to be as relentlessly self-improving as Wipro.

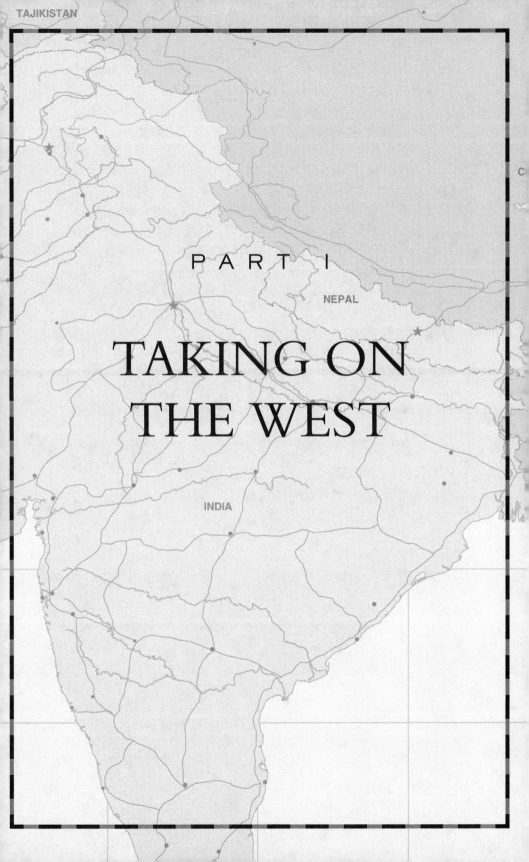

PART I

TAKING ON THE WEST

1

WHY WIPRO MATTERS

Wipro matters the way Wal-Mart matters. Wal-Mart has transformed the retail business for consumers. It's everywhere, with a wide selection of merchandise and low prices. Wipro and its Indian brethren are doing the same with tech outsourcing and back-office services. Western companies that hand off any of that wide array of tasks to Wipro and the other top Indian firms can typically expect to get better service at a lower cost. Some domestic U.S. outsourcers offer a similar array of services, but the Indians have trumped them with lower labor rates. So, Wipro is like Wal-Mart. It's everywhere, offers a wide selection, and charges low prices.

Wipro matters for another reason. In some ways, it's a model for the twenty-first century corporation. Wipro shows how to flourish in a rapidly changing business environment where companies are faced with new competitors from around the world. It's following a new operational blueprint, the transnational model: A company's work is performed at the places in the world where talent can be tapped most efficiently. At the same time, Wipro strives relentlessly to achieve operational excellence, running its services with all of the quality and efficiency of an ultramodern factory. These are the key ingredients in the new formula for global competition.

Why Wipro matters depends on who you are. For large, established corporations, it's a valuable service provider and partner that can make you more efficient and competitive. For Western companies that are under pressure to globalize, it's a map to a brave new world where employees and operations must be distributed in new ways. And, for up and comers in emerging markets, Wipro is a big brother who can guide the way.

Enabling the Virtual Corporation

The way large companies organize themselves and operate is undergoing a huge transformation. The primary big-company model for much of the twentieth century was the vertically integrated corporation. Its epitome: Standard Oil. The company, run by the legendary capitalist J. D. Rockefeller, not only extracted oil from the ground but also transported it in its own pipelines, refined it in its own factories, shipped gasoline in its own trucks, and sold gas at its own service stations. That model broke down over time, and, in the early 1990s, management gurus dreamed up the antithesis of the vertically integrated company: the virtual corporation. Rather than do everything for themselves, companies would examine how they did business and identify the parts that were crucial to their success. Anything else—they were better off finding a specialist to perform that work for them.

While few companies took virtualization to its radical extreme, some have made it a key element of their success. A prime example is Dell Inc. The company, today's number one personal computer (PC) company, was started by Michael Dell in his college dorm room. Other established PC companies had large research and development (R&D) operations, giant marketing departments, and multiple channels of distribution. Michael Dell relied on the makers of electronic components to perform his R&D. He bought the components they designed and manufactured, and then he assembled PCs out of them and sold the PCs over the phone. Dell Inc. is a much more complex and multifaceted company now, but it still puts most of its effort into what it can do best. It concentrates on understanding its customers' needs, managing a superefficient network of suppliers, and selling primarily via the phone and Internet. It farms out other work to firms in Silicon Valley, Taiwan, and India.

In 2003, Dell changed its name from Dell Computer Corporation to Dell Inc. This reflected how it had refined its view of itself. It concentrates on building its brand, managing a supply chain, and selling via the phone and the Web. Today, Dell sells Dell-branded computers, networking machines, printers, cameras, and TVs. Tomorrow: Who knows? Dell can tap into a network of designers, component builders, and product manufacturers to help it bring new products to market that may have very little or nothing to do with computing. The brand, the supply chain, and the product assembly points are Dell. Everything else can be virtual Dell.

These days, hundreds of companies are virtualizing their operations. A major breakthrough came in 2003, when A. G. Lafley, CEO of Procter & Gamble Company (P&G), started applying the concept to his company. Once, during a lunch with IBM CEO Samuel J. Palmisano, Lafley asked Palmisano to estimate how many of P&G's more than 100,000 employees it really needed to keep on the payroll. Palmisano wouldn't venture a guess, and Lafley shocked him by saying it might be possible for P&G to get by with only one-quarter of that workforce. Ultimately, Lafley didn't go nearly that far, but he ended up outsourcing much of the company's information technology operations, human resources functions, and customer service—and a big chunk of its product development.

When high-profile CEOs like P&G's Lafley publicly consider radical changes in the way they run their companies, people listen. Since P&G began its outsourcing project, there has been a steady drumbeat of corporations figuring out what operations they can farm out to others and what they should keep for themselves. "People will find better and better ways to do this," says William Davidow, the legendary Silicon Valley venture capitalist. "It's happening with engineering. The same will happen with financial services. You're creating massive global markets for services."

Indeed, the numbers are already impressive. Information technology outsourcing blossomed in the 1990s, and by 2004, it accounted for $300 billion of the $1.1 trillion tech industry, according to tech market researcher Gartner Inc. Still, tech outsourcing has a lot of room to grow. It's done predominantly by large corporations in the United States. Gartner expects the pace to pick up on other continents and in smaller companies, powering market growth of more than 7 percent per year to $440 billion in 2009. Business process outsourcing has even more headroom. IDC, another tech industry market researcher, estimates that, worldwide, companies spend about $22 trillion annually on basic business functions, while they spend about $1.6 trillion annually on farming that work out to specialists. The market researcher estimates that the outsourcing market overall will grow by about 10 percent, compounded, between now and 2008. That's faster growth than the Chinese and Indian economies. "Companies are becoming more willing to outsource or rethink how they handle their business processes," says Frank Gens, a senior vice president at IDC.

A New Sort of Outsourcing

Here's where Wipro comes in. It's an enabler of the virtual corporation. While Wipro began its foray into information technology in 1980 as a traditional maker of computers, most of its success has been in the outsourcing ranks. Wipro began offering software programming services in 1992 and a short time later provided electronics engineering services for hire. Now it has a full array of information technology outsourcing services, including testing of products and managing clients' computer data centers. In 2003, with the acquisition of Spectramind, one of the Indian pioneers of customer call center services, it plunged into the rapidly growing call center outsourcing business. And, soon after, it broadened out to offer a wide variety of so-called transactional BPO services, including accounting, travel and entertainment expensing, insurance claim processing, and real estate mortgage processing. It even operates a small group of radiologists in India who evaluate X-rays of patients for American hospitals for a fraction of the cost of the hospitals doing it themselves with in-house talent.

Why the push to broaden out? To be seen as a major outsourcing player, Wipro needed to be able to offer clients a wide variety of services. Outsourcing clients don't usually want to depend on a single supplier to handle all of their tech-related services, but they like to have just a few "throats to choke," as they say in the outsourcing business. So they often expect a supplier to handle several services for them. By constantly broadening its array of services and capabilities, Wipro is increasingly seen as a strategic partner for its clients. Take Royal Dutch Shell, the Anglo-Dutch energy giant. It signed an outsourcing deal with Wipro in February 2004—starting off relatively modestly. By the end of 2005, however, this amount of business had grown into a huge flow, including a variety of software programming and business process outsourcing (BPO) services. By the end of 2005, among accounts that were worth more than $5 million a year, 65 percent of them included more than one of Wipro's services. "We're becoming an end-to-end supplier," says Girish Paranjpe, president of the Financial Solutions strategic business unit. "We're going from smaller pieces to bigger parts. It shows we have arrived."

As recently as 2003, Wipro was still considered primarily a low-cost provider of routine software programming services. But since then, it has emerged as one of the most capable tech services outfits in the world. A 2005 "Technology Audit" by the Butler Group business analysis firm credited Wipro with having industry-leading processes, a proven ability to blend offshore labor with on-site client services, a range of services to compete with the largest service providers, targeted consulting services, and the right formula to be able to repeat the offshore delivery model and expand into additional geographies. Tech behemoth Hewlett-Packard in 2005 chose Wipro as one of its global services partners—on the same level as Western giants Accenture and Capgemini.

While few major companies will virtualize to the maximum, some of them are tapping into external services as part of their strategies for rapidly launching new products or services. These companies understand that their main strengths are their brands and their customers. They're expert at slicing and dicing market data and spotting new opportunities for selling new products and services.

They typically set up small SWAT teams to pursue these projects. Speed is of the essence, so they reach out to service providers to supply much of what it takes to build a business—everything from design services, to technology, to manufacturing, to distribution. These aren't the rigid supply chains of old, but agile, built-on-the-fly networks that are created, expanded, and contracted as needed. The result: low risk and speed to market. Depending on which industry it is utilized in, this instant-business technique can deliver new products and services, from concept to market entry, in six months to a year. Some leading practitioners are Virgin Group, Procter & Gamble, and Best Buy.

Wipro has emerged as a key participant in these new supplier networks. You see it most clearly in its engineering R&D business. Wipro designs semiconductor chips, creates real-time operating systems, writes software applications for new devices, and designs user interfaces. Often, consumer electronics clients simply give Wipro a short description of what they want built and a bill-of-materials cost—and Wipro does the rest. While it doesn't manufacture finished products, it works with contract manufacturers to build prototypes. "There's a need for somebody who ties together the technology from the United States, the manufacturing from China, and, perhaps, the intellectual property from Israel. That's us. We're a product integrator," says Ramesh Emani, president of Wipro's Product Engineering Solutions group.

Here's an example of how it works: Wipro played an essential role in the rapid development of a digital video set-top box for a telecommunications company in the United Kingdom. Wipro came up with the basic design, and it selected a microprocessor from the United States, software from the Netherlands, and a tuner from Japan. It designed the application software and did the system integration work in India. Then it oversaw manufacturing in Korea and helped out with field trials in the United Kingdom.

Wipro can also help start-ups launch rapidly. These are virtual companies in the purest form. Take E-OPS, in Miami Lakes, Florida, which bills itself as the first 24/7 paperless loan processing business.

It was formed in 2005 to provide essential processing services for tens of thousands of independent mortgage brokers across the United States. E-OPS itself had just six employees when it began doing business. All of the rest was done by Wipro. Its employees in India gathered and processed every loan application, appraisal, title, inspection report, and insurance document—and sent them off to the banks. "It's amazing that you can run a national company with just six people," says E-OPS CEO Joe Machado. "But, thanks to Wipro, we're twice as fast as the competition at half the cost."

Multinationals Beware: Here Come the Transnationals

At one time, the West's multinationals ruled supreme. Some, like General Motors (GM) and Ford, are now reeling. And while many of the other multinationals remain strong, they, too, are scrambling to adapt to a rapidly changing global business landscape. Their old ways of doing business aren't working so well anymore. And, worse, in many cases, those ways have become liabilities, burdening them with excess costs and bureaucracy.

GM makes the point. In the second half of the twentieth century, it expanded globally. In each major region, it created a mini-GM. It replicated all of the functions of the mother corporation, including headquarters, sales, marketing, support, and manufacturing. All of this effort was designed to serve that one market. This approach, the multinational model, worked well for many years. And then it stopped working well. Competitors such as Toyota and Honda emerged, first as lower-cost producers, then as high-quality producers, and finally as superior designers and marketers. In order to compete more successfully, GM has changed the way it designs and manufactures vehicles. Now, it has design centers and manufacturing plants throughout the world. But they don't just serve their regional markets. Instead, GM has centralized control over where it designs and builds cars and trucks. It used to build vehicles within the regions where they were designed. Now decisions about where to build a vehicle have three variables: available capacity, proximity to market, and lowest costs. GM is starting to behave less like a multinational and more like a transnational.

The transnational business model is based on the idea that a company should perform various corporate functions and types of work at the locations in the world where it can be most efficient. That mix of places provides it with an available workforce, access to capital, the right expertise, the right level of face-to-customer contact, and an effective mix of wage rates. The transnational concept is at the core of Wipro's strategy. While Wipro has sales offices in 14 countries, it has software, hardware engineering, and BPO centers in nearly as many. In addition to its vast engineering factories in India, Wipro taps the brainpower and expertise of people in Japan, China, Taiwan, Dubai, Australia, Canada, the United States, the United Kingdom, Germany, Sweden, Romania, and, soon, Vietnam.

A second crucial step for transnational corporations is setting up an infrastructure that facilitates communication and collaboration between their far-flung outposts. While it's still necessary for people who work in transnational organizations to meet face-to-face from time to time, the best of these outfits operate quite well via the network, on e-mail, teleconference calls, and collaboration Web sites. In fact, in some cases, a heightened awareness of the problems inherent in long-distance communications often results in interactions that are crisper, more efficient, and more effective than the face-to-face kind.

The Art of Global Collaboration

Wipro has mastered the art of global collaboration. Its thousands of software programmers work in teams whose individual members are sometimes scattered across continents. Yet, in spite of great distances and multiple time zones, Wipro managers keep those teams running smoothly. They achieve this through a combination of superior technology and superior business processes. At Wipro, nothing is left to chance. Its services are run with the efficiency of a modern factory. Its core customer service business processes describe how every step in a customer engagement is to be handled. Each of the approximately 2,000 projects it has on its plate at any given time is tracked in its project management system. Project leaders and team members can log in from any computer equipped with an Internet browser and keep up to date with requirements, progress, and customer feedback.

Wipro treats its staff like a vast pool of brainpower and expertise from which its project managers can pluck at will. This is crucial to its ability to operate globally. From the day employees are hired, a digital dossier is created in a vast database that stores all of the pertinent information about them, including their array of skills, the projects they have worked on, and what they're working on at any given time. Project managers choose their teams for a particular project via an internal Web site called TED (Talent, Engagement, and Development) Web—searching for the skills they need and then selecting from among people with those skills. Because the company tracks how long it typically takes to perform any particular task, project leaders know when a given employee with a particular skill will be available to take on a new assignment.

Here's how it might work: A project manager in Boston and a service delivery manager in Bangalore team up to complete a job for a Boston client. They select business analysts in Boston, software architects in Seattle and Bangalore, and programmers in Bangalore and Hyderabad. The result: a global, virtual team.

The team members keep in touch and share work using a handful of sophisticated technology tools. They have computing programs that allow them to check out and work on individual software components, all under tight controls and review processes. Every Wipro office is equipped with teleconferencing equipment so widely scattered groups can hold virtual meetings. The company even runs what amounts to its own telephone company. Whenever one Wipro employee calls another, the connection is handled using so-called voice over Internet protocol (VoIP) technology. All those calls are free. Right now, the company is testing technology that could allow all employees to have video conferencing setups on their desktops or laptop PCs. In the future, a virtual team meeting could connect somebody in her living room in Dallas with somebody at a departure gate at Narita airport outside of Tokyo with somebody at his office in Bangalore.

Wipro is a model for how to operate as a transnational organization. It also builds technology and business processes to help its clients operate the same way.

If You Don't Constantly Improve, You Constantly Fall Behind

Rich Garnick will tell you one of the keys to Wipro's success: intensity. Before Garnick, an American, began to work for Wipro in 2001, he had worn out colleagues at a handful of tech companies with his relentless work ethic. But at Wipro, where he was president of North American operations for four years, he more than met his match. There, executives and managers sometimes work 20 hours in a day. Plus, they often work on weekends. Because the company operates in so many time zones, meetings take place at every hour of the day or night. Often, Wiproites in America are up at 5 a.m. teleconferencing with colleagues in Bangalore. They use airplane flights to catch up on their sleep. Garnick, who is now president of North American operations at Keane Inc., a smaller rival (he grew weary of the long trips to India, he says), used to catch naps whenever the opportunity arose.

What drives all of this intensity? There's a hunger for success that permeates the Wipro culture. Part of it comes from years of disappointment in India. Independence from Britain in 1947 was followed by decades of confrontation with Pakistan and stifling bureaucracy. With the liberalization of the 1990s, and after the initial tech victories on the global stage, people at Wipro and other Indian companies saw they could compete as equals and win. "Wipro unleashed the energy of all of that talent to deliver a compelling value proposition to its customers and, at the same time, to give hope to a whole country," says Garnick.

Now Garnick is trying to retool Keane, a $1 billion company with 9,000 employees, in the Wipro mold. He's not only expanding his operations rapidly in India, to take advantage of the inexpensive talent, but he's trying to re-create the intensity of the Wipro employees. His task is to convince Keane's people that the company's future is brighter than its past. Then he has to convince them to work tirelessly to make that happen. That may not be easy in the United States, where a sense of entitlement to success is firmly embedded.

While Wipro's employees come to their jobs with a lot of enthusiasm, it's the company's techniques for channeling that energy into productive activity that lay the foundation for its success. At every step, Wipro stresses the importance of constant improvement. "You don't stand on the roof top and say, 'I'm a leader. I don't have to learn,'" says Suresh Senapaty, the company's chief financial officer. "We have always been humble. We admit to ourselves when we're not the best at something. Then we set out to change that."

It starts with the individual. Standards are high to start with. About 1.2 million people apply to Wipro per year, but fewer than 20,000 are hired. Wipro recruiters make the rounds of the country's 150 engineering colleges each year and allow only the top students to take the aptitude test, which culls relative few who land face-to-face interviews. Once they are hired, all "freshers"—new employees coming right out of college—take 8 to 10 weeks of classroom training that teaches them how to take their school knowledge and apply it to the world of work in the Wipro way. Once the freshers are established, Wipro helps them manage their careers, offering programs in leading a small team, running a business, and senior management. In addition, there are online courses offered for each skill area, be it software programming, hardware engineering, or telecommunications. Every employee is required to complete 10 days of training annually. These sessions often include Saturday sessions. "When it comes to training, they hardly ever say no," says Pratik Kumar, the senior vice president in charge of human resources.

The constant-improvement approach is also essential to the success of Wipro's project teams. This is achieved, in large part, through adoption of best business practices and ever-improving business processes to achieve operational excellence. By its very nature, the constant-improvement imperative can never be fully satisfied. The effort must be regularly renewed. The organization needs a kick in the pants to avoid complacency and inertia. "When we launch a big, new initiative, we get big step improvements," says Sambuddha Deb, Wipro's chief quality officer. "After three years, you hit a plateau. So you need to look for the next new thing."

Innovation Should Be Like Breathing

Quality and efficiency programs are aimed at improving *the way things are done.* Innovation is aimed at *what is done.* At Wipro, innovation is not left for technical druids laboring off in some expensive laboratory. It's practiced by nearly everyone in the organization. And it's a routine daily activity. As a technology company, Wipro creates new information technology across a wide swath of areas of expertise, from software architectures for corporations to wireless technologies embedded in microchips. As a services company, Wipro creates new solutions for its clients. That's technology components, packaged with business processes, delivered as a service.

The company's technology and solution innovations come in three ways. On a grassroots level, they bubble up from engineers who are immersed in working on projects for customers. Rather than keeping these ideas to themselves, employees are encouraged to submit them to the company's seven-member Innovation Council via the employee Web site. The best of the grassroots ideas are turned into special Innovation Initiative projects, often with the employee who suggested them invited to participate in bringing the ideas to fruition. At the same time, Wipro has set up an organization made up of people whose job it is to produce innovations in specific areas. It operates about 40 Centers of Excellence, where programmers and engineers focus on emerging technologies, including things such as wireless communications or grid computing. As these technologies grow up, they're transferred into practices in the company's business units, and the Centers of Excellence are disbanded— only to be replaced by new ones targeting the latest emerging technologies. Last, the members of the Innovation Council visit with customers to discover their problems, their priorities, and even their ideas for harnessing new technologies.

Success Is an Act of Will

Ultimately, what makes Wipro so successful is its aspiring culture. "There's a sheer will and determination to be in the top three in whatever we do. We'll do whatever it takes to make things happen," says A. L. Rao, the company's chief operating officer, a 25-year veteran. In order to grow and thrive, Wipro had to become a world-class organization capable of competing with the legendary giants of the tech industry. It set off on this journey the way a mountaineer takes on a 20,000-foot peak, by preparing thoroughly and taking one step at time. It keeps moving along at a rapid pace because many of its employees, from Premji on down to the youngest paper handler, keep their eyes on the goal and drive toward it. Wipro is not just a company. It's a quest. And, in a fiercely competitive and rapidly changing business environment, no company that is not also a quest can succeed for long. Bottom line: Wipro matters because it challenges other companies to strive for excellence.

2

A TEXTBOOK CASE OF
TRANSFORMATION

On October 9, 2005, about 65 people gathered at Wipro's head-quarters in Bangalore to celebrate the twenty-fifth anniversary of the company's information technology business. These were members of the intrepid band that planted the seeds of a global tech powerhouse in a small vegetable oil company in western India. About 25 of them still worked for Wipro, but the rest had moved on. People came in from all over the world—the Wipro diaspora. Even Leland Cole showed up. He was the American who licensed key software technology to Wipro in 1980 that became the core of its original computer business. Chairman Azim Premji made a short speech and handed out mementos. Then the group heard comments from Sridhar Mitta, the first tech person that Premji hired. He was Wipro's long-time chief technology officer and is now founder and CTO of e4e, a Bangalore tech services company. Mitta reflected on how far the company had come since 1980, and why. "We did 12 things right. If we did 11 things right, it would not have been a successful company," Mitta remembers saying. "It was partly design and partly luck." This chapter chronicles that amazing journey from cooking oil to bits and bytes.

Squeezing Profits from Peanuts

August 11, 1966: The date would forever stick in Azim Premji's memory. He was 21, a senior at Stanford University in Palo Alto, was studying for his summer school exams, when a call came through from his mother, Gulbanoo Premji, in India. The news was shocking: His father, M. H. Premji, just 51 years old, had died of a heart attack. Azim Premji quickly arranged to fly home to Bombay, now called Mumbai. When he departed from the San Francisco airport, he expected that he would be back at school in time to start his fall semester. He was just two quarters short of graduation. Instead, his father's death marked not just a family tragedy but a fateful change of life direction for the young Premji. Instead of pursuing his dream of helping to develop the Third World as a policy maker at the World Bank, he would be plunged into the nitty-gritty of saving one failing company in a backwater economy.

Fortunately, entrepreneurship ran in his blood. Premji's grandfather had started from scratch and built one of the largest bulk rice trading companies in India. His father worked for his grandfather but later branched out on his own by starting a manufacturing and distribution company called Western India Vegetable Products in 1945. He wasn't very attentive to the basics of the business, however. He preferred to play the role of policy maker, lobbying the national government in Delhi for deregulation of the food grains industry and serving on a handful of industry boards. When the young Premji arrived home on August 15, 1966, he found the family businesses in shambles. He also learned that his father had selected him to run it—a duty he felt he could not shirk. "It's like being thrown into a swimming pool. To avoid drowning, you learn to swim quickly," says Premji.

He plunged right in. The company had a weak management team, though the managers immediately transferred their loyalty from father to son. It had about 350 employees, mostly in and around Bombay, and only $3 million in revenues. The company was publicly traded—one of the first to list on an exchange in India—and not long after Premji took over, it came time for a general shareholders' meeting. The investors were restless. Premji remembers that one of them stood up, complained about the poor rate of returns, and said, "There's no way a twit like you can run it." He demanded that

Premji sell the company to the highest bidder. "More than anything else, that made me determined to prove him wrong," says Premji.

It was time for a crash course in capitalism. Premji had never taken a business class in school, nor had his father taught him anything. So he visited a professor at a leading management school in Bombay and asked him to recommend a list of textbooks. He bought a pile of them, and over the next year, he read them all, mainly late at night and in the early mornings. Out of that reading he learned business basics and systematically built a company based on modern principles and practices. He also got advice from his father's former lieutenants. While they weren't dynamic executives, they knew the vegetable oil business in and out.

Premji's experience at Stanford had prepared him to be a different sort of leader. Unlike Indian engineering programs of the time, Stanford's program required engineering students to take a wide range of liberal arts courses, including English literature, Western civilization, philosophy, and psychology. Premji says this made him a thoughtful person. His years at Stanford also gave him an appetite for competition. When he arrived in Palo Alto, he found that he lagged way behind his classmates, so he raced to catch up. Once he accomplished that, he set his sights on always being in the top 20 percent of the class. "You were constantly questing for excellence," he says.

In those first difficult years, Premji established a management style and a corporate culture that formed a solid foundation for everything that would come later. While his father's top men had based their decisions on tradition and instincts, he brought numerical measurement and analysis to play. And way before it became de rigueur for Western businesses, he benchmarked each of his managers against the others.

The company's business was buying peanuts from farmers and crushing them to produce shortening and edible cakes. The key employee was the buyer, who would evaluate a farmer's harvest by taking the seeds in his hands and biting them and estimating the oil content—then setting a price based on it. Premji replaced that system with a very simple process for getting samples from farmers, drying the nuts, weighing them, and calculating the oil content. He transformed what had been an art into a technology-based business process, which ultimately became one of the company's core competencies. That changed the company his father had left him from a money-losing business to a profitable one.

The shift left the buyers feeling devalued, but Premji quickly gave them something more important to do: manage the business. They monitored the sales of their retailers, got a better measure of supply and demand, and learned to price more sharply. To drive weekly improvements, Premji began holding staff meetings every Monday morning—something Wipro continues to do to this day. This was before telephone conference calls—or even direct dialing—were available in India. So he set up his managers on a series of operator-assisted calls, listened to their reports, and set new goals for the following week. He empowered his managers. They were free to set prices in their regions as they saw fit. But they were also held accountable for their performance. These were innovations for India, which had been straitjacketed by bureaucracy, tradition, and government control.

Leading by Example

Premji led by doing. He was willing to work long hours under sometimes unpleasant conditions, and he expected his employees to do the same. Even now, he sometimes works more than 10 hours a day, plus weekends. But that's positively a pampered existence compared to the company's early days. The original manufacturing plant was in Amalner, a small town about eight hours' drive from Bombay. During the summers the temperature would get up to 112 degrees. The cash-strapped company couldn't afford air conditioning, and every summer production dropped off. Premji wouldn't accept that as a given, so he moved to the town for three months one summer. "After that, one never heard that productivity had to fall in the summer," he says.

The most important foundation Premji built in the early days was his stand on ethics. In the late 1960s and early 1970s, corruption was rampant in the Indian economy. Government officials often demanded bribes for granting permissions. Customers asked for kickbacks. Farmers bribed clerks to tamper with weighing machines. Premji decided that, henceforth, his company would live by a higher standard, which he believed would ultimately enhance its stature with customers and employees. He set a zero-tolerance policy for bribes and any form of corruption or corner-cutting. This policy went for everyone from top managers to laborers. "We said anybody committing an act of breach of integrity would lose their job overnight. It's open and shut and black and white," Premji says. It took several firings before people believed it. But finally, they did. The company stood out, and not just from local Indian outfits. Some of the multinationals had fallen into the trap of paying bribes as well.

Finally, the cooking oil business thrived, and Premji broadened his horizons. He had no grand vision of what Wipro could become. But he saw opportunities and didn't want to miss out on them. In the 1970s, Western business giants were rapidly buying up unrelated businesses to form conglomerates. The idea was that by placing bets in different industries, with different up-and-down cycles, a company could smooth out its earnings. He diversified into soaps and beauty products and into manufacturing hydraulic components for construction equipment. Western India Vegetable Products became Wipro Ltd., a miniconglomerate. It was now a $30 million company, diversified, and comfortably profitable, but still not even a blip on the world's business radar screen.

From Vegetable Oil to Bits and Bytes

Premji's next diversification move set him up for success beyond anything he could have imagined when he returned home for his father's funeral. In 1977, the Indian government passed new rules that required foreign companies to operate through local, Indian-owned affiliates. IBM, then the world's dominant computer company, packed up and left the country. "When IBM left, it created a vacuum," recalls Premji. "So we decided to zero in on info tech."

Premji and his lieutenants knew nothing about computers, but that didn't stop them from starting a computer company. When Premji interviewed Sridhar Mitta, then a technical manager specializing in satellite tracking at the government-owned Electronics Corporation of India Ltd., Mitta warned him against getting into the business. "They didn't listen to me," Mitta says. Not only that, but Premji and his lieutenants also convinced him to join the company as its head of R&D. Mitta didn't even have a computer science degree.

Mitta went to school on the computer industry, just as Premji had studied business when he first joined the company. He rented a 4,000-square-foot office in Bangalore, home to several of India's top technical and management colleges, and started casting around for a product idea. This was before IBM introduced the PC, so it wasn't clear what path computing would take. After months of study, Mitta decided to build a so-called minicomputer, based on microprocessors and aimed at the business market—a first for India. It would be a lot less expensive than an IBM mainframe, but could do similar kinds of work. He and Premji licensed a computer operating system from Sentinel Computer Corporation in Cincinnati, Ohio, hired a staff of seven people, and set out to build a computer business. Wipro became one of the early Indian tech companies to set up in Bangalore, which was then a sleepy retirement town known mainly for its balmy weather.

Within one year, Wipro shipped its minicomputer. It was the first computer made in India that did not require programmers to write their applications on huge decks of punch cards. When the company showed it off at a computer show in Delhi in 1981, "it sent shockwaves through the Indian market," says A. L. Rao, the company's chief operating officer, who had joined in 1980 as one of its first tech employees. Wipro later got into the PC business and quickly became the leading computer company in India. It succeeded by being first out with new technology and delivering top-class customer service.

But the good times would not last. In the early 1990s, India liberalized its business regulations. This development essentially invited the world's top tech companies to flood into the country—which they did. Wipro faced a crisis. There was no way it could beat Compaq, Hewlett-Packard, and IBM in the PC business over the long haul, Premji and his lieutenants believed. The big brands had vast R&D resources and huge sales volumes that would allow them to underprice and outengineer Wipro and the other homegrown Indian PC outfits.

The Making of a Global Tech Powerhouse

What Wipro did next was to set the stage for its eventual emergence as a player on the global stage. It was Mitta's idea to begin selling engineering expertise to the world's top tech companies—an engineering lab for hire. "We saw that while the door was open for others to come in, it was also open for us to go out. So we decided to become a global company," says Mitta. Wipro's first target was software programming, designing embedded applications for telecom gear and computers. But it quickly followed with hardware and chip design. Texas Instruments and Motorola had opened their own software shops in India to get top-quality programming on the cheap. Wipro's leaders saw that they could set up similar operations and sell their services to a wide range of Western corporations—not just technology companies but banks, manufacturers, and retailers.

But would the giants of Western capitalism turn to a tiny, no-name Indian outfit to perform some of their important brainwork? The answer was: not very fast. So Premji and his colleagues decided they needed to do something to give them credibility. Their solution: aggressively adopt international quality standards. That led to the program of spotting up-and-coming standards and quickly adapting them to software programming and hardware R&D.

Wipro began in 1995 by receiving certification in the International Organization for Standardization (ISO) 9000 quality standard.

This is when it only had a few hundred tech employees. Then it focused on Carnegie Mellon University's Software Engineering Institute standard for software programming just as it was taking shape. In 1999, Wipro became the first software services company in the world to achieve the top certification, Capability Maturity Model (CMM) Level 5. Wipro was quick to adopt Motorola's Six Sigma quality program, which improves and maps out business processes to make them repeatable and dependable. Now Wipro is swarming with black belts—the top-ranked Six Sigma experts. And, just now, it's busy taking the lean manufacturing techniques that Toyota has used to such advantage and applying them to software programming and running business process outsourcing operations. (For more about these quality and process-improvement programs, see Chapter 14.)

That description makes it all sound so easy and smooth, but it wasn't. Practically every move Wipro made was a battle against the traditional way of doing things. This is part of what has made it such a determined organization. Subroto Bagchi, the longtime Wipro executive who is now chief operating officer at MindTree Consulting, remembers what it was like to gain a foothold in Silicon Valley. First, he had to apply to the government in Delhi to get a foreign exchange permit. His case officer would allow him to buy only $10,000 in U.S. dollars to pay the first year's expenses. With that paltry sum, he moved his wife and two daughters to a two-bedroom apartment in Cupertino, near the Apple Computer campus. He set up a home office in the dining room. He bought a PC and a fax machine at Price Club, using a friend's credit card, and began churning out proposals as quickly as his fingers could type. His youngsters would be watching cartoons in the next room, but when they heard the phone ring, they knew to put the TV on mute so Dad could pick up the receiver and say, "Wipro Technologies."

As they spread out across the United States in search of customers, the Wiproites were like nomads. They got leads from technical people—often other Indians—whom they knew in companies such as Intel, Seagate, and Sun Microsystems. They'd go to a city and stay in the cheapest hotel and look through the telephone directory to spot potential customers. Then they'd sit in the hotel room and make a bunch of calls to prospects. "Nobody had heard of us," says Sudip Banerjee, president of Enterprise Solutions, one of the company's three large strategic business units. "We'd make dozens of phone calls. Nobody would return them."

The big breakthrough came with General Electric (GE). In 1990, the two companies had set up a joint venture, Wipro GE Medical Systems, to sell GE's medical equipment in India. So GE was familiar with Wipro when it decided to shift some of its software development to India. The entire Wipro management team, including Premji, pitched in and won the deal—first to maintain some of GE's applications and, later, to develop custom software. "It was a large piece of business and gave us credibility," says Banerjee, who was instrumental in the development of Wipro's software business. He started key alliances with the likes of Adobe, Netscape, and Macromedia, and, when software became an independent business, he was its first president.

So twice in a little more than a decade, Wipro was able to spot fundamental shifts in the business environment and then scramble to create whole new businesses. "It's a core competency for us," says Premji. "We're able to evaluate opportunities at the right time and put together an act to make a commercial success of it."

The Hypergrowth Years

Azim Premji and Sridhar Mitta set the table; a colleague, Vivek Paul, served dinner. In 1999, just as the demand for software fix-ups for the millennium bug known as Y2K was peaking, Premji hired Paul as his vice chairman and president of Wipro Technologies, the tech subsidiary. The goal was to accelerate growth. Paul already knew Wipro well—and vice versa. He had been recruited from management consultancy Bain & Company in 1990 as the first employee and leader of that medical equipment joint venture. He ran it for six years before returning to the United States to run GE Medical Systems. GE Chief Executive Jeff Immelt called him in to his office and questioned why he would give up a bright future at GE to join a small company in Bangalore. But Paul had seen the capabilities of the Wipro employees in India, and he jumped at the chance to run its global tech business. "I saw the opportunity to take what was then a cottage industry and corporatize it, making process excellence a core competency," says Paul.

Wipro was a company in transition. During the dot-com boom, which swept over India as well as the United States and Europe, a number of the company's top executives—Mitta among them—left to join start-ups. Wipro's service businesses didn't seem very sexy at a time when people saw the opportunity to raise money, launch Web sites, and become rich practically overnight. The people who were left behind wondered about Wipro's future—and their own.

Paul knew he had to do something to change the mood, but he didn't know what. Then, one day, when he visited a circus on the outskirts of Bangalore, he noticed a large elephant that was tethered to a very small peg in the ground. The elephant could easily have pulled the peg out and broken free, but it didn't even try. Paul asked the trainer why. The answer: The elephant had been tied to that peg since it was an infant. At first, it tried to pull away, but it couldn't. Over time, it stopped trying. "The lesson I learned was you can't limit yourself," Paul says. He decided Wipro simply wasn't thinking big enough.

Set Audacious Goals

To inspire the company, Vivek Paul and his lieutenants came up with an audacious goal. Wipro would be a $4 billion company by the end of 2004. It was the "4 in 4 plan." He expected half of the growth to be organic and half to come from acquisitions. That was it—a big, bold goal that challenged everybody to do his or her best. "We decided to dream big, and people had the confidence we could actually achieve it," says Paul.

Paul knew that setting a mind-blowing goal wasn't going to be enough, by itself. He set about tuning up the company so it could actually achieve it. If Wipro was going to grow rapidly, it needed to have a stronger foundation to build upon. It needed to be able to rapidly scale up its staff and business activities without collapsing under its own weight. Under Premji, the tech business had been organized in independent business units, each with its own corporate functions. Paul created a set of strong central corporate functions that the business units shared. For one, he created a central staffing pool from which managers in different businesses could draw. He put in place a business scorecard, so he and his managers could closely track their performance on their PCs and benchmark it against the competition. Also, he knew the company would have to add service lines if it was to grow rapidly, so he shifted from having just one major reorganization a year to being flexible enough to reorganize three or four times a year—without creating chaos.

The pace quickened. Wipro aggressively expanded its capabilities in a half-dozen industries that it targeted. It became a major player in business process outsourcing (BPO). And it beefed up its consulting, systems integration, and computing data center management businesses.

By the time Paul decided to move on, in the spring of 2005, Wipro Ltd. had grown into a $1.9 billion corporation with more than 40,000 employees. It fell far short of the $4 billion revenue goal that Paul had set out, but nobody begrudged him that. A worldwide economic slowdown in 2001 and 2002 slowed the pace of growth for the entire tech industry. Plus, Paul decided against an aggressive acquisition strategy after a couple of small buys he made in the United States proved hard to digest. His legacy is that he woke Wipro up to the possibilities, and he retooled it into a company far better able to capitalize on them.

A Time to Recharge the Company

After Paul decided to leave, his Wipro colleagues took a deep look at themselves and their company and decided things had to change—again. Tata Consulting Services, an offshoot of the giant Tata Group, had gone public. Not only was it larger than Wipro, but it started making big splashy deals, especially in Europe. Infosys Technologies, long Wipro's little sibling, had grown faster and pulled ahead in revenue size. Meanwhile, Wipro's American competitors had woken up to the threat from the Indians and were adopting the global delivery business model. Accenture, IBM, and others had set up operations in India and were rapidly hiring thousands of programmers and engineers. Competition was keen. And it was coming from new places—China, for one. The People's Republic started its foray into tech as a low-cost manufacturing center, but it quickly branched into product design and software outsourcing. At the same time, salaries in India were rising, but Wipro and the other Indian tech outfits couldn't simply pass their increased costs on to clients. "They're going to have to reinvent themselves," Rahul Merchant, head of global business technology at Merrill Lynch and Company, says of the Indian tech companies.

Premji was anything but complacent. "The concept of global delivery and partnership has changed the nature of business," he says. "Nobody can take their success for granted. If we don't sustain our motivation, the Chinese will eat us up."

Premji had taken his company global. He was immensely wealthy. He could have hired somebody else to take Paul's place and run the tech business—or the whole company. Instead, he was energized. "We face plenty of challenges," says Premji. "You have to be continuously innovative to keep ahead of the curve." To attack those challenges head on, Premji chose to personally lead the technology business. He decided Wipro had to be more aggressive about revenue growth, both through organic expansion and acquisitions. And he felt the company's practice of making incremental innovations in both technology and business processes would not be sufficient anymore. Wipro needed to learn to make "quantum" innovations. He restructured his executive staff, both to avoid overloading his own plate and to shake up the organization. He hoped that all of these moves would pay off within a few years and produce more than a $5 billion company. "We're significantly more risk taking than we were a year back," he says. "We're willing to take unknown paths. We saw that if we didn't, we'd lose a lot opportunity."

A key maneuver was promoting A. L. Rao, long the leader of the company's telecommunications industry group, to chief operating officer. Part of Rao's new job was overseeing technology innovation. Twenty-five years earlier he had been one of the company's first technical hires, heading up product development, with an initial staff of four fresh university graduates. When Premji handed Rao the job in July 2005, he made it clear what he wanted: bigger innovations. One of Rao's first moves was to strengthen the technical competency of the company's service delivery teams. The idea was to use pay incentives to encourage top employees to advance their careers as technical leaders as an alternative to pursuing the business leadership path.

A bigger step was to foster those quantum innovations that Premji had in mind. He was looking for combinations of technology and services that could create new $100 million to $200 million businesses within a matter of years. "We don't want to just come up with ideas for how to use grid computing. We want to come up with the equivalent of grid computing—but in the services realm," says Rao, referring to technology for harnessing together many computers to perform a complex data processing job—like genomic research. Wipro does not suffer from the "not-invented-here" syndrome of many U.S. technology firms. It knows when it needs help and is grateful to get it. So one of Rao's first moves was to engage the services of a consulting firm, Erehwon Innovation Consulting, in Bangalore. That was the beginning of a major effort to turbocharge the company's innovation engine. It was classic Wipro: Study it. Follow a process. Come up with something new.

The Wipro Way

At the same time, Premji and his executive team decided to formalize the company's core philosophy and give it a name: the Wipro Way. Like the well-known HP Way, established by David

Packard and William Hewlett, legendary founders of Silicon Valley's Hewlett-Packard Company, the Wipro Way gives managers and employees alike a clear target at which to aim. It identifies Wipro's four pillars of strength: customer centricity, process excellence, people management, and career development. Then it sets a high bar for each—for instance, to have the best customer satisfaction ratings of any company in its industry. "This is how we build a culture of excellence," says Sambuddha Deb, Wipro's chief quality officer. "We see this as a journey, and the journey will never be over."

Can Wipro make it to the next level and become a $5 billion and then a $10 billion company? That's not assured. Often in business, the leader who can guide a company to the $1 billion revenue level doesn't have the skills to manage the next stage of growth. We'll now see if the self-taught Premji can keep up his impressive track record for learning and adapting on the job. And what of the people around him? Many of Wipro's executives have been with the company for 10, 20, or even 25 years. That has some pluses. They're deep in experience and know how to work together. But tight knit can also mean insular. In a business like Wipro's and in a world undergoing such rapid change, insularity can lead to missed opportunities and aversion to risk.

The Wipro Way is a work in progress. So is globalization. And that's all the more reason to study Wipro, learn how it operates, and understand what it has done right—and wrong. Think of Wipro as an advance scouting party on a journey across a new frontier.

3

HOW TO LEAD IN
MULTIPLE MARKETS

There are no gimmicks to Wipro's tech strategy. It's brute force. During the first five years of the decade, its goal was to build out a comprehensive portfolio of tech services, and to deepen its expertise both in technologies and how different industries use them. The mission was accomplished. Wipro now offers an array of services including software programming, tech support, engineering R&D, product testing, systems integration, information technology (IT) consulting, and call centers and other flavors of business process outsourcing. It's taking advantage of the beachheads it has established with software development services by cross-selling its clients additional services from its long menu. At the same time, it has organized around more than a dozen vertical industries, including telecommunications, manufacturing, and retailing. Think of it as a breadth and depth strategy.

Spread Out, but Don't Be Scattershot

Few $2.4 billion companies are in as many businesses as Wipro. It ranges from soaps, lightbulbs, hydraulic machinery parts, and, yes, still, vegetable oil, to all the tech stuff. And that includes selling PCs in India. Much of that sprawl is a result of its forays in decades past into conglomerate-style diversification. But for the moment, forget the nontech businesses. They're just 10 percent of revenues. When it comes to tech services, Wipro's strategy is ultracohesive. As it grew, it steadily expanded its array of services. In most cases, it's serving the same customers with an ever broader and more sophisticated menu. Rather than sell a British-based bank only software programming, it can also sell the bank IT consulting, manage its desktop computers, and even run its consumer credit card accounts receivable department. In this way, Wipro can focus on a fairly concentrated market—the world's top 1,000 corporations, or so—and spend quite frugally on market development and advertising. That's the mantra: Less on selling; more on serving. This helps explain its high customer satisfaction numbers.

Here's the roster of Wipro's tech services:

- *Software maintenance and development.* Wipro programmers write new custom software programs for clients, such as a branch banking application or a system for managing relations with dealers for an auto manufacturer. In addition, they fix flaws in programs and make improvements in software features and functions.

- *Package implementation.* The company handles installation and configuration of large run-the-business applications such as accounting, human resources (HR), customer relations, and supply chain management from software makers such as SAP and Oracle.

- *Infrastructure outsourcing.* This service involves management of computer servers, networks, and personal computers. It's primarily done by employees in India, but some of the work is performed in the clients' offices.

- *Business process outsourcing (BPO).* From offices in India and elsewhere around the world, Wipro employees handle tech support calls for global computer companies and customer service and marketing calls for banks and insurance companies. It also handles core business processes such as health insurance claim processing.

- *IT consulting.* Wipro consultants advise clients on how to improve their business performance by applying new technologies or improving their business processes.

- *Product engineering.* Its engineers design everything from chips and circuit boards to whole consumer electronics devices or components of autos or airplanes.

- *Testing.* Wipro handles quality assurance processes not only for corporate customers who are about to deploy new custom-written software, but also for commercial software makers.

The growth rate for the company's core software programming and maintenance services has slowed from the torrid rates of the late 1990s, but Wipro believes it can maintain a very healthy 25 to 30 percent overall annual growth rate because its portfolio includes fast growers such as tech consulting, BPO, and infrastructure outsourcing. In fact, in fiscal year 2006, the company's global tech services grew 33 percent and sales were accelerating. The fourth quarter produced a 39 percent jump.

Wipro's Diversified Portfolio of Businesses

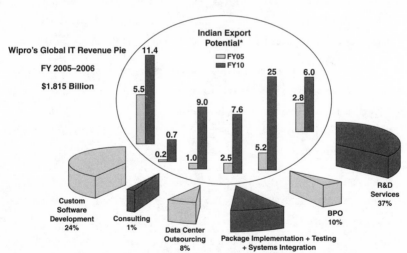

Note: Percentages below the pie chart represent Wipro's distribution of revenues for the fiscal year ended March 2006.

*Source: McKinsey-NASSCOM Study 2005. Company estimate (all figures in U.S. billion dollars)

Here's where things start to get complicated. Some of the software programming and maintenance services are delivered by independent business units, including BPO and consulting. Some specialty software services are housed within the chief technology officer's organization. And at the same time, some services are integrated into the company's three large strategic business units: Enterprise Solutions, Finance Solutions, and Product Engineering Solutions. Product Engineering Solutions is both an array of services and a vertical business unit aimed at the telecommunications and IT industries. Here's the breakdown of the three strategic business units:

- *Enterprise Solutions.* This unit includes energy and utilities; manufacturing; retail, consumer packaged goods, and distribution; health care and life sciences; and media and travel services. The unit's share of Wipro's total global tech services revenues is 42 percent.

- *Finance Solutions.* This unit is concerned with securities and capital markets, banking and financial services, and insurance. It makes up 21 percent of the company's total revenues.

- *Product Engineering Solutions.* This unit encompasses broadband communications; wireless communications; voice and data communications devices; telecommunications solutions, embedded systems (software within machines); computer systems and storage; semiconductors and consumer electronics; and software products. Its share of total revenues is 37 percent.

To cap it off, there's a third organization: Sales. Selling is organized along geographical lines, with three main groups: one for the United States and Europe, one for Asia Pacific, and another for Japan.

The company operates a three-dimensional (3-D) management matrix to coordinate the three types of organizations. The industry verticals dominate. They're essentially business integrators that combine multiple service lines, add particular industry expertise, and take the entire solution to the customer. They have program managers and service delivery people on location in the customers' offices. An even larger part of their workforces are the project managers and software programmers in development centers in India and scattered elsewhere around the world. When they need to, they tap into the independent service organizations to bring additional capabilities to bear for their customers.

Salespeople report up through their geographical sales organizations, but most of them are aligned with one or two verticals, and they also report to managers in the verticals. Unlike traditional software companies, where the salespeople are the only ones who regularly face the customers, all three Wipro organizations deal directly with customers. That makes customers feel well tended to.

Turn Complexity into a Virtue

The 3-D matrix also makes for some complex interactions. The salespeople make first contact with prospects, but once a company shows interest, they work closely with the verticals to evaluate the opportunities, assess staffing needs, and generate proposals. When customers visit Wipro facilities in India, which are run by the strategic business units or the service lines, their sales representatives often take the lead in arranging the itineraries and sometimes even accompany them. All three organizations get involved in account planning. They might work together to identify the top 25 prospects in a geographical area and then zero in on the service lines they hope to sell to them.

This is when disagreements can pop up. What if the BPO service line spots a promising customer about which the vertical business unit isn't so excited? These conflicts are resolved through discussion. The verticals have the last word. But, often, they'll heed the advice of the sales managers, who are closest to market trends. "The issue isn't who controls the account. The heads of the various groups work together to deliver a solution," says A. L. Rao, Wipro's chief operating officer.

To encourage the three organizations to play nicely together, Wipro has developed a shared credit system. In addition to its regular financial accounting, the company tracks functional profit-and-loss tallies for its verticals and its service lines. Individuals and groups get credit for their role in landing new contracts and in participating in ongoing services. Their performance is measured and they are paid partly based on those shared credits. Of course, salespeople are compensated based on what they sell. They're paid a premium for lining up fixed-price contracts rather than time-and-materials deals, and they get paid more for arrangements with a larger offshore labor component. But, in addition, they'll be more likely to make their quotas if they collaborate closely with the service lines and vertical business units.

The ever tighter integration of Wipro's three organizations is paying off. For instance, in mid-2005, the company reorganized its go-to-market strategy for the BPO service line. Previously, it had been independent, with its own salesforce. But, that July, the BPO salesforce was merged into the main salesforce. Not only did the global salesforce start selling BPO alongside other services, but it actually started in some cases leading with the BPO pitch. The idea was that if they could win a customer with the BPO services, they had a good chance of later getting additional contracts for writing new software programs to support improvements in the business processes. Thanks to these shifts, the BPO business landed six new customers in the second half of the year. That compared to just seven customer wins in the entire previous year.

This BPO move fits hand in glove with Wipro's major strategic goal of penetrating deeper into the accounts where it has already established a foothold. The rationale is it's much cheaper to sell more services to customers who already know and like you than to find new customers who may still not understand the Indian proposition. Wipro aims to sell each customer more kinds of services and to go deeper within each service line. To do so, the Wipro people who work closest with each client do rigorous assessments of the customer's business, its use of technology, and the likelihood that it will seek additional outsourced services. This information is fed into Wipro's computerized planning systems, where the company keeps close track of its current business with each client and new business opportunities.

One of the keys to Wipro's success is how well it integrates its capabilities and presents itself to its customers. Some of the business units have created hybrid sales and service delivery people who combine business development and ongoing service roles. An example is John Hackmann, an Anglo-American who is a strategic relations/program director addressing the capital markets business of a European-based investment bank. He's both a salesperson and a service program director. He has played both roles, separately, when working for other tech companies over the years. For Wipro, he's the primary liaison to the customer. He has a program director counterpart in India who arranges to send employees to work on site at the bank—under Hackmann's supervision—and also supervises any work that is done for the client in India. Part of Hackmann's role is to understand the bank's business, its budgets, and its priorities—and help it reduce its multibillion-dollar annual IT budget.

Hackmann's job is strikingly different from most traditional sales jobs. "You are responsible end to end," says Hackmann. "A salesman often doesn't know the technical ins and outs, and isn't responsible for the end results. A traditional salesman can make promises and walk away. I can't walk away."

Another way Wipro integrates its pieces for customers is through consulting. In fact, consulting services is the newest of its service lines, organized in 2004. The idea was to use consulting to showcase Wipro's broad array of services, including BPO. "We're the marines who can help spearhead an operation and then bring in the army behind us," says Sanjay Joshi, the co-chief of Wipro Global Consulting, who was formerly a senior consultant at McKinsey & Company. Previously, the company had added consultants to several of its verticals, and had about 200 consultants of this type at the beginning of 2006. Later it decided to create a separate consulting organization as well. The independent consulting outfit is small, with fewer than 75 professionals.

It operates quite differently than the traditional Wipro business model—where customers ask Wipro to complete well-defined tasks and its engineers go back to their cubicles and do the work. In consulting, 90 percent of the work comes out of discussions with clients about problems they are facing. Typically, small consulting teams consist of three to five people, including some experts pulled from the verticals and service lines. Wipro doesn't do corporate strategy consulting. It's all about helping clients achieve operational excellence in IT or business processes. "It may not seem glamorous, but we don't fall for glam easily. And what people want most is improvements to their operations," says Joshi.

While Wipro's organizations constantly interact and coordinate with one another, Premji also encourages independent thought and actions. He treats each of the company's three strategic business units like mini-Wipros. The leaders of the businesses have profit and loss responsibility. They have to come up with a strategy, hire and promote executives, and decide what training to give their people.

To get a clearer idea of how these businesses operate, consider the Finance Solutions vertical. When Girish Paranjpe took over as president in 2000, the business unit had just 1,000 employees and $50 million in annual revenues. At the conclusion of the fiscal year ended in March 2006, it had nearly 6,000 employees and $350 million in revenues. When Paranjpe took over the unit, the company was struggling in its effort to line up capital markets clients. To gain expertise rapidly, Paranjpe took risks. He hired some top Wall Street talent and bought a boutique Boston consulting company that focused on financial services. Neither the hires nor the acquisition worked out as well as he had hoped, but they helped deepen Wipro's knowledge of an industry in ways that paid off almost immediately. As a result, the capital markets piece of his business grew fast, and it now accounts for 40 percent of Paranjpe's revenues. "You have to be entrepreneurial," he says. "The strategy grows from the ground up. I get advice from corporate people, but they don't tell me what to do. In the end, it's my call."

The Wipro organization chart looks a bit like a patchwork quilt, but the organization works. As chairman, Premji oversees the company's subsidiaries, including information technology, the consumer care unit, the hydraulics manufacturing unit, and the Wipro GE

The Key Players in Wipro's Technology Business

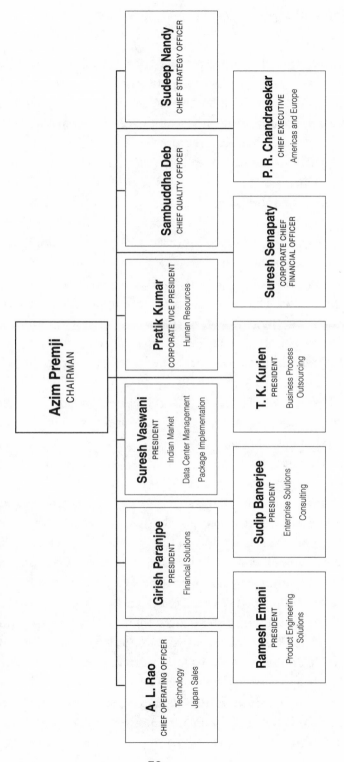

Medical Systems joint venture. Technology, however, is the core business. The chart on page 53 shows how responsibilities in the tech business are carved up among the company's top 10 tech and corporate executives. Suresh Vaswani oversees not just the Indian and South Asia geographical regions but two of the horizontal service lines: software package implementation and infrastructure management. Chief operating officer A. L. Rao oversees overall technology development plus sales in Japan. Another point worth noting: chief quality officer Sambuddha Deb reports directly to Premji. This arrangement signals the importance the chairman gives to quality and operational excellence.

A key element of Wipro's management structure is the IT Strategy Council. It's the high-level committee where the company's entire technology business comes together. The council handles strategic planning, and it gives the thumbs-up or thumbs-down on major new initiatives that require large investments and significant risks. It typically meets once every three months and includes Premji, the five business unit leaders, the chief strategy officer, and the heads of marketing, overseas sales, and consulting. A second group, the IT Management Council, made up of Premji and the tech business unit leaders, meets every three to four weeks to consider shorter-term operational and tactical issues.

Wipro's organizational structure and management philosophy produce a company that is cohesive and, at the same time, more entrepreneurial than you would expect of a services company of its size and maturity. The structure is complex. The relationships are multifaceted. It helps a lot that many of Wipro's executives have been with the company for many years and have played a variety of different roles—so they know each other, and each other's jobs, very well. "We think about streamlining. Is there a way we could make it better? But we haven't been able to come up with anything. It works pretty well," says P. R. Chandrasekar, chief executive for the Americas and Europe. That's a testament as much to Wipro's leaders as it is to the mechanics of the organization. But put them both together, and you have a powerful model for a collaborative corporation.

Go Deep to Address Specific Industries

In the late 1990s, many tech industry leaders started to recognize that when it came to their customers, one size didn't fit all. Sure there were commodity products that would be widely used—such as desktop computers and powerful server computers. But when it came to software and services, the better the tech company understood its customers and sculpted offerings for the customers' particular needs, the better off everybody would be. Thus began the era of verticalization. Software companies began creating industry-specific versions of their software packages, and services companies began to create industry-specific groups of services.

Wipro's global technology business was the first Indian services outfit to go vertical, and it was among the first worldwide. The initiative started off in 1999—think of it as Vertical *Lite*. It was mostly about organizing the salesforce along industry lines. But, before long, the company began rebuilding itself fundamentally to address industries. The first ones were financial services, retail, utilities, manufacturing, telecommunications, and high tech. But as its knowledge of industries grows, and as it adds capabilities, the number of verticals addressed grows too—currently, the number is 16. These are the vertical businesses that are divided up among the three strategic business units.

Wipro has created subverticals within these 16 categories. Each is treated as a separate business, with its own profit and loss tracking. For example, manufacturing, within the Enterprise Solutions unit, has five subverticals: automotive and avionics, chemicals and pharmaceuticals, high-tech, industrial and general manufacturing, and process industry. "The degree of focus and specialization goes deeper and deeper, and there is scope to go deeper still," says Sudip Nandy, the company's chief strategy officer.

How deep does Wipro go? Pretty darned deep. One aspect of depth is the technology itself. Different industries require different kinds of technology expertise—everything from Radio Frequency Identification (RFID) tags for tracking inventory in the retail business to highly specialized chip design for the computer games industry. In the RFID realm, Wipro went so far as to set up its own employee stores with RFID technology. Each item of merchandise was implanted with an RFID tag—a small chip that transmits a radio signal. If employees wanted to know if a certain item was in stock, they'd be able to check a computer and get the answer, plus be directed to what shelf the item was on. Wipro not only got a wealth of knowledge from this experiment, but it also got a tremendous marketing tool for prospective retail customers visiting its Bangalore campuses.

A lot of this is cutting-edge stuff. For instance, a California startup came to Wipro asking it to design a "physics chip" that could be used in computer gaming. To make games more realistic, the startup wanted a chip that could assess the impact of physical things on each other within the game and provide instructions, on the fly, on how to express those impacts graphically. For instance, how would debris fly if a bullet hit a wall? Wipro did the job, allowing its client to concentrate on marketing the chip to the makers of PC graphics accelerator cards and to game software makers so they'd design games to include this kind of realism.

The ultimate expression of Wipro's strategy is to package up technologies into an industry-specific solution and offer the solution as a managed service. That's what it aims to do with its Data Synchronization solution for the retail industry. While doing programming jobs for consumer goods manufacturers and retailers who distribute their products, Wipro's engineers came face-to-face with one of underlying problems in retailing: Handoffs of information about merchandise were often faulty. In particular, there was a lot of difficulty in matching purchase orders and invoices. Overall, 60 percent of such invoices have errors on them, and 30 percent of product and part catalogs have at least some incorrect model or part numbers, according to research by management consultant A.T. Kearney. These kinds of errors cost industry more than $40 billion a year in inefficiencies and lost sales.

In 2002, a solution started to present itself. A number of industry organizations had begun to publish technology and terminology standards that could be used in common by manufacturers, distributors, and retailers. Wipro saw the opportunity to create a suite of software products that would help retailers create new systems of organizing and tracking their inventories and communicate more accurately with the suppliers. In addition, it would prepare them for a time when technology and terminology standards became more widely adopted. An essential element of the package was software that would create an interface between a retailer's merchandising, planning, and inventory tracking software applications, and those of its suppliers. Wipro's initial offer—taken up by a number of retailers—was to sell the service of implementing its Data Synchronization software package. The next step is much more ambitious. Wipro plans on offering retailers the option of subscribing to a data synchronization service. For each supplier with whom a retailer wants to synchronize, Wipro will handle setting up and maintaining the connections, and customers will pay on a per-transaction basis.

But vertical specialization isn't just about technology and service solutions. Wipro has hired specialists in all sorts of roles, from consulting to project management. They're steeped in industry knowledge and are so familiar with their customers' strategy and competitive position that they can give smart advice about how best to use technology to improve their performance. In addition, Wipro gives employees who work in the verticals specialized training. Every employee of a given vertical business line is required to take a short course in all of the business aspects of that industry within six months of being hired. Project managers take more specialized and advanced-level courses. An entering employee will take a financial services course, for instance. Someone requiring more detailed knowledge will follow up with an insurance course and then, perhaps, a life insurance course. Even basic software programmers take these courses. "We have to teach programmers about their industries. Otherwise they're blind to what they're doing," says Selvan Dorairaj, Wipro's vice president for talent transformation and staffing.

The idea, ultimately, is to be so close to clients and their businesses that they begin to see Wipro as a partner in arms. This strategy is still in the early stages. Paranjpe, head of the Finance Solutions division, uses face-to-face human relationships to foster Wipro-to-client bonding. In late 2003, he created the concept of the client engagement manager for key accounts. Each client engagement manager is responsible not just for communicating with the client but for managing an integrated team of Wipro employees. This includes Wipro people working in the client's offices, the service delivery people in India, plus any consultants on the case. In a sense, the client engagement manager is the CEO of a virtual company. Each has a profit and loss responsibility. Their compensation is based on meeting revenue and profit goals. For one U.K. insurance client, Wipro's business went from zero to $50 million a year in two years, and it now has more than 600 people dedicated to the account. By early 2006, Finance Solutions had seven client relationship managers. It aims to eventually have a dozen or so client relationships built on this model.

One of the rewards of the verticalization strategy is it cushions Wipro against cyclical demand swings in particular industries. While, broadly speaking, each of its verticals has done well, some have weak quarters, and a few, telecommunications among them, have had years of relative weakness. By serving so many industries, Wipro's global technology business gets one of the benefits of being a conglomerate without actually being a conglomerate.

Breadth and depth. It's Wipro's one-two punch. The beauty of the company's strategy is that it can expand in both dimensions incrementally, yet achieve superior revenue growth overall. At the same time, it has relatively low risk of failure.

4

GROWTH: KEEP A THOUSAND FIRES BURNING

To keep up a healthy revenue growth, Wipro continuously places bets on new businesses and new geographical markets, and penetrates ever deeper into industries and geographies. Premji has adopted and modified a rule of thumb for deciding whether to be in a business, one developed by Jack Welch, ex-CEO of General Electric. Welch decided that GE would enter or stay in a business if it could be number one or number two. Premji is a little less stringent. He'll enter a new market—or expand more aggressively—if Wipro has a chance to rank in the top three over the long haul. He has to see the potential for long-term revenue growth rates of at least 20 percent per year. And he wants to be able to match Wipro's operating profits, which typically are in the 20 percent-plus range.

Since Wipro is in services, it's difficult to grow as fast as a traditional software products company. It typically sells a relatively narrow set of products in relatively high volumes, and it gets most of its money up front. Wipro and its Indian tech brethren have to do a long courtship with customers, customize their offerings for each one, and then staff up to do the job. That makes their ability to achieve outstanding revenue growth all the more impressive.

How to Expand Fast without Stumbling

Rather than placing one or two big, risky bets at a time, Wipro, like many companies, places many bets of different sizes. It approaches market expansion the way it constantly improves its own business processes through its quality and operational excellence programs. Victory is won by making many incremental improvements, continuously, all over the place. In this way, Wipro grows rapidly even while it keeps its risks low. In early 2006, the company was expanding operations in Canada, Germany, France, Eastern Europe, the Middle East, and China. It was investing in consulting, infrastructure outsourcing, and data security practices, among a slew of others. In addition, it was making one relatively small acquisition after another.

The company's expansion strategy for Europe shows how it's done. Wipro was one of the first Indian tech services companies to establish a foothold in Western Europe, in the early 2000s. But it had concentrated most of its resources in the United Kingdom, where companies were quicker to adopt outsourcing in general and offshoring of work to India in particular. Having knowledge of English was an advantage. The new targets for expansion were Germany, France, the Benelux countries, and the Nordic countries. Large corporations in those countries tended to have expensive local workforces, and they were under pressure from leaner U.S. and U.K. competitors to reduce costs. To satisfy the needs of those corporations from the European continent, Wipro had to modify its usually ultralean staffing model and place more employees near its prospective customers. P. R. Chandrasekar, in his capacity as the chief executive for the Americas and Europe, added staff in Munich and Düsseldorf, in Sweden, and in Paris. In the past, Wipro served many customers by parachuting in staffers from India for short stints. Now it's clustering people in its key markets—seeking to create critical masses of sales, sales support, service delivery, and consulting people. In continental Europe, Wipro and the other Indian services outfits lose the advantage of having English as their country's second language. So Wipro is also training software programmers in Bangalore in French and German, and lining up continental translation agencies for massive, long-term engagements. Plus, it has engaged language translation agencies in Europe to do large amounts of document translation work.

The linchpin of its European push has been opening a large service delivery center in Bucharest, Romania. Wipro shopped around for months, sizing up Prague, Budapest, and cities in Russia. It chose Romania for its strong tech workforce, low labor costs (just a bit higher than India), and the availability of multilingual employees. Once Premji okayed the plan, in October 2005, Chandrasekar and the service line chiefs moved quickly.

There's a fundamental rule of engagement at Wipro: Move ahead in measured steps. You build a foundation, watch for demand, and quickly respond to it. China is a case in point. While other Indian tech companies have announced huge and rapid expansion plans there, Wipro has not—yet. As of mid-2006, it had established two offices, in Beijing and Shanghai, with a combined staff of 60, primarily to serve multinational customers with whom it already has relationships. Wipro believes that China will be a difficult market in which to build a strong services business. That's because of the shortage of people with English-speaking skills, the high costs, and the high attrition rates—much higher than attrition in India.

This decision to go slow was made in late 2005, and it wasn't taken lightly. "We had a lot of debate. Some people wanted to ramp up right now. They wanted to have a leap of faith," says Ramesh Emani, president of the Product Engineering Services division. "In the end, we decided to grow organically, in response to demand. We didn't want to dramatically scale immediately."

Because Wipro is constantly watching so many different markets, there's always something happening—an opportunity, a decision, an investment. If it's able to put the right foundation pieces in place in China, correctly calibrate demand, and respond quickly when it emerges, its cautious approach will look mighty smart half a decade from now. The key, overall, is to make a lot of right moves, big and small, and keep the whole thing moving ahead at a healthy pace.

Fill in the Gaps

Wipro spots new opportunities for services by constantly looking for gaps between what it offers and what customers are asking for. Think of this as fill-in growth. A lot of the ideas for fill-in services come from the grassroots—its employees. For example, the company's Product Engineering Services unit in 2006 got clearance from Premji to spend $3 million on a chip testing lab. Previously, when Wipro designed a chip for a client, it would send the designs to a foundry to be manufactured in test quantities. Then it would send the chips to one of several specialized chip testing shops in India or Taiwan. Testing could add three months to the development process.

By testing the chips itself, Wipro can knock two months off the process. Time-pressed customers appreciate that time savings, plus Wipro gains by charging for the service. The idea bubbled up from a team of five people in the chip design unit. As a result, Wipro hopes to have created a new $30-million-a-year business within three years. Now, a $3 million investment isn't a lot of money. But the rule at Wipro is to spend wisely—even the small amounts. Also, the goal is to make sure the potential rewards are worth the effort and they're likely to be achieved.

Redefine Established Markets

Often, Wipro is able to create sizable new businesses for itself by changing the rules of the game in well-established markets. That's the case in tech infrastructure services—which is monitoring and maintaining the whole array of computing devices and networks and software applications. The traditional outsourcing model, established by American services outfits, was for a tech services company to buy a client's hardware and software and take over their staffs of techies, then figure out ways of cutting costs. It's commonly called "your mess for less."

Wipro does things differently. When it expanded into global technology outsourcing, starting in the early 2000s, it didn't want to commit capital for the old way of doing business. Nor did it want to employ thousands of people within clients' offices thousands of miles away from India. So it began offering outsourcing services a different way. Within its technology infrastructure management business, it doesn't buy the gear. Clients remain in charge of strategy and purchasing decisions, so they retain control over their technology fate. It's a situation that suits many clients who felt they gave up too much control to traditional IT outsourcers in the 1990s. So that takes care of the capital side of the equation. On the staffing side, Wipro has created a portfolio of automated monitoring and maintenance software and process that allow it to perform 90 percent of the work from India and only 10 percent on-site.

Customers were wary at first. They didn't think sprawling and complex computing systems could be managed from India. They were nervous about handing minute-by-minute control over their data centers to people 12,000 miles away. And they worried about security. One by one, Wipro dealt with their concerns. It demonstrated basic competence, showed how its remote monitoring and management tools made long-distance services feasible, and, for those who were most concerned about security, set up separate offices within the Wipro campuses for each client.

The financial results for clients are quite impressive. Wipro has been able to deliver initial cost savings for customers of 25 to 30 percent. One Wall Street client achieved a 50 percent savings. But the Wipro advantage isn't just measured in monthly billings. It's about quality of services as well. Here's a before-and-after comparison of one Wipro infrastructure services engagement—laying out both quantitative and qualitative improvements.

Attribute	Before	After
Nature of team	Not dedicated to these tasks	Dedicated
Location of team	On-site	On-site and in India
Time coverage	Partial, weekdays	24/7
Computer uptime	Not defined	99.8% for critical systems
Feedback	Random, infrequent	Monthly, from all users
Cost to client		Savings of 30%

Wipro's own financial results for this business are just as impressive as those of its customers. Between 2000 and 2005, revenues for the infrastructure outsourcing business outside of India grew at an average compounded rate of 62 percent, hitting nearly $100 million in fiscal 2005. It built up a staff of 2,700 people, and lined up more than 140 customers. The business unit's advanced remote-management techniques have landed many first-time Wipro customers, which provides an entrée for Wipro to sell them additional services. And sweetest of all, it's a very profitable business with operating margins slightly higher than the healthy mid-20s margins achieved by its software development business.

Future prospects are bright too. NASSCOM, the Indian software and services trade group, estimates there's a potential $55 billion market for infrastructure services delivered remotely. "We're going into a big ocean with a teaspoon," says G. K. Prasanna, vice president in charge of Wipro's global infrastructure services group. "Our opportunity isn't limited by the market size. It's only limited by how many people I can hire and train, and how many centers I can open."

Wipro's efforts have earned it recognition as one of the top providers of remote infrastructure services. In a 2005 study, Forrester Research, one of the leading tech industry market research outfits, listed it among the top 10 global players in this category. Forrester noted that while Wipro is ahead of its Indian competitors, it needed to beef up automation. It was relying too much on labor arbitrage. Wipro took the message seriously. In late 2005 it upgraded the capabilities of its Global Command Centre in Bangalore. Many of the improvements were aimed at improving security measures. For instance, a "password vault system" automates the process of providing or changing passwords for a client's computer users, and it prevents Wipro technicians from actually seeing temporary or permanent passwords.

While this business is really clicking now, Wipro doesn't limit itself to just one way of providing services. Starting in mid-2004 some customers began asking the company to offer a wider array of IT outsourcing services in a package—including taking over their IT staffs and buying and managing their computer equipment. So Wipro launched a new business, called Total Outsourcing Services, in India. In late 2005, after proving it could succeed with the business model, it decided to begin offering the service in the United States and Europe. "We were missing out on one segment of the market," says Anand Sankaran, vice president of Total Outsourcing Services. "Now we're able to participate in much bigger deals."

Still, Wipro's version of total outsourcing services isn't a carbon copy of the traditional model. For example, rather than building up large, on-site workforces in clients' offices, it's keeping staffing lean and tapping into local partners to provide most of the hands-on services.

Mergers: The String of Pearls Strategy

Mergers are one of the fastest ways to get big fast. Wipro does acquisitions judiciously and keeps them small. "You do a string of pearls, not a big bang," says Emani. That's a wise approach, since many analyses have been done showing that most big acquisitions fail to pay off for shareholders.

Wipro's most important acquisition was Spectramind, one of the pioneers of India's call center outsourcing industry. In 2002, Wipro paid about $100 million for the company, which had 2,700 employees in Delhi and Mumbai. The decision was to buy its way into the

BPO realm rather than trying to build its own organization from scratch. It was quite an unusual move for Wipro, which usually builds its core businesses organically. In the next three years, Wipro's BPO unit grew to become nearly 10 percent of revenues. In mid-2005, the Spectramind founder, Raman Roy, and a handful of his top lieutenants, quit to form a new company. Fortunately, Wipro has a deep bench. Premji promoted one of its own to run the service line: T. K. Kurien, then a seven-year Wipro veteran. Kurien had previously been chief financial officer of Wipro GE Medical Systems. He settled on a strategy of building up the transactional BPO sector—running corporate back-shop operations such as accounting and travel expensing.

Wipro made a handful of small acquisitions to help get a foothold in the North American IT consulting business. The key one was paying $19 million for NerveWire Inc., a boutique financial services firm, with about 90 consultants, in Newton, Massachusetts. The idea was to gain expertise in financial industry consulting. That part worked. But, while several of the managers did well at Wipro, many of the consultants quit—apparently over concerns about working for a little-known Indian company. By late 2005, only about 25 percent of the NerveWire consultants had stuck with it. "Now we focus on organic hiring of American consultants," says Wipro's Financial Solutions head Pranajpe, who was the architect of the merger.

One of Wipro's core skills is to learn from its mistakes. The big lesson that former vice chairman Vivek Paul took away from the consultancy acquisitions was that, for Wipro, at least, the old style of assigning a large number of consultants to work directly with each client would not work. Instead, Wipro would employ a thin layer of consultants but rely on its other services as its money makers. Once it got into the consulting business, it saw that the activity provided only about 10 percent operating margins. Meanwhile, operating margins in software development were in the mid to high twenties. So, in the future, consulting would be an ingredient for Wipro, but not a large business on its own.

In late 2005 and early 2006, after a two-year hiatus, Wipro fired up its mergers and acquisitions (M&A) activity again. It had the means, with $800 million of cash in the bank and a richly valued stock. The plan was to focus on small strategic deals that would add expertise and intellectual property, help open new markets, or enhance service lines. A prime example of its strategy was its December 2005 purchase of NewLogic, for $56 million. The Austrian company was a leader in semiconductor design services for complex wireless applications such as wireless computer networks. In the deal, Wipro got 120 engineers, 20 customers, and 25 core technology patents. Just two days later, Wipro agreed to pay $28 million for mPower Inc., a Princeton, New Jersey–based company that provided payment services for banks out of facilities in Chennai, in India. mPower also ran a joint venture with MasterCard International to provide payment processing services. Wipro's plan was to use this merger as a foundation for selling financial services clients application development, infrastructure services, package implementation, BPO, and software testing. In February 2006, it paid $20 million for cMango Inc. of Sunnyvale, California, to strengthen its tech infrastructure services capabilities.

In March 2006, Premji anticipated that Wipro would have to make another 8 to 10 acquisitions in the following 12 months. "As we made these acquisitions, we gained a higher degree of faith in ourselves," he said. "You do one, and you succeed with the integration. Then it feeds on itself. It gives us the confidence to do many more."

Premji's Pet Projects

When you ask Premji what was the biggest mistake he made in his business career, the answer comes quickly: overdiversification. He fell prey to a 1970s fad. One disappointment that stands out was the company's entry into the industrial finance market. It provided capital for customers who were buying equipment or building factories. That adventure ended with a whimper after five years of struggle. Few of his forays have been complete disasters, though. And several have done quite well, though they account for only a sliver of the company's revenues. "The global IT business is 90 percent of the company. The other 10 percent is my hobby," says Premji. "It's fun. I spend maybe 10 days a year on it—the consumer part. It produces some excellent people for us in finance, logistics, and branding."

The largest of the nontech pieces is Wipro Consumer Care and Lighting. It sells a wide array of consumer products in India, including toilet soaps, hair care soaps, cooking oil, baby care products, and lighting products. The business is profitable, and Premji appreciates the extra revenues. He also cross-pollinates between his consumer and tech organizations. For instance, branding has never been a strong suit in the tech business. By and large, it's an engineering-dominated organization with a tin ear for marketing. But Premji is determined to change that. To train and sensitize its techies, the company has included a section on consumer branding in its Business Leadership program—a short course designed for promising managers.

Even more promising, longer term, is Wipro Infrastructure Engineering. It's the business Premji established in 1976 that manufactures hydraulic cylinders and other precisions components for use in construction equipment and industrial plants. It dominates the Indian market, with a 44 percent share. With India's economy booming and construction taking off, the business is growing at 40 percent per year, even faster than Wipro's overall growth rate. Now, it's starting to distribute components for use in overseas markets. Premji believes the business can be a global leader over time, following in the footsteps of his info tech business.

Only the Paranoid Thrive

Where will Wipro's path take it? There's certainly no restraint on its ambitions. Executives there talk about what it's going to take to turn the company into a $10 billion global business someday. While its sheer size now means it won't have the astronomic revenue growth rates of the past, there's still a big, long ramp for Wipro not only in its core tech services but in BPO. In fact, the marriage of technology and business processes could be the key to the company's future. Both skill sets take it ever deeper into its customers' businesses. And they reinforce each other. Over the long haul, BPO will be less and less of a manual labor business and more about technology automation and the science of recrafting operations.

There's plenty of mileage left in shifting jobs to India. Premji believes that labor arbitrage will continue to be a significant advantage for Wipro and its Indian companions for a long period of time. It's simple math. If the salary for an Indian engineering graduate grows at the current average of 12 percent per year from a base of $7,500 in 2005, while Western engineering salaries rise an average of 2 percent per year from a base of $60,000, then it will take more than 20 years for the salary level in India to catch up. He points out that the cost of living in India is determined not by the supply and demand characteristics of the 1 million tech industry employees, but by the economics of the entire 1.2 billion population.

Still, there's no complacency at Wipro. The company has adopted the philosophy of Andy Grove, the longtime chief executive at American chip giant Intel Corporation, who declared that, in the tech industry, "only the paranoid survive." Western tech services outfits are rapidly building up their own capabilities in India. That puts intense pressure on Wipro to continually refine its service delivery model so it offers just the right mix of Indian labor and on-site handholding. "We have a feeling that the platform we're on, offshoring, with price arbitrage, is a burning platform. It's only good for a few more years," says Chief Strategy Officer Sudip Nandy. "We need to do things differently to compete against international competition."

Wipro is perpetually in transition. Right now its focus is on stepping up from the role of low-cost IT service provider to that of highly valued advisor and business partner. It's like shifting from being an electrician to being an architect. The idea is not just to boost quality and lower costs for clients, but to help the company tune up its performance by analyzing its operations and helping it come up with improved processes, better use of information technology, and, in the case of Wipro's engineering R&D clients, better product development. "We're starting to sell transformation," says Nandy. If Wipro succeeds in this quest, it will increasingly compete with the likes of Accenture and IBM for mindshare of the executives at the world's largest corporations.

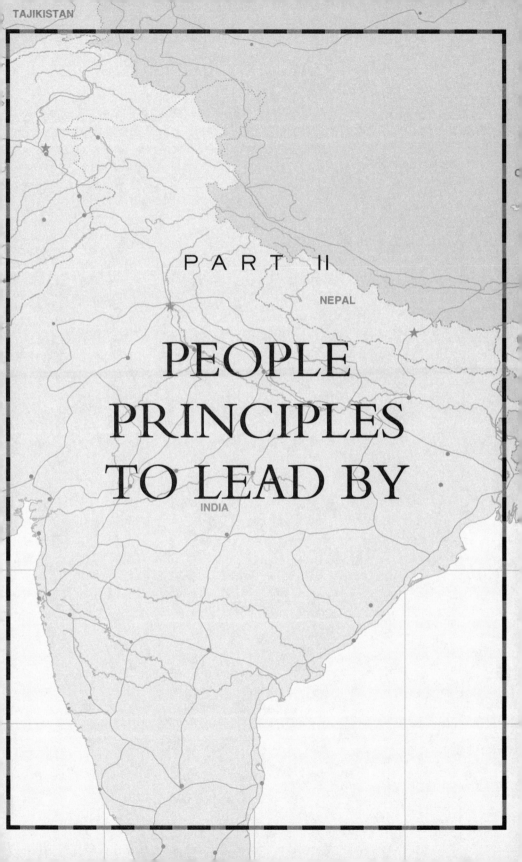

PART II

PEOPLE PRINCIPLES TO LEAD BY

5

ADOPT ULTRASTRICT ETHICS
TO BUILD A STERLING BRAND

Azim Premji tells a cautionary tale to illustrate the company's stand on business ethics. The story goes like this: Once, a Wipro employee traveled from Chennai to Bombay by train. Because of his rank, he was entitled to ride in the first-class compartment. But instead, he traveled second class. Yet when it came time to make an expense claim with the company, he improperly asked for compensation for a first-class ticket, so he could pocket a few rupees. The company found out and fired him. The man was a union member, and the union called a three-month strike in protest. Premji didn't back down. "At Wipro, there are no exceptions," says Premji. "And there is no price you're not willing to pay for doing the right thing."

Do Well by Doing the Right Thing

Where did this righteousness come from? Premji's mother is one source. Gulbanoo Premji was one of the first Moslem women to get a medical degree in India, and though she didn't practice medicine professionally, she was a person of stature in society. She set up a charitable hospital for children with polio and was involved with its governance from ages 30 to 75. When Premji returned from California to run the company in 1966, she gave him stern advice. He recalls her saying: "If you believe in something, stay with it. Don't waver. Honor your commitments. If you owe money to people, pay them. If you don't have enough money to pay them now, set up a schedule and pay over time." This advice turned out to be crucial during the first difficult months that Premji ran the company.

Since those early days, Premji has made values an essential part of Wipro's corporate culture. This topic is much bigger than business ethics. It's a broad set of beliefs about how the company and its employees should behave. Over the years, Premji and his executives have developed, refined, and codified the company's values. They have also produced simple statements of values that they want to be foremost in employees' minds when they're on the job. They're printed on the back of their business cards—a constant reminder to them and also something they show to clients, suppliers, and prospective employees. Here's the current one:

The Wipro Spirit
Intensity to Win
Act with Sensitivity
Unyielding Integrity

At Wipro, values aren't just empty platitudes that are framed on the wall, or once-a-year code-of-conduct statements that must be signed to collect a paycheck. They're living, breathing things. The company publishes its values and its detailed rules of conduct, it teaches them to employees, and it frequently issues reminders. And when people violate the rules, there are consequences. Premji sees values as a thread that weaves through and binds the organization— no matter how fast it grows or how far-flung are its operations. "It builds muscle tone in an organization. It builds pride. It gets better customers and suppliers," he says.

As business increasingly goes global and everybody trades with everybody else, values are going to become an essential element of every successful company's portfolio of assets. In many emerging global markets, commercial and governmental corruption are rampant. Yet these markets are where a lot of the growth opportunities lie, so the temptation is to play by local rules. Premji and Wipro show that it's possible to thrive even while refusing to play along. In fact, by setting and heeding a higher standard, a company can create an aura of righteousness around its brand. And righteousness is an extremely valuable brand attribute.

Early on, Premji saw that by insisting on ethical behavior from everyone in his organization, he could differentiate his company from the competition. And in those early, difficult days, his company needed all the help it could get. In the first two or three years, Premji fired several managers and laborers over ethical violations. Finally, people got the idea.

There's a potential financial downside to behaving ethically, of course. You risk losing some business opportunities. In the medical equipment market in India, for instance, some suppliers maintained hidden accounts for paying kickbacks to purchasers and winning their business, says Premji. The gimmick was to place bribes for doctors in offshore accounts. In spite of those practices by some competitors, Wipro GE Medical Systems, a joint venture of Wipro and General Electric, has achieved a 40 percent share of the medical equipment market in India.

There are some financial benefits to following strict ethics too. Think of corruption as a tax. If you don't pay bribes, you don't pay the tax. "Particularly in government, officials know how to prioritize their time," says Premji. "If they know a certain company is fanatical about this issue, they know it's not worth their time to fight this company. They'll get nowhere. Then you don't even get asked for bribes." Sometimes corrupt officials and businesspeople even make a point of handing some business to Wipro—just to give themselves protective cover.

Still, maintaining ethical standards requires constant vigilance. As recently as April 2005, a senior project manager was fired for violating the company's ethics guidelines. He claimed, incorrectly, that he had worked for a high-profile consulting firm before joining Wipro. The company's human resources department doesn't leave much to chance. It engages outside research firms to verify the information on job applications. In this case, the man's claim was found out, and, after confessing, he was fired. There was no delay, even though the man played a crucial role in a project Wipro was working on for a customer. Wipro notified the client, explained the situation, got its assent, and moved ahead.

How Wipro's Values Came to Be

In the mid-1970s, Premji decided to formalize the company's belief system. Wipro was still a tiny company, with 450 laborers and 75 white-collar staff at the factory, and a skeleton crew of 12 people, including Premji, at the headquarters in Bombay. But Premji had begun hiring formally trained managers out of the Indian Institute of Management, and as he began to diversify into new markets, he was hiring people from other companies. "We said we must be sure we stand for something as a company. We must be sure we know what we're looking for when we hire," he recalls. The company examined the ethics and values statements of high-profile companies worldwide and talked to business ethicists in academia. Group discussions were held within the company, drawing in not just managers but rank-and-file employees. "We asked, 'What do you think is true to us? What is the quest we should build the company around?'" Premji says.

Ultimately, they came up with a list of six Wipro beliefs:

1. Respect the individual.
2. Be a business leader.
3. Accomplish all tasks in a superior manner.
4. Maintain the highest ethical standards.
5. Serve customers well.
6. Measure performance based on long-term profitability.

Every few years, Premji would reexamine the company's beliefs. It was a way of engaging the management team and employees in an exercise that would put them in touch with one another on a fundamental level and force the entire organization to take stock.

By the late 1990s, the company Premji had taken over in 1966 had undergone a complete transformation and was suffering a bit of an identity crisis. Vegetable oil was less than half of the business. Tech was dominant. But Wipro was also selling everything from lightbulbs to facial soap. Meanwhile, it was hiring like mad—thousands of fresh-faced college graduate engineers with only the foggiest idea of what they were getting into. What was Wipro? What should it mean to employees? And what should it mean to customers and partners? Premji had hired a marketing consultancy, Shining Strategic Design (SSD), to improve one of his soap brands, but he later decided on a complete brand makeover.

SSD is run by Shombit Sengupta, a Bengali who had gone to Paris as a young painter in search of the bohemian life and who isn't afraid to shake up his clients. One of his first moves was to have a survey firm interview Indian customers about their opinions of Wipro. The news was not good. While people had positive views of Wipro's products, they saw the company itself as low-profile, cold, and hard to do business with. There was a lot to fix. Ultimately, a project that had begun as a brand touch-up would evolve into a major revamp of the company's brand and beliefs—a process that lasted for two years.

It was a massive effort. Externally, SSD performed a series of in-depth focus groups with people in each of India's regions. Then it held a series of discussions with the company's executives and came up with a proposal for a new brand identity. The idea was to develop a new values statement tied in with the new brand identity. Rather than being inwardly focused, as the earlier beliefs had been, it would encompass employees, customers, and business partners.

Much care was given to each element of the makeover. SSD proposed replacing the company's old logo, a large black W, with a multicolored flower, which the company calls a "rainbow flower." Each color in the new logo had a symbolic meaning—thoroughly vetted with customers. Yellow meant prosperity; blue, openness; and red, integrity. Sengupta even modified the petals of the flower when people in focus groups said they were too sharp. He wanted Wipro to seem soft and approachable. The tag line went through many iterations before they settled on "Applying Thought." As part of its effort to be seen as a global company, Wipro vetted its logo with

Western customers including Microsoft, Cisco Systems, and Allied Signal. The same level of scrutiny was used when it came to reworking the company's values statement.

The proposed changes were debated throughout the company. Some employees recoiled at the idea of changing the beliefs. Several members of the senior management team objected to the new logo and slogan. A flower didn't seem to them to be an appropriate symbol for a tech company. And they thought "Applying Thought" might give employees the idea that they could sit around all day thinking rather than getting things done. "The brand team had a harrowing time convincing top management," says Vineet Agrawal, now the president of Wipro Consumer Care and Lighting, who spearheaded the overhaul.

Even Premji balked at some of the changes that were proposed, and that caused a bit of drama. Anand Kumar, now a general manager in the BPO unit, recalls that the proposal was presented to Premji at a Thursday afternoon meeting that lasted until 10:30 p.m. "Premji was fuming—and even threatened to call off the whole project, stating that the beliefs were core to Wipro," Kumar recalls. The next day, Premji met with a small group of executives for breakfast. At the meeting, which took place at Premji's house, they laid out their rationale for all the changes. Premji went along with some, but he would not agree to one: the idea of dropping integrity as one of the company's values. Customers surveyed had expressed the opinion that Wipro's commitment to integrity went without saying. Premji disagreed. "Mr. Premji made the inclusion of integrity in the values nonnegotiable," says Agrawal.

The new code, renamed Wipro Values, had four pieces, as they were stated on Wipro's Web site:

1. *Human Values.* We respect the unique needs of customers and employees. We are sensitive to their differing needs in our interactions with them.
2. *Integrity.* We deliver what we commit. With honesty, fairness, reliability, and uprightness in whatever we do.

3. *Innovative Solutions.* We consistently offer novel and superior solutions to satisfy the needs of the customer.
4. *Value for Money.* Delivering higher value to the customer through continuous improvement in quality, cost, and speed.

The values were later boiled down into the Wipro Promise, a short and simple phrase that could be memorized easily and printed on the back of business cards. It said: "With utmost respect to Human Values, we promise to serve our customer with Integrity, through Innovative, Value for Money solutions, by Applying Thought, day after day." At the same time, Wipro launched a massive ad and marketing campaign to make the world aware of its new identity and values.

Don't Set the Way You Express Your Values in Stone

At Wipro, nothing stays the same for long. In late 2005 and early 2006, the company embarked on yet a third values exercise. "We're asking ourselves, Are we practicing it, are we true to it, have the circumstances changed?" says Premji. Indeed, a lot *had* changed. In 1998, the company had just 6,000 employees. At the beginning of 2006 there were 60,000. In 1998, it had just $444 million in revenues. For the fiscal year ended in March 2006, revenues topped $2.4 billion. The company is much more global than it was in 1998, and as a result of all of the boom-times hiring and the addition of call centers, the average age is dramatically lower, 25 compared to 35 back then. "It's an accelerated life cycle. We do a shift in five to seven years that most societies go through in 50 years," says Anurag Behar, who heads up Wipro's Values and Community Initiatives programs.

The latest values quest started off with a broad survey of employees. There were two lines of questioning. The first set was about the then-current values. Were they being practiced? Where they still relevant? The second set was about the future. If employees had a blank slate to write on, what should the company's values be for the years ahead? More than 28,000 employees responded to the survey, so Behar felt he got a good sense of the pulse of the organization. An outside research outfit then conducted 80 focus groups drawing on about 1,100 employees pulled from across the organization. It also did a series of one-on-one interviews with a smaller number of people. This resulted in a report to the executive team in November 2005. They discussed the matter in a series of meetings and finally came up with a proposal. But it wasn't until the end of January, after a thorough review by employees, that Wipro formally adopted its new values statement. Here it is:

Intensity to Win
- Make customers successful

- Excel through innovation and teamwork

Act with Sensitivity
- Respect the individual

- Be thoughtful and responsible

Unyielding Integrity
- Deliver on commitments

- Be honest and fair in action

- Conduct an unwavering search for truth

The leaders wanted to keep the new statement rooted in the values of the past. The statement hits hard on respect for employees and customers, and sensitivity to society and the natural environment. Yet they also wanted to signal Wipro's aspiration to play an ever larger role on the global stage, hence the "intensity to win" line. "The context of the company has changed. Customers and stakeholders expect new things from us. We have become significantly Westernized. We had to address those changes," says Premji.

All of this attention to values may seem a bit over the top to some Western readers. The tendency in the United States is to stick to the basics: make the product, advertise the product, sell the product, and when your brand needs some sprucing up, hire an outside expert to handle it. No icky navel gazing. Yet for Wipro, this focus on establishing a group identity, group values, and a common aspiration for the future is as essential as giving new employees desks, PCs, and telephones. These truly are values to live by. They also lead very concretely to goal and strategy setting. Each time Wipro has undertaken a values exercise, it has followed up with a visioning exercise. These visioning exercises meld the company's aspirations with detailed analyses of market opportunities and competitive dynamics to yield a set of ambitious growth goals for the following five years. In turn, each of those exercises funnels into the company's rolling three-year strategic planning process. So at Wipro, values aren't empty slogans dreamed up by the CEO and top execs at their annual golf-and-Chardonnay retreat. They're the lifeblood of the company.

The other top Indian tech services companies share Wipro's belief in the importance of fundamental corporate values. Infosys founder N. R. Narayana Murthy started his company in 1981 with $250 in cash and one customer. In June 2006, when he stepped down as the company's executive chairman, he reflected back on what had made it possible for the organization to grow to $2.5 billion in revenues and 52,000 employees. He never imagined in the early days that the company would come as far as it had, but he was certain of one thing from the beginning: Infosys' values.

He established those values at his very first meeting with the six people he invited to help start the company. During a meeting in his bedroom, they spent their first four hours together discussing what the company's primary goal would be. Would it be revenues, profits, or market capitalization? Finally, Murthy told his colleagues that it would be none of those things. The best path to success was for the company to seek respect from each of its stakeholders. "My view was if we sought respect, we'd automatically do the right things by each of them," he said. "We'd satisfy our customers, be fair to our employees, and follow the best principles with respect to investors. We wouldn't violate any laws, and finally, we'd make a difference to society. And I said if we did these things, automatically we'd get revenues and profits and all that."

When I interview the founders of Wipro, Infosys, and TCS, I sometimes get the feeling that I'm talking to members of a family of brothers who were separated at birth.

Make Values Part of the Daily Rhythm of the Company

When new employees start their jobs at Wipro, the first order of business is values training. The half-day session starts off with a series of videos: one on business ethics in general, a second showing Premji explaining the company's values, and the third laying out the process of reporting violations to the ethics ombudsman. To make sure recruits get the message, each one is required to read and sign a code of conduct, including rules on conflicts of interest, handling of intellectual property, privacy, and insider trading. Many of Wipro's new hires are in their early twenties, so the company engages them with an interactive computer game that tests their knowledge of the values and rules. They have to answer 15 questions. For each correct answer, a piece is placed into a jigsaw puzzle on the screen. They must answer at least 10 of the questions correctly to show they have absorbed the lesson.

The company slips refresher courses into many of its career training programs. When John Hackmann, an Anglo-American who works in the United Kingdom, participated in a management training program shortly after he joined Wipro in 2005, he was surprised to see the importance placed on ethics. It was the first session in a five-day program. He had previously worked at several tech companies, including American stalwarts Hewlett-Packard and NCR, both known for their attention to values and social responsibility. "It was an eye-opener," he says. "At another company you start off by talking about sales or financial performance."

The company posts ethics messages on the employee Web portals and sends out e-mails with reminders. These cover not only matters employees encounter in the normal course of doing their jobs, such as cheating on promotional tests, but also their behavior in the off-work hours. One example: Don't travel without a valid bus pass. In addition, the company posts extensive descriptions of dos and don'ts on the values page of the employee Web site. This is very detailed stuff. It includes warnings against keeping people waiting for appointments, and it cautions managers to refrain from criticizing subordinates in public.

In most Wipro offices there are "whistleblower" boxes. This is the most visible manifestation of the company's ethics ombudsman program. Employees are encouraged to drop notes in the boxes or send e-mails to the ombudsman when they see any of the many ethics rules and regulations being violated. For example, let's say that a team leader in the BPO operation circumvents steps in a regulatory compliance process to make the group's performance figures look better. That's a violation for the ombudsman to check out.

Does all this values stuff really get through to employees? Apparently so. Rudra Pratap, a 24-year-old support analyst in one of Wipro's software programming shops, calls the values program indispensable. "The values involve each of us," he says. "They come into play day in and day out in what we're doing. They make us try to do better."

Wipro doesn't stop at policing its own employees' behavior. It asks dealers in the domestic Indian tech market to sign a code of conduct as a condition of doing business. If a dealer does something improper and Wipro finds out, it can result in divorce. "We'll terminate them, no matter what the losses," says Suresh Vaswani, president of Wipro Infotech. If Wipro learns of ethical problems in a partner, customer, or even a government agency, it reports them to higher-ups. Vaswani, or even Premji, will pay a visit to the top people and ask them to take corrective action. As a result, Wipro's policies don't just keep its corner clean; they have impact throughout the world of business.

Reach Out beyond the Corporate Borders

Companies run social responsibility programs and rich people have their charities, but Azim Premji and Wipro go at it with considerably more intensity than most.

Wipro Cares, the corporation's social responsibility initiative, combines company money with employee volunteerism. It focuses on improving public education, safeguarding the environment, and responding to natural disasters. The education program provides training for teachers, administrators, and parents—with the goal of fostering more creative and analytical curricula in public schools, rather than rote learning. In an effort that targets underprivileged children, Wipro volunteers spend two hours every Saturday tutoring and encouraging these kids. Volunteers have contributed many thousands of hours to disaster relief. In October 2005, for instance, they were among a small army of people who planted 174,422 saplings along the shore of the Bay of Bengal to commemorate the loss of life in the South Asian tsunami and also to help restore the coastline.

When it comes to the environment, the company, once again, doesn't just mouth platitudes. Through conservation efforts on its campuses, it has reduced water consumption by 60 percent, food waste by 38 percent, and energy consumption by 10 percent.

The Azim Premji Foundation is an attempt to help transform Indian society through improving public education. Premji established the foundation in 2000 and it became operational in 2001. To date, he has contributed $125 million in Wipro stock—and has pledged to keep replenishing as money is spent. The main focus is on convincing educators that they need to retool their approach to education and on giving them the tools to do it. So far, one Indian state has agreed to switch to analytical learning. In a second program, the foundation has distributed curriculum-enriching computer CDs to 14,000 schools and trained 25,000 teachers how to integrate the material into courses.

In a sense, with his focus on social responsibility, Premji has come full circle from where he stood in the summer of 1966 when his father died. He had hoped to take his Stanford degree and go on to a career of helping people in developing nations. Well, that's just what he's doing. His detour to run a failing cooking oil company turned out not to be much of a detour at all, in the end. He's helping to lift India. "What we're focused on is quality education," says Dileep Ranjekar, a former head of HR who is now CEO of the Azim Premji Foundation, Premji's charity. "Unless India fundamentally addresses the quality issue and shifts from rote learning to analytical learning, it can't realize its dream of becoming one of the world economic superpowers."

There's obviously a crucial side benefit for Wipro. Unless the Indian public education system improves dramatically, Wipro won't be able to fulfill what it sees as its destiny—becoming one of the world's great companies by offering up India's brainpower to the world.

6

EDUCATE NEW HIRES AND
HOLD ONGOING TRAINING

There are some distinct advantages to being in a service business. Relationships with customers tend to be close-knit. Revenues typically come in a steady, predictable flow. But the downside is that it's a people-intensive enterprise. When you grow, you have to add people. And if you grow really fast, like Wipro, you have to add a lot of people all the time. Wipro global tech business added about 14,000 people in the fiscal year ending in March 2006. So how is Wipro able to grow its workforce so fast without stumbling? "It's our strong emphasis on process," says Premji. "We have made recruitment, induction, and training into core competencies." Indeed, Wipro has turned HR into something approaching a science—yet without making people feel like they're cogs in some huge, churning machine.

Most Western companies aren't growing fast enough to face the hiring and training challenges Wipro handles as a matter of routine. They're adding people slowly—if not paring back. But for Western managers, Wipro still offers lessons on how to orient new hires to their jobs and provide them with continuous performance-enhancing learning. And for rapidly expanding companies in emerging markets, Wipro provides a blueprint for how to get big, fast.

The Wipro Brain Transplant

There's no simple way to sum up how Wipro works, peoplewise. None of the usual metaphors tells the whole story. To some extent, it's like a giant ant colony. You have swarms of people, split off in small groups, working away furiously on a thousand projects. It's also a bit like a factory production line. A lot of the work is broken down into chunks, organized as a process, and results in finished products whose quality is closely monitored. It's like a university. Bright people are brought in and provided with a course of study that gradually turns them into experts and life learners. But it's also like a pressure cooker. The heat is turned up, and the steam is blowing out the top.

With all of those demands, pulls, and pressures, it's not easy to be a Wipro employee or manager. Some smart people just aren't cut out for it. They're better off somewhere else. Others have the right combination of skills, smarts, discipline, and ability to work well with others. But even they don't just come off the street and go right to work for Wipro. New college graduates, called "freshers" in Bangalore, go through up to five months of orientation and training before they start their regular jobs. And even experienced recruits are typically reoriented and retrained to some extent.

Going to work at Wipro requires something akin to a brain transplant. Everybody is expected to adopt the values, soak up the culture, follow the established work processes, and write software or design circuits the Wipro way. "You hire bright people who are amenable to your culture. They don't have bad habits in software coding and work style. You can mold them in the way you want," says Ramesh Emani, head of Product Engineering Services. "Our philosophy is you don't expect to get people already trained. You have to train them at every level."

In fact, youngsters who go to work for Wipro right out of college get a second education that prepares them to succeed in a global information-centric corporation. The company has identified 24 "competencies" that are essential for individuals and the company, which it teaches to employees. The list is as instructive as it is long, including initiative, persuasiveness, problem solving, customer service orientation, delegation, developing staff, specialist knowledge, innovation, interpersonal sensitivity, teamwork, self-confidence, relationship building, integrity, flexibility, cross-cultural awareness, decisiveness, and global thinking. In addition to being taught in Wipro's training courses, these competencies are the basis for part of the company's performance appraisal system. In annual reviews, employees are rated on a 1-to-5 scale in each competency that's particularly relevant to their job and then given the tools to improve their performance.

It's a stretch-goal culture. Wipro believes in giving people the basic technical and social skills they need—then asking a lot of them. "It stems from a basic philosophy," says HR director Pratik Kumar. "You grow on the strength of the people you have. If you give the right training and show them a big challenge, giving them a job when they're 70 percent ready, then, 9 times out of 10, they'll rise to the challenge and deliver."

One of the keys to Wipro's success in human resources is the importance that Premji places on it. Kumar reports directly to him rather than to a COO or chief administrative officer—like you'd see in many other companies. Kumar says Premji actually spends more time on HR matters than he does on finance. He participates in many of the training programs for managers. When people throughout the organization see how seriously Premji treats HR, they take it very seriously themselves.

Wipro has long had strong training programs, but things really took off in the early 2000s. It was partly out of necessity. Because of rapid growth in demand for services, it had to hire and train thousands of employees per year. But another factor was the arrival of an inventive manager, Selvan Dorairaj, as vice president in charge of training. He had previously run one of Wipro's vertical industry business units, and before that, he had been one of the leaders of the company's Six Sigma quality initiative. At the time, Wipro offered only technical training—and just eight weeks for freshers. As a former business unit leader, Dorairaj saw that a lot more had to be done to prepare employees to work effectively in teams on large, complex, global projects. As a Six Sigma "black belt," he was tuned into the value of listening to customer feedback to identify defects in a business process. So in 2002, he invited in 300 Wipro line managers to get their ideas on how training should be changed.

The result was a more holistic view of what training could be. It's not just technical but professional and behavioral, and not just initial but continual. Dorairaj introduced "talent transformation" as the company's guiding concept. Since then, the HR department has built up a massive infrastructure of classrooms, courses, and curricula for career-long and career-enriching learning. It has 120 full-time faculty members, many with doctorates. On any given day, the company can train 5,000 people, if all of the seats in its e-learning and classroom training centers are put to use.

Wipro's training programs match or beat what's available at most other companies, in any country and in any industry. The company was a winner of the BEST Award from the American Society for Training and Development in 2004 and 2005.

Recruiting with a Vacuum Hose

When you hire more than 10,000 people a year, you need to have a strong methodology or you'll go nuts—not to mention, fail. About half of Wipro's hires each year come from college campuses. The other half are "laterals," people hired from other companies with in-demand technical or management skills. Because there's so much competition among India's 500 tech companies for the brightest college prospects, college recruiting now takes place more than a year before graduation. In fact, Wipro recruits who began reporting for duty in July 2006 got their job offers in the spring of 2005. This is far from ideal, since it's hard to predict a year ahead exactly how many new employees you'll need and in what categories. But Wipro's an adaptive organism. It makes the best of very challenging situations.

Recruiting starts with an assessment and winnowing process. Before a team of a dozen Wipro recruiters arrive at each of the country's top 150 engineering colleges, they eliminate from consideration anybody with a rating of less than 6.5 on a 10-point grading scale. The recruiters load testing software on the colleges' computers and run applicants through a series of aptitude and knowledge tests. The top performers rate interviews later that same day. The best of the best get job offers—on the spot. The whole process is completed in a single day, starting at 7 a.m. and finishing at 9 p.m. Then the recruiters dash off to the next campus.

While there's a lot of competition for the brightest college prospects, Wipro more than holds its own. Rivals Infosys and TCS and dozens of others also have aggressive recruiting programs, and they have excellent reputations among college students. One thing that gives Wipro a leg up is its reputation as a nurturing place. That's why Apeksha Kawri, a computer science graduate of the RV College of Engineering in Bangalore, decided to join the company. "Our graduates who were already working at Wipro said the people there were very encouraging and supportive and treat freshers well," she says. That tipped the balance. She decided to work there, even though the pay and benefits weren't better than at some of its competitors.

In Wipro's BPO unit, the pressure is even more intense to recruit rapidly and right. These employees are hired to handle customer service and technical phone calls or to process paperwork rather than for their technical skills, so evaluating them is more difficult. Yet, at the same time, it's crucial for Wipro to make sure it is hiring people who will fit in, and, if they're top performers, who will stay a while. Throughout India, the BPO industry has been roiled by high attrition rates—often more than 50 percent a year. It's a tough job. Many employees work the graveyard shift. They're under pressure to get jobs done quickly. And because this industry is booming, competitors are constantly luring away each others' employees with better salary and benefit offers.

These BPO jobs are especially demanding at Wipro because it's constantly improving business processes and upgrading staff skill requirements. The unit hires about 2,000 people a month. So each month it screens about 15,000 applicants out of a pool of about 3 million recent college graduates.

To deal with that deluge of applicants, the BPO organization launched a unique remote-recruiting program in late 2005. If that sounds impersonal, it is. But extreme situations call for extreme tactics. Wipro advertises for applicants in national and regional newspapers. It secures space in about 60 technical and English language training facilities around the country. Applicants come in at an appointed time, sit at a computer, and take a series of tests—including a psychological profile to see if they're suitable for this kind of work. Then, if they pass, they're instructed to go into a nearby room where a Web camera has been set up. A Wipro recruiter, whom they see on a PC screen, interviews them. If they're right for the job, they get an offer immediately. The entire process is handled without Wipro people leaving their offices.

Boot Camp, Bangalore Style

Every July, Wipro's training engine roars to a start as hundreds of 21- and 22-year-olds show up at the Bangalore campuses for boot camp. They come in waves. Every two weeks a batch of 300 to 400 young people reports for the Fundamental Readiness Program. This process runs through November. The freshers start off with a three-day orientation session—with the first day and a half dedicated to values. There's also a bit of fun. In team-building exercises, they're divided up into small groups that compete with one another. In Kawri's case, the groups took turns trying to convince the captain of an imaginary sinking ship that they were the ones who should be rescued by the single helicopter that was on the scene.

With orientation completed, they then move on for 8 to 10 weeks of classroom training. Since many of them are not computer science majors, this course includes a lot of basics. But even computer science grads get a refresher course in the tech fundamentals. Then they drill down on particular topics, such as computer operating systems, networking, Web site programming, and digital electronics. The new employees are introduced to the company's quality processes. They spend three days learning the basics of business, including finance, sales, marketing, and HR. And they get behavioral training. This is when they're introduced to the 24 competencies they'll be measured on for the rest of their Wipro careers. To keep their jobs, they have to pass a battery of tests with a minimum score of 70 percent.

After new hires complete what amounts to basic training, they move on to more specialized material—the Project Readiness Program. By now, they have been slotted for a service line, such as software programming or product engineering, and they're assigned to an industry vertical. In Product Engineering Services, for instance, every new employee goes through two to three months of technology training, with separate tracks in such areas as the Linux and Windows computer operating systems. For Kawri, who was assigned to the telecom vertical, some of the most useful training was in building self-confidence. She and other freshers were assigned to prepare reports on technical topics and given two to three days to gather information and prepare their talks. Then they presented before a group of 20 colleagues, including managers, who peppered them with questions. It was sink or swim. Kawri swam.

In addition to technical training, each vertical business unit teaches its new employees the basics of that industry. Some of the individual client account teams teach new employees about their client's strategy and competition.

New call center employees get special training in the cultures of the countries where their clients' customers are based. They learn history, current events, pop culture facts, and even regional weather patterns. They're trained to speak English with a neutral accent. Wipro's cultural training has such a good reputation that, in 2005, two young women who were hoping to marry Indians who were living in America joined the company just to take the program. When they were done, they quit—but then felt guilty and offered to pay for the classes.

Training doesn't end when new hires leave the classroom. A lot of it takes place on the job. In Product Engineering Services, new employees are assigned to a team, typically of 10 to 15 members, where they learn the day-to-day routine. They're introduced to a knowledge database called EagleVision, built up over 15 years, which employees use as sort of a cookbook for completing assignments. It's full of hundreds of ideas and blueprints for how projects should be done. "It's a way to bring people up fast, with common knowledge," says Emani, the service leader.

New hires who already have work experience get a miniversion of Wipro boot camp. They attend two to three days of orientation, and then, often, take a few weeks of training in their areas of specialization before starting their regular jobs. Within their first six months at Wipro, they'll typically attend a session where Premji talks about the company's values and answers any questions the new employees want to put to him.

Perhaps the company's most innovative initial training program is the Wipro Academy of Software Excellence (WASE). It's a university within a company. Through a partnership with the prestigious Birla Institute of Technology and Sciences in Bangalore, Wipro offers a full course of study and awards master's degrees in software engineering. The program, which takes four years to complete, is offered free of charge to a select group of new employees with bachelor's degrees in science or math. This way, Wipro is able to broaden the pool of job candidates and, over time, convert top science grads into very loyal professional computer scientists. "It's a win–win," says talent transformation boss Dorairaj. "We're able to retain good people for four years, and they get a degree."

Indeed, the program provides immediate payoffs for both Wipro and the employees. Participants work a normal five-day workweek in the office, then spend from 9 a.m. to 6 p.m. each Saturday in the classroom. Their studies and their work-a-day duties cross-pollinate. "When I'm studying, I run into things I'm seeing in my projects. Or with work, I see how I could handle things better," says Rudra Pratap, 24, a participant in the master's program who has worked for Wipro for three years. He had planned on seeking a master's in engineering after he wrapped up his undergraduate program, "So this is a golden opportunity for me," he says.

Ongoing Talent Transformation

After investing all that time and money in initial training, Wipro doesn't want to see its top employees quit and sign on with rivals. That's one of the reasons it offers employees ladders of training that they can climb through the years, both to help earn promotions and expand their knowledge into new areas. There are two formal career ladders: technical and management. But in addition, the company offers a whole range of courses designed to improve employees' performance and enrich their professional lives, no matter what career track they follow. Education isn't just an option; it's a requirement. All employees must complete the time equivalent of 10 days of training annually. They're more than happy to do so. In fact, they average 12 days of training per year.

Wipro employees plan and manage their careers—and identify the training they need—using a computer program called Career-Mosaic. It maps the organization and describes common career paths and the requirements for each level. Open jobs are posted online for all to see. Meanwhile, the managers in each business unit use the Talent Review and Planning system to keep track of the talent pool and match current assets against anticipated needs in the future.

The most basic form of technical training is certifications. Most large tech firms with widely used technologies offer certification for various levels of expertise, and customers want to know that Wipro employees assigned to their projects are qualified to do the work. An independent training industry has grown up to provide this kind of course material, but because there's so much internal demand at Wipro, it runs many of the programs itself. Most of the certification training is done through online interactive programs conducted via PCs and the Internet—even the tests. Wipro enriches the experience by employing a team of "mentors," who stand ready to answer questions put to them by employees while they're online. Employees type their questions into an instant messaging system and get an answer back within two minutes. That way, they don't lose time being confused. During any given month, an average of 15,000 Wipro employees are involved in certification courses or other online training programs.

The training programs are more formal for the more advanced technology roles—architects, solution builders, and consultants. Architects have a deep understanding of a single technology area. Solution builders understand an array of technologies and pull them together to create a solution to a customer problem. Consultants combine broad knowledge of technology with an in-depth knowledge of a business or even a particular industry. The program for architects combines classroom sessions with hands-on experiences. These folks are responsible for being expert at cutting-edge technologies, many of which are developed far away in Silicon Valley or other tech enclaves. Wipro has forged partnerships with a dozen key tech firms, including Microsoft, IBM, and Cisco Systems, to set up and operate specialized technology labs. Wipro provides the space and the computers; the tech giants supply software and training materials, either for free or at a discount. Employees get proficiency certificates when they complete the programs.

Prepare the Leaders of the Future

While Wipro is a technology company at its core, it doesn't give short shrift to management training. The company organizes itself in building blocks. The smallest component is the project team, made up of 10 or 15 engineers. They're run by project leaders. Two, three, or more project teams are combined to handle larger jobs, and they are run by project managers. Delivery managers oversee several project groups and coordinate with salespeople and program managers who work directly with customers. Just as the company has defined 24 competencies for its rank-and-file employees, it has laid out 8 leadership qualities. These are the factors on which it focuses in leadership training, and they're some of the key elements in the managers' annual performance assessments. They are:

1. Strategic thinking
2. Customer orientation
3. Self-confidence
4. Global thinking and acting
5. Commitment to excellence
6. Working in teams
7. Building future leaders
8. Aggressive commitments

With each increment of greater responsibility, managers need more business and general-management knowledge, so Wipro has established training programs for each step of their career journey. The steps in the leadership training ladder are the Entry Leaders Program, for people who want to become project leaders; the New Leaders Program, for first-time managers; the Wipro Leaders Program, for more experienced managers; the Business Leadership Program, for client-facing program managers and other business-oriented leaders, and the Strategic Leaders Program, for business–unit leaders who have strategy and planning responsibilities. These programs tend to be one-week modules where managers are excused from their regular duties and fully immersed in classroom sessions.

To see how training feeds advancement, consider the career path of Satish Hariharan. He's a 32-year-old lead consultant managing a team of 10 presales consultants in Bangalore who help salespeople prepare project proposals. Hariharan is the typical ambitious Wiproite. He started his career there right out of college, rose within five years to project manager, did some on-site programming in the United States for a couple of years, returned to India to work as a technical architect, and began his present job. Next, he plans on getting a sales assignment in the United States or Europe. He completed the New Leaders Program in 2000 and the Wipro Leaders Program in 2005. He also completed a 2½-year part-time course, Post-Graduate in Software Enterprise Management, that was offered jointly by Wipro and the Indian Institute of Management in Bangalore.

Hariharan says all this training has smoothed his advancement in the organization. It helps him do his current job more effectively and prepares him for the next one. "You learn to see things from a customer perspective and an industry perspective," he says. "It brings you a breadth of knowledge. It has helped me become a better manager and leader."

While Wipro's weeklong management training modules can't offer a lot of depth, the company immerses participants in the material, so they're true learning and shaping experiences. During a Business Leadership session in Bangalore in December 2005, the 50 participants divided up into teams to play a business simulation game similar to Carnegie Mellon University's Management Game, where teams from universities around the world compete with one another based on how well they run imaginary companies. The Wipro teams ran small manufacturing companies. Over a three-day period, they made group decisions about strategy and tactics. It turned out that the winning team was similar to Wipro. It didn't make any huge investments at first, but when demand picked up, the team rapidly increased factory capacity, and its virtual sales soared. The game gave the Wiproites a taste of business leadership that they hadn't had in their careers so far, and it gave them a sense of whether they'd enjoy and excel at general management.

For middle managers who decide they want to become senior managers, Wipro offers what it calls a mini-MBA. This is typically for people with at least seven years at the company. It's a part-time program that lasts four months. Employees attend classes from 4 p.m. to 8 p.m. on two weekdays, and then a full day on Saturdays. The classes are taught by faculty members at local universities, including the Indian Institute of Management. Every year, 150 to 200 people complete the course.

Not all management training can take place in the classroom. Some has to be done on the job. Wipro's BPO unit found that many of the young managers it trained formally would forget what they had learned under the pressure of real-life situations and conflicts. The unit has dealt with this by creating a coaching program. It assigns senior managers to newly hired or newly promoted junior ones. Now if a problem comes up, the junior managers can call their mentors or even ask them to come to the office and help deal with a situation. The coaches get deeply involved when new situations crop up, but gradually they let their charges fly solo.

Self-Improvement for All

The company offers a wide array of self-improvement programs for employees of any rank. These include cross-cultural training for every major country in which Wipro does business, and language training for a handful of key countries. Part-time programs in German, French, Japanese, and Chinese are offered in 180- and 360-hour versions. In addition, there's a full-time, full-immersion Japanese program that lasts for nine months, which prepares people to work in a service delivery center outside Tokyo. There's a behavior development program that all employees are encouraged to take, called CRISP, for Communications, Relationship management, Interpersonal skills, Self-realization, and Personal effectiveness.

And when business experts visit India from around the world, Wipro invites them over to give lectures, called Expert Talks. Past talks included such stars as Jack Trout, the American advertising guru, and C. K. Prahalad, the management expert from the University of Michigan's business graduate school. The company videos the talks and Webcasts them so employees at any of its campuses can tune in.

Wipro doesn't neglect the spiritual and emotional sides of life either. Some of the training programs include lectures and exercises addressing mental health and life-balance skills. At a Business Leadership program conducted in Bangalore in late 2005, the last session was conducted by Dr. Thimappa Hegde, director of the Narayana Institute of Neurosciences in Bangalore. He spoke to 50 middle managers about how he deals with suffering and death among his patients. Then he led the students through a yoga exercise. They then split up into small groups, and he asked them to relate personal experiences that had been especially meaningful to them. John

Hackmann, a program manager who works in the United Kingdom, recounts that several people in his group spoke about the death of family members, and some even shed tears.

He was impressed with the openness and honesty of his colleagues and with Wipro's care for its employees' psychological well-being. "In our job you have a lot of stress," he says. "You have to create a balance between your job and your inner self. Finding that balance is how you become a complete person."

A company that helps employees become complete people? Well, that's the goal. And it's not some silly indulgence dreamed up by HR people with too much time on their hands. For Wipro to succeed against fearsome Indian and Western competition, it needs to essentially create new people from the raw talent of its employees, equipping them with a set of values, skills, and behaviors. There's no room for unproductive friction within the organization. Employees up and down the ranks must know what's expected of them, work with energy and enthusiasm, collaborate with one another, and be willing to learn and grow.

The major challenge for Wipro is upgrading itself from offshore supplier of cheap labor to trusted advisor and partner to its clients. Only through continuous talent development will it be able to complete that journey.

7

SOLICIT SUGGESTIONS AND EVEN CRITIQUES FROM EMPLOYEES

Chains of command are useful things. Information and decisions should flow through the proper channels. Yet we all know that often rigid chains of command prevent what's really going on in an organization—and with customers—from reaching the top dogs. Wipro is designed so this kind of thing won't happen. Information flows freely in both directions, from employees to bosses and vice versa. Wipro's executives hold extensive question-and-answer (Q&A) sessions when there's news and, sometimes, even when there isn't. Employees are surveyed and solicited constantly on everything from the menu in the company cafeteria to the next tech innovation. And at Wipro, the open-door policy that many companies talk about but few actually practice really is an open door.

Open Multimodal Communications with the Staff

At Wipro, internal communications are more than a two-way street: It's like the Los Angeles highway system—eight lanes, and snaking in every direction. This isn't just feel-good stuff designed to prop up morale. Internal communications are the lifeblood of an organization that is spread worldwide, growing at 30 percent per year, constantly expanding into new markets, and depending on collaboration to get its work done. Here are some of the ways the company reaches out:

- *Face-to-face meetings.* With more than 60,000 employees, Wipro long ago stopped being the kind of place where the top executives know all their employees' names. But it tries to retain some of the intimacy of a smaller organization. Premji and other executives address training classes, have lunch with groups of rank-and-file employees, and mix with people in informal situations. They even answer e-mails from regular folks.

- *Outgoing information.* The employee Web site, Channel W, is a "virtual campus" where, in addition to the usual HR self-service features, employees get the latest company news, receive reminders on policies such as the ethics rules, and see Webcasts of executive presentations.

- *The feedback loop.* This is called Wipro Listens and Responds, or WLR. The company conducts a major employee perception survey about once every 18 months, and then does smaller quarterly surveys. It also conducts spot surveys on timely topics on the Web site and conducts open online chats and forums involving executives. Employees are encouraged to submit suggestions via e-mail, the Web site, or boxes in offices on how the company can improve quality practices and business processes.

- *Welcome to whistleblowers.* Employees who learn of any violation of company rules, or simply have a complaint, are actively encouraged to tell the company about it via e-mail, phone, or fax. Confidentiality is assured. A group of "ombudspersons" investigates and ultimately turns the matters over to compliance committees for deliberation and action.

Beyond the company's formal employee communications channels, it fosters a participatory spirit. You see this most clearly in its sprawling office complexes in Bangalore. With all the 20-somethings on the staff, these places take on some of the flavor of a college campus. They even have clubs, everything from dance and music to literature and sports. The idea is to have fun and build a sense of community, but these organizations also bring together people from many levels who can share career and success advice.

One group, called Fun at EC, organizes events for the Electronics City campus in Bangalore where approximately 15,000 Wiproites work. To celebrate New Year's Day in 2006, the group built a stage, erected a huge projection screen, and put on five days of live rock music, performing every day from 4 p.m. to 9 p.m. It was a blast, of course, but the organizers also saw it as an opportunity to learn business skills that will come in handy as they rise in the ranks.

Open Communications Start at the Top

As with many things at Wipro, the philosophy about employee communications begins with Premji. Even though in 2005 he added the task of running the company's technology business to his long list of duties, he spends a considerable amount of time communicating with regular employees. Premji speaks to the entire staff via Webcast at the beginning of each fiscal year, where he explains the strategy and the business plans for the upcoming 12 months. That's typically followed by a lengthy Q&A session. In addition, he addresses new management employees about the company's values and participates in many of the leadership training programs—often mingling with participants during informal gatherings at the end of sessions.

At a Business Leadership program in Bangalore in late 2005, for instance, he spoke to a group of 50 middle managers for 2½ hours, where he talked about what makes Wipro a business leader and about the investments he planned on making. Unlike some American CEOs, he doesn't make passionate speeches or browbeat people with tirades. He's soft-spoken and matter of fact. "He's a very natural speaker. He's not rah-rah—none of that nonsense. He just talks," says John Hackmann, one of the participants.

During Q&As, Premji invites employees to ask tough questions, but out of respect for him, they rarely do, according to numerous employees I spoke to. He's open about the company's challenges though. If he feels Wipro has hard work to do to improve margins or match a competitor's capabilities, he'll bring it up himself. And if he's asked about this kind of thing, he speaks frankly. During a management training session in November 2005, a midlevel manager told him he thought Wipro needed a visionary goal to aim for, like former vice chairman Vivek Paul gave the organization in 2000. Premji agreed with him but asked for patience. He said his executive team needed to spend more time on improving efficiencies and boosting margins—then they'd do some soul searching about the company's longer-term future. During his Q&A sessions, if there's a question Premji can't answer on the spot, he'll write it down and make sure employees get their answer later.

Premji also responds personally to e-mails. Satish Hariharan, a lead consultant in the company's financial services business unit, was concerned in early 2004 that Wipro was losing too many good employees who were being lured away by rivals. He wrote an e-mail to Premji warning him about this matter and suggesting that Wipro keep closer tabs on industry pay comparisons and try to keep ahead of the curve. He got a response from Premji the same day, April 30, 2004. The chairman told him the top managers were reviewing the matter and were considering a salary hike, which they later implemented. "We have been much better since then," says Hariharan. "We have been able to retain a lot of talent. We're on par or better."

With word and deed, Premji signals to subordinates that he's approachable. "He's a humble guy. He doesn't put himself above everybody," says Rich Garnick, the former head of North American operations. "He works as hard if not harder than anybody else. Other CEOs act like they want to be treated like royalty. He's not like that."

Premji sets the communications standard for his lieutenants to follow. The business unit bosses hold quarterly communications sessions where they talk about their performance and goals and take questions from the rank-and-file employees. They'll typically have 500 people in a room and many others tuned in via Webcasts. For

Suresh Vaswani, president of Wipro Infotech, the South Asian operation, the quarterly Webcast lasts four hours. The first hour is his presentation. The next three hours are Q&A. When he travels, he not only meets with customers but arranges lunches and dinners with employees who are sometimes three and four levels below him on the organization chart. "We want to make sure we have heard everybody's perspective. Anybody can walk into anybody's office and have a discussion. We're not hierarchical. Senior managers don't just talk to the layer next to them," he says.

To make sure that all managers have enough face-to-face interactions with employees, the company has created the Meet Your People Program. The company studied activities of some of its most highly regarded managers and came up with a set of best practices for all supervisors. They're required to inform their staff members regularly about the company's goals and their individual roles in accomplishing them, to help their people set and meet career goals, to meet with people regularly to help them increase productivity, and, while they're at it, to have a little fun in the workplace.

About that open-door policy: Several Wipro employees told me that they have walked into the office of senior executives without invitation—and without trepidation either. One of them is Sangita Singh, who heads Wipro's software package implementation business and was formerly head of marketing for the global tech unit. Back in 2000, when she was a junior marketer, the marketing chief took a transfer and the replacement only lasted a few weeks. Nobody considered her for the top job. She was just 30 years old, in a company whose top leadership was dominated by middle-aged men. But she wasn't deterred. On May 9, 2000, she marched into then–Vice Chairman Vivek Paul's office and introduced herself to him. She told him about her ambitions and asked for a chance to prepare a presentation that would detail how she would change the tech division's marketing. He gave her a shot. And two weeks later, after reviewing her pitch, he gave her the job.

Stories like that get around. They send the signal to all: If you want something badly, go straight to the boss and ask for it.

When in Doubt, Ask Your Employees

In a services company, when there are problems, they're typically rooted in personnel matters. So any effort to solve them must begin with a deep understanding of root causes. This is one of the key reasons why Wipro managers spend so much time with rank-and-file employees. They need to know what employees are thinking before they can fix things.

The BPO unit's struggle with attrition in 2005 is a case in point. T. K. Kurien, head of the service line, was faced with 90 percent attrition rates among the 15,000 people in his call center operations when he was promoted to run the unit in the spring of the year. He literally couldn't hire and train people fast enough to keep up with demand and turnover. Rival call center operators were standing outside his operations in Delhi offering his people salary raises and hiring them on the spot as they left work at the end of a shift. With all the investment he put into training, he'd lose money if a new hire didn't stay with Wipro for at least nine months.

Something had to be done. But before he could hope to start to solve the problem, he had to understand it better. Kurien had never headed up a call center operation. So to bring himself up to speed, he essentially took the staff to lunch. Over a two-week period, he held a series of lunch and dinner meetings in the company cafeterias with groups of 15 to 20 employees from his offices in Delhi, Bangalore, Kolkata, and Mumbai.

These people were not like software programmers. Most programmers are motivated more by technical challenges than money, and they dream of rising through the ranks and becoming architects or project managers. When he spoke to his call center agents, he found that they were primarily interested in spending money on things like the latest cell phones, $300 sneakers that automatically adjust to their feet as they walk, and expensive perfume. When he asked them about their aspirations, he says, "It was all very short term. They're saying, 'I'm making money now, and I don't know what I'll be doing next month.'"

At the end of two weeks, Kurien thought he had a partial answer. He had to train supervisors so they did much more for their young agents than show them how to do their jobs. They had to teach their people to aspire to something and show them how they could gain, long term, from working at Wipro. They needed to become career counselors.

What Kurien had done is classic Wipro. When it comes to dealing with employees, the motto is simple: Listen and learn.

Don't Just Ask, Do Something about It

In addition to all those face-to-face meetings, Wipro aggressively surveys employees looking for emerging concerns and problems. The company began by conducting these surveys every two years, but then it switched to an 18-month interval and, by early 2006, was considering switching to 12 months. The pace of change was just too rapid to wait so long between pulse takings. Originally these surveys were done by third parties, including Gallup, but, to save money, Wipro's internal staff now conducts them.

The survey itself is just the start. After it's completed, the HR department analyzes and interprets the results and then holds focus groups with small collections of employees to explore particular issues in depth. When that process is finished, HR posts the results of the survey on the employee Web portal and presents a list of actions the company plans on taking in response. Then before the next survey is conducted, representatives of functional departments, including HR, information technology, administration, and security, hold focus groups to make sure they have responded to the issues raised in the previous survey and have improved their service levels. One of the questions on the new survey is how well the company responded to the previous one. "That particular question has a lot of weight," says head of HR Pratik Kumar.

Here are some of the issues that were raised by employees in response to a 2005 survey, and the company's responses:

- Employees felt the company had become too driven by numbers and had lost some of the personal touch. In response, the HR department asked managers to spend more time face-to-face with employees in a mentoring role. Now all supervisors have to give their own supervisors a tally of the amount of time they spend on mentoring.

- Overseas employees said the company was too India-centric. To get important decisions made, they had to appeal to managers back in India. In response the company gave more decision-making authority to the geographical operations. Now, in the United States and Europe, more decisions can be made in those locations without their consulting India.

- Overseas employees complained that they were not able to participate in training programs as much as they wanted. The company's response was to create short, portable versions of many of the technical and behavioral courses and assign itinerant trainers to travel around the world and present them. Because many of the U.S. and European employees were stationed in customers' offices, it was difficult to spring them to participate in a weeklong course, so most of these are one- and two-day offerings and are done over weekends.

Often, personnel issues come up suddenly and have to be resolved quickly. In those cases, Wipro does "dipstick" surveys, testing to see the level of employees' satisfaction with a particular practice. For instance, in early 2005, the Indian government changed tax policy to begin taxing employers on the value of pension benefits. Wipro surveyed employees online, then conducted a series of employee focus groups and found that while managers typically preferred to keep their traditional company pensions, many of the younger employees wanted more flexibility, including the option to spend the pension contribution money on more immediate needs. After taking stock, Wipro opted to offer two programs. It retained the traditional pension program for managers and began paying taxes on it; and it paid cash contributions to junior employees. They had the option of investing their cash in retirement programs offered by third parties. If they did so, Wipro didn't have to pay taxes on the contributions. To help employees make wise decisions, the company also launched tax and retirement advice services for them.

On the employee Web site, Channel W, employees have multiple avenues to express themselves, not only to the HR department but to the quality people and the folks in charge of innovation. This is a key element of the Wipro Listens and Responds program. The results are distributed to the appropriate people in the organization for consideration and response. The challenge is to cull through all the input and figure out the reasons they are hearing one criticism or another. "We have weekly meetings to talk these things over. If it's a quick fix, we'll do it immediately. Otherwise, we'll get input from all the appropriate people before we respond," says HR chief Kumar.

All of this listening and learning keeps Wipro's HR professionals mighty busy. For instance, Rajesh Sahay, the HR general manager in Enterprise Solutions strategic business unit, made about 20 policy modifications in fiscal 2006 as a result of suggestions from employees. One example: Employees had complained that the travel expense limits for hotel accommodations were not keeping up with the costs of rooms. It was hard to find a decent hotel at the allowed rates. The HR department surveyed hotel rates in various Indian cities and concluded that its allowances had to increase between 5 and 10 percent, depending on the city. So it made the adjustments.

Sometimes, employee feedback can yield dramatic changes. For instance, in early 2005, American consultant Mikelle Fisher told her boss that she wouldn't likely stay with the company long term if it didn't improve the basic benefits package. There was no maternity leave beyond what was required by law, there was no flexible or dependent-care spending account, and the health-care package was not competitive. Later that year, she got a call from an HR representative who was concerned that fewer than a dozen of Wipro's consultants were women and wanted to see if anything could be done about it. Fisher laid out her complaints. She even gathered some comparative data from friends who worked at other consulting companies. By the end of the year, prompted by feedback from many employees including Fisher, Wipro had revamped its benefits significantly. It introduced an extended maternity benefit in the United States, including eight weeks of paid time off and the option of an additional six months of unpaid leave. In addition, a flexible spending account was added, which provided tax savings for medical and dependent-care expenses. The company also came up with a creative way to boost the medical plan. American employees who need nonemergency surgery now have the option of traveling to India, all expenses paid, and having surgery done there.

A Suggestion Box for Quality Improvements

Wipro's quality improvement programs, Six Sigma and lean, would only be window dressing if the company didn't go to great lengths to get employees to suggest changes in the way it does business. Who better to know what needs to be fixed than the people who live and breathe a service delivery process every day? To encourage the flow of information, the company has placed suggestion boxes in many of its offices. Employees are urged to drop notes in the boxes or to send in suggestions via e-mail. It's a sure way to qualify for one of the team participation awards that the company lavishes on the staff (see Chapter 8). In addition to the suggestion boxes, there's a quality section on the Channel W Web site. There are open forums for discussion of quality issues, and employees can submit their suggestions via online forms.

Employee feedback is especially crucial in the BPO unit. After all, the service they provide is handling and improving their clients' business processes. To encourage big ideas, each BPO office holds a "Lean Day" every month. People who have ideas for major process improvements go before a panel and present them. If the proposals past muster with the panel, they are turned into lean projects.

With so many suggestions coming in from so many different sources, one of Wipro's challenges is to manage them all and sort out the bright ideas from the stinkers. Ideas proposed as Six Sigma projects are reviewed by black belts, the company's top-level Six Sigma experts, to see if they're worth the considerable effort of being handled as formal projects, which draw on numerous people and can take weeks or months to complete. "You don't want to have excessive enthusiasm and turn everything into a Six Sigma project. You don't want too many," says HR boss Kumar.

When they're handled correctly, these interactions with employees not only improve services but energize staff members. Srikanth Vittal Murthy, 26-year-old accounting associate in the BPO operation, has soaring ambitions. "I plan on being the top accounting guy at Wipro some day," he told me when I toured a BPO office in Bangalore. Anxious to prove himself, he looks for processes in need of fixing. In late 2004, soon after he joined Wipro, he was assigned to handle import payments for the company's own domestic business. Because of delays in getting documents and approvals from the government, he'd end up paying bills late. On his own initiative, he contacted Wipro procurement officials and learned that the problem was getting a series of government approvals handled properly and quickly. So he asked for a meeting with the procurement people to try to sort things out.

The problem was serious enough to warrant a Six Sigma project. Though Murthy was a fresher, he was invited to join the team, which was headed by a black belt and included representatives from the procurement and logistics departments. Ultimately, they worked out a solution that involved setting up a control sheet that listed all of the steps that needed to be taken and making sure the documents were routed to the proper people to handle them. As a result, they cut in half the time it took to shepherd documents through the import duty process.

Looking for Trouble

From the beginning, Premji had encouraged employees to come forward to report ethical breaches. In 2003, the company formalized this practice in its ombudsman policy. It has eight ombudspersons assigned to its various business units and geographies. They're responsible for receiving complaints from employees, investigating them, and handing the matters over to compliance steering committees for resolution. Employees can raise any concern, from an ethical or legal violation to dissatisfaction with the personnel evaluation process. "The organization had reached a size and we felt we needed to have a channel where employees could raise issues to somebody outside their business who is not in their line of command," says Ishwar Hemrajani, the chief ombudsman. "And second, we have a strong set of values. It's an effort to make sure the values are being practiced." The company's shareholders, business partners, and customers are also invited to participate. Ultimately, each quarter, a summary report is presented to the audit committee of the board of directors, in part to assure that serious problems aren't being bottled up within the ranks.

Confidentiality is assured. The ombudspersons are senior managers who are nominated by the senior business leaders, so they're trusted to be discrete. To add an extra layer of privacy protection, they can only see the complaints that are brought or assigned to them as individuals. The ombudspersons log each complaint they handle into a computer tracking system. Only Hemrajani and an administrator see them all.

The ombudspersons investigate by interviewing the complainant and the person who is being accused and gather information from other employees and company records. Once they have the facts, they present them to their business unit compliance steering committee. Minor matters are often handled by the ombudsperson and one or two members of the steering committee. More substantial ones are heard at a monthly committee meeting. And the most serious matters are kicked up to a corporate steering committee. About 80 percent of the cases are resolved within 15 days. Most are wrapped up within six weeks.

In the first three years, more than 500 complaints were filed. These ranged from minor matters such as clarifying a personnel policy to major offenses for which a person could be fired. About 12 percent of the cases resulted in terminations. In July 2005, for instance, five people lost their jobs for downloading pornography onto their company computers.

When problems are uncovered, the company doesn't just punish rules violators; it tries to prevent that particular violation from happening again. For instance, in 2005 an employee complained that two managers in the BPO unit were violating the company's transportation policies. They had company cars that were being used by their families in their hometowns, but they were assigned to temporarily work in other locations, and they were using company transportation there as well. Through an investigation, it turned out that these managers had been allowed to operate this way when they worked for Spectramind, the BPO pioneer that Wipro purchased in 2004, and they were not aware of Wipro's transportation reimbursement rules. The ombudsperson found that other managers were also violating the rules. In the end, the company did a better job of communicating policies and came up with a new process for assuring that its policies were conveyed to employees of companies it acquires.

The ombudsman policy sometimes raises issues that set in motion much broader self-examination projects among the company's executives. Chief Ombudsman Hemrajani aggregates and categorizes all of the cases, which makes it possible to spot patterns that indicate that something is wrong on a large scale and needs to be fixed. This happened with some recruitment and hiring issues. The company came upon a series of instances where college recruits or lateral hires had falsified their experience and training. Eighteen people lost their jobs within the space of 12 months. The company came up with new policies aimed at discouraging applicants from falsifying their records, and it hired outside firms to do background checks. But it also began discussions of recruitment in general. "We are asking ourselves, Are we getting the right candidates? We're thinking about that now," says Hemrajani.

Wipro's Must-Do List

While Wipro is in some ways a model for communications with employees, it's by no means perfect at this sort of thing. Over the years I have spoken to several employees who, while they were very positive about Wipro overall, felt it needed to improve some aspects of its internal communications. One example: While it's quick and thorough when it comes to talking about its financial performance, it's less transparent about management changes. Employees sometimes hear from their clients, rather than directly from the company, when client-facing personnel changes are on the way.

Wipro's biggest challenge is communicating well with the 20 percent of its tech staff that's scattered around the world outside of India. Often these people work out of their homes or in customers' offices or in small Wipro offices. They are separated from headquarters by thousands of miles and a dozen time zones. Often, too, they're Americans or Europeans, unfamiliar with Indian culture in general and Wipro's ways in particular. Typically, when non-Indians are hired to work in North America and Europe, they get only the most perfunctory orientation. So it's no wonder that they feel disconnected. The challenge for Wipro is to go the extra mile to link up with these people, and, perhaps, to make the investment in bringing new foreign hires to Bangalore for bonding purposes. Several Westerners who eventually visited headquarters said it made a big positive impact on their attitude toward the company.

Another Wipro shortcoming is the paucity of Western managers in its ranks. "If it wants to create a truly global model, it has to bring into the company truly multicultural individuals, not just people who understand a language, but who come from a different culture. Otherwise you're superimposing an Indian business culture on very different environments," says John Hackmann, a program manager in the United Kingdom who is, in general, enthusiastic about Wipro.

Wipro is on the road toward becoming a transnational organization. To accomplish its goal of being recognized as one of the world's outstanding global corporations, it will need to do more to broaden its ethnic and cultural mix and to connect well with people in its far-flung outposts.

8

REWARD EMPLOYEES WITH RECOGNITION AND RESPECT

Wipro promises its customers high-quality services at significantly lower prices than they're accustomed to paying. That creates a conundrum. High quality is costly. Yet charging low prices, it would seem, makes it very difficult to achieve and maintain high quality. Wipro accomplishes this partly through a combination of frugality and continuous business process improvements. The other part: a package of rewards designed to compensate employees fairly and motivate them, but without breaking the bank.

Doing this is no easy task. Since nearly 50 percent of the company's costs go to salaries and benefits, a misstep on the compensation front can immediately show up in slimmer profit margins. On the other hand, if the company underpays relative to rivals Infosys and TCS, it will lose good employees to them, which results in the company incurring additional recruitment and training costs. It takes a lot of creativity and vigilance to stay on top of this. Wipro does it though a combination of cash compensation, stock, and nonmonetary rewards.

Boost Morale with Creative Rewards

When Srikanth Vittal Murthy, a 25-year-old associate in Wipro's finance and accounting BPO unit, showed up for the customary Friday afternoon staff gathering in the unit's Bangalore office one day in the spring of 2005, he was surprised and pleased to discover that he was one of the guests of honor. About 100 of his colleagues clustered around, and he was given a gift, a check, and a cake with his name written on it in honey. It was all in recognition of his role in starting and participating in that Six Sigma quality project, described in Chapter 7, that resulted in an improvement in the way the office handled accounts payable processes that involved government import duties.

Murthy had spotted a problem and took the initiative to get it fixed. The black belt from his Six Sigma team had arranged for the prizes and certificate, and other members of the Six Sigma team from other departments attended the little ceremony. "I was happy to have everybody else hear about what I had done," says Murthy. "It's a motivation. Now if I see something that can be improved, I'll do it. I want to do more projects."

Handing out awards is a key morale-boosting tool in the BPO unit. The business employs thousands of young people, many of whom perform repetitive tasks and get significantly less in pay than their counterparts in the software programming ranks. Attrition rates are high. So the organization is under pressure to come up with creative ways to make people's work lives more enjoyable and to make them feel appreciated. In fact, celebrating and handing out prizes aren't just a nice extra—they're required. Every team leader is supposed to celebrate on a weekly basis, provided somebody has done something worthy of a prize. And when employees are promoted, their supervisor calls up their spouse or parent to spread the good news. "One of the big push-backs we get from families is that stress levels are so high, and they hardly see their spouse or child. These touches soften things," says Wipro's BPO leader T. K. Kurien. "You can be hard, but if you don't recognize people and have a softer side, you're running a slave camp."

Kurien offers more substantial rewards for people who have done outstanding things—say, coming up with an important process change or achieving dramatic improvements in customer satisfaction levels. They're sent on all-expenses-paid trips to Singapore, where a handful of theme parks are very popular with South Asians.

About 10 to 15 people win these trips per quarter. He'd like to send more, but the budget won't allow for it.

While the BPO unit is most aggressive about rewarding employees in this way, each Wipro business unit has its own rewards and rituals for handing them out. Most have adopted a standard set of awards as a starting point. These awards are crafted to reward behaviors that are vital to the health of the business. Here are the basic awards:

- *Feather in My Cap:* For an outstanding effort by a small team of employees.

- *Thanks a Zillion:* For helping a colleague on another team handle a difficult situation.

- *Dear Boss:* Given to managers who are nominated by their staffs.

- *All for the Best:* For learning an important lesson as a result of making a mistake.

The awards include a diplomalike certificate. They also often include gift certificates at local stores, pendants, pens, and small glass statues.

In addition, Wipro Technologies also hands out divisionwide awards. The Best People Manager Award, for instance, is given to those managers who create a better workplace for their team members. These leaders produce a remarkable record of high employee satisfaction, high productivity, and low attrition.

All of these awards may seem quaint—or even silly—to a Western corporate warrior, but clearly, at Wipro, they're important and they make a difference. Typically, the awards are handed out at team meetings, and notices are published in newsletters—which, in some cases, even customers see. Winners proudly pin their certificates to the walls of their cubicles. Some even create little shrines to personal achievement. "This is a very good program. You get a lot of visibility. It shows you have something unique in you," says Rudra Pratap, a tech support analyst who has worked at Wipro for more than three years.

Learn How to Celebrate Victories

For many Indians, I'm told, celebrating doesn't come naturally. And among the older generation of Wipro's leaders, there's a strong tendency to skip the confetti and get on with business. The attitude: Sure, hand out the little awards, but if it costs real money or takes time, don't bother. As a result, if the company wins a major new contract, a leader will typically send out an e-mail with the news, but close with an admonition to work harder to keep more wins coming. In contrast, when Infosys hit the $1 billion revenue mark in 2004, it celebrated with a now-legendary party including performances by Indian pop singers and gala dinners. It also handed out $25 million in bonuses—between $500 and $5,000 for every employee. Wipro hardly paid heed when it crossed the same threshold. Its explanation: It had never looked at $1 billion as a special target or milestone, so why throw a party? Former Wiproite Vikram Gulati, now the chief executive of Intelligroup, a New Jersey–based IT services outfit, says Wipro needs to celebrate more. He should know. He worked there for 17 years before leaving in 2005. "They didn't know how to have fun," he says. "It's not a grim environment. They're professional and to the point. But you need a little bit of levity."

HR boss Pratik Kumar agrees with Gulati. Employees have sent him the same message in surveys. The company has a birthday and anniversary calendar, and it sends out little congratulatory notes to employees. This effort is commendable, but it's not nearly enough. "We can do better at this. We have to let our hair down," he says. "We have two generations coexisting, and 65 percent of the employees are from the younger generation. We have to respond to their expectations. If we don't, we'll have more cracks in the organization."

Still, Kumar points out that celebrations are far less important than creating an enriching work environment. Wipro's leaders put a lot of effort into making employees feel they're respected and they have prospects for rising in the organization. The company also gives them important and challenging work to do, and opportunities to shift from one type of work to another. "I don't think people stay on in an organization if they don't enjoy what they're doing. It's not about hanging balloons and having a party," Kumar says. "Fun is a state of mind. Do I feel free? Can I reach out and express myself to somebody? Fun is how well you're engaged, and do you see meaning in your daily life."

That's not just the HR guy rationalizing either. Employees I interviewed spoke of getting ample rewards and fulfillment apart from pay, stock, and awards ceremonies. "You get a lot of exposure here to a lot of technologies and industries. No other company has it. I wouldn't sacrifice this," says Pratap, the tech support analyst.

Package Pay with Job Satisfaction

When it comes to salaries and other compensation, keeping up with the Joneses (in this case, the Infosyses and TCSes) is one of the biggest challenges Wipro faces every day. Because of rapid growth in demand for tech employees, salaries are rising fast in Bangalore and across the country. Entry-level salaries at India's tech companies rose about 15 percent in 2003 and 2004, while salaries for midlevel managers rose 30 percent annually during the same period, according to NASSCOM, the association of Indian software and services employers. Wipro and its Indian rivals have to be extremely careful about salary levels. Since nearly half of their costs are in human labor, if they give a salary increase of 10 percent, it wipes off 5 percent of their bottom line.

Wipro modifies its pay tactics based on shifting competitive dynamics. If Infosys makes a run at a slew of Wipro's middle managers with higher salaries, Wipro will respond by raising salaries. But, typically, it pays in the fiftieth to sixtieth percentile of each job category in India, where 80 percent of its employees are based. It does separate calculations in the United States and Europe, responding to local competitive pressures. The basic message to employees is, "This is a strong, stable company that's value-driven. You won't see exponential growth in your pay, but you'll never be embarrassed by your compensation," says HR general manager Rajesh Sahay. Employees I spoke to agreed that they were paid fairly, though not lavishly.

It may sound odd to have one of the top three tech outfits only paying in the middle of the salary range. Wipro is able to manage this because it offers other compensations to employees, such as working for an industry leader and being treated with respect. The company's retention program has three pieces: organizational alertness, supervisory engagement, and job satisfaction.

- *Organizational alertness.* Wipro keeps an eye out for shifting trends. It tries to get out ahead on an issue so it can be proactive. That creates the impression in employees of an organization that doesn't have to be forced to do good things for them. For instance, while the conventional wisdom in 2005 was that the Wipro workforce is mostly young single people, the company analyzed its medical expenses and discovered that 52 percent of its medical bills were for pregnancy, childbirth, and pediatric care. That signaled that a large percentage of its employees were now in the family-rearing stage, so the company began taking measures to serve that kind of employee, such as expanding child-care programs.

- *Supervisory engagement.* Managers are expected to spend a significant amount of time helping individual employees. "We say, people join good companies but leave bad managers," says Sahay. Wipro's managers are expected to be coaches in addition to being supervisors. Apeksha Kawri, who joined the company as a fresher in 2005, says coaching was vital to her in her first months on the job. She had not studied telecommunications technologies in college, yet as a junior engineer, suddenly she was helping to design state-of-the art systems for providing broadband Internet connections over telephone lines. "My project leader teaches me on the job," she says. "It's a challenge for me to learn so quickly, but with help, I'm able to manage it."

- *Job satisfaction.* Every element of the company's HR policies and interactions with employees is crafted to build strong and lasting bonds between the company and employees. For instance, the personal evaluation system is designed not just to improve performance and establish compensation levels but also to fulfill employee's ambitions. Supervisors help their staffers map out their career goals and then get the training they need to achieve them.

All this people work pays off. When Accenture opened a gleaming new software programming center in Bangalore in 2003, Wipro initially lost a lot of employees who left for Accenture. They were drawn away by the lure of working for higher pay at one of the world's most respected tech outfits. But within six months, Wipro says, it was hiring more people from Accenture than it was losing people to its rival. "In the end, money takes a back seat to these other factors," says Sahay.

Still, a flexible pay system is crucial to Wipro's success. It's totally merit based. That's a Wipro hallmark. The top 25 percent get the biggest salary hikes and get restricted stock grants. Some of the top performers in 2005 got 40 percent salary increases. The people in the middle got the average salary increase, which was 11 percent in 2005. The bottom 10 percent get little or no raise. The company sometimes bends the rules and doles out spot salary increases to specific individuals, which are separate from any general salary increase. U.K. Program Manager John Hackmann says he got a small raise just two months after he started working for Wipro in mid-2005. "I wasn't expecting it or asking for it. There's a sense they value you as a person," he says.

While the company is flexible about bending compensation rules when need be, it has a strict policy against making counteroffers when employees come to their supervisor with an offer from a competitor. "That would set an unhealthy precedent. Otherwise a lot of people would come and ask for it," says Sahay. Instead, starting in 2004, Wipro came up with a program of dealing with this challenge preemptively. It now offers retention bonuses to absolutely critical employees—not just to managers but also to top technical people. Typically, once an employee is awarded one of these bonuses, he or she gets paid in two chunks, one after six months and one after a year.

Wipro's business unit leaders are given considerable leeway to run their outfits as they see fit, and this includes tinkering with the compensation system. T. K. Kurien is one of the more adventuresome among them. Starting in June 2005, just months after he took over the BPO unit, he restructured the compensation to include a substantial chunk of incentive pay. Up to 30 percent of every employee's salary is based on meeting a set of benchmark goals. The incentive pay of every team member, including managers, is linked to customer satisfaction results, and managers' pay is linked to employee satisfaction.

Wipro has an array of creative incentives for salespeople. It pays richer commissions for deals that include a very high ratio of offshore labor. It also pays more for fixed-price deals, rather than the traditional time-based business model. The company prefers to do fixed-price work because that makes it worthwhile to bring innovation to bear, which gives the client improved efficiencies and gives Wipro richer profit margins. That compensation program has helped shift the amount of Wipro's business that is fixed price from 10 percent at the beginning of the decade to 25 percent in mid-decade.

Still, in spite of its incentives, Wipro faces challenges in attracting and keeping top salespeople. Accenture and IBM simply pay better, in some cases. When Wipro recruits in the United State and Europe, it still has to overcome the image of Indian companies as low-cost, labor-arbitrage operations. That perception is starting to change, as corporations ask the Indian outfits to do more and more sophisticated work—and the Indian companies prove themselves worthy. There's also the attraction of working for a fast-growing up-and-comer. "I talked to McKinsey, IBM, and Wipro—and I chose Wipro," says Theo Forbath, head of tech strategy consulting. Recruiting is "easier than it was five years ago," says P. R. Chandrasekar, the chief executive for Americas and Europe. When it comes to awards and trips for salespeople, though, Wipro is a laggard. It's not that it's against that kind of thing. "We just haven't gotten around to it. Everybody is so stretched, and some things slip—the softer things," he says.

Wipro's pay for executives is pegged to market conditions—with little or no frosting on top. During the last year that Vivek Paul was vice chairman, the 2006 fiscal year, he made $1.3 million in salary and bonus. Paul's fat paycheck reflects the fact that he was a high-profile executive on the world stage and able to command global-scale compensation. Premji himself made $403,000. The next tier of Wipro executives were paid between $160,000 and $180,000 in salary and bonuses. Those pay packages are substantially lower than what a senior vice president at an American tech outfit could expect to make, but they reflect both the lower cost of living in India and the dynamics of the local market for executive talent. It also helps explain why the Wipros of the world can price their services so much lower than their Western competitors.

Use Stock to Share the Wealth

Three decades after Wipro established itself as one of the pioneers of Indian capitalism by going public, it broke new ground again. This time, in 1985, it was the first Indian company to grant stock options to employees. Options were commonly handed out by tech companies in California's Silicon Valley, but Wipro wasn't closely tracking Silicon Valley trends in the early 1980s, and it came to the idea on its own. Options are shares of stock that are granted to employees at the market price on the day of the grant, and they can be sold later for the market price on the day of the sale. In a fast-growing successful company, where the stock price appreciates rapidly, options provide a strong incentive to stick around until they vest and can be sold.

At first, Wipro's stock option plan was just for senior executives, but over time, the company showered options on outstanding middle managers and technical leaders. It made many people wealthy by Bangalore standards. At the end of the 2002–2003 fiscal year,

Wipro had granted more than 14 million options to about 5,000 employees. It stopped granting stock options in 2003 while it considered what to do about upcoming U.S. accounting rules changes; these rules required companies listed on American exchanges to expense stock options.

When Wipro revised its stock compensation plan in October 2004, it became one of the first Indian firms to grant restricted stock. The goal is to identify important contributors and bind them to the company for years. Wipro's restricted shares are granted at a set price, and they can be sold at that price when they vest, 20 percent at a time, over a five-year period. About 500 senior managers get large stock grants worth two to three times their annual salary. And in late 2005, the company decided to increase the stock awards proactively for this core group to keep ahead of the competition. Each year, when 20 percent of their grants vest, they'll be replenished with even larger grants of stock. "We need to grow rapidly over the next three years. To get a fair shot, we need to keep our leadership team intact" says HR boss Kumar.

Stock grants aren't just for top management, however. The company hands out warrants for restricted shares to 8 to 10 percent of its employees each year, including about half of its managers and many highly skilled technical people. It's a motivator, for sure. Several lower-level employees I talked to said that while they did not receive stock yet, they didn't resent it, and they hoped to qualify in the future. Others who have received grants were positively giddy about them. "It's considerable. You can't buy a big mansion, but the Indian market is doing really well, and it's a good incentive to stick with the organization," says Satish Hariharan, a 33-year-old lead consultant in the financial solutions business unit. He has been able to buy a plot of land near the company's campus in Bangalore's Electronics City and plans on building a house on it.

At most long-established American corporations, compensation for white-collar employees seems like a settled matter. Sure, there's tension between employees' expectations and the willingness of their bosses to pay, but America's knowledge workers haven't faced the same pressures that have squeezed pay for their blue-collar counterparts over the past three decades. Until now. As the march of globalization continues and American firms face off with lower-priced outfits from India, China, and elsewhere, there will be considerable pressure on them to reduce compensation costs. That's for everybody from managers to software programmers to business analysts to administrative workers.

Soon Wipro's struggles with finding the right balance between cost cutting and compensation won't seem so, well, foreign. American companies facing these new challenges would be wise to study how Wipro does it, particularly its techniques for improving employee satisfaction and loyalty.

9

SPEND THE MINIMUM ON FRILLS AND PERKS

Compensation isn't the only place where Wipro has to walk a tightrope. The company's executives constantly monitor every kind of expense and look for ways they can do things more cheaply, or spend more wisely. Since tech services are still essentially people businesses, Wipro doesn't enjoy some of the advantages of a traditional software product company. When those companies sell software by the disk, it takes the same number of engineers to develop a product for 1 million customers as it takes to produce the same package for 100 customers. It's simple: The more they sell, the higher their profits. But when you're selling services, you have to add people for every new contract you get. So, to improve profit margins, Wipro and its Indian peers have to continuously squeeze out costs. Wipro looks for annual productivity gains in each of its businesses, depending on the situation. In this way, it achieves operating profit margins in the mid-20s for its technology business, which is comparable to some of the top traditional software makers. That's a remarkable feat.

There's a guiding principle that underlies all of Wipro's spending decisions: value for money. When managers and employees size up a spending situation, they cut out waste at every opportunity. Wipro doesn't scrimp when it comes to its employees' health and safety. It gives the staff good equipment and a pleasant working environment. They're comfortable when they travel. But perks and frills? No way.

The Boss Sets the Tone

When I interviewed Azim Premji for the first time in late 2005, I asked him about a story I had read: He was so tightfisted that he counted the rolls of toilet paper used at Wipro's headquarters. While he said those reports were "completely overdone," he acknowledged that he's very careful about how he spends the company's money. (It's the same in his personal life. While he's the second-richest person in India, he drove a white 1996 Ford Escort for nine years before replacing it in 2005 with an equally modest Toyota Corolla.) He's even cautious about creating the appearance of lavish spending. For instance, even if airlines offer him an upgrade to first class, he won't take it. "It's a philosophy. I apply the same standard for myself as I do for everybody in the organization," he says. "We build an approach with our employees where they consider the company's money as their own money. They apply the same standards of expensing to company money that they apply to their own money. We want people who set policy to walk the talk too. We don't believe in a five-star culture."

A lot of Wipro's reputation for parsimoniousness originated in the early years, when it had difficulty getting foreign exchange for overseas expenses. Back in those days, everybody, even executives, traveled in economy class when they took the 20-hour trips from Bangalore to New York or San Francisco. When engineers and program managers were working in clients' offices, they'd pack two or even three people in a hotel room. Since many projects lasted for months or even years, employees would rent inexpensive apartments. In the early 1990s, one apartment complex in Silicon Valley, Santa Clara's Halford Garden, became a home away from home for many Wiproites. Typically, three engineers would share a flat. The three would budget about $900 monthly for food, and they'd share a car. They'd stifle homesickness by cooking up huge pots of spicy *vindalu* and *masala*. "Wipro was built with the blood, sweat, and tears of those guys," says Subroto Bagchi, the COO of MindTree Consulting Company, who set up Wipro's first operations in Silicon Valley.

In recent years, the company has loosened up its spending policies just a tad. Top executives can now fly business class on overseas trips, though they all—including Premji—still fly coach within India. People are allowed to stay one to a room in hotels. The tightwad culture is so firmly ingrained, however, that some employees still follow the two-to-a-room practice even though it's no longer Wipro law. "I don't think we do anything extreme now," says Premji. "Because of globalization, we have gone more liberal on it, but we still value money. At the same time, we respect that Western culture is different."

Still, stories circulate through the staff about Premji's penchant for penny-pinching. It has been widely reported, for instance, that he sometimes prowls the corridors shutting off lights in unoccupied rooms to conserve electricity. Rich Garnick, former head of Wipro North America, says that while some stories of Premji's frugality are exaggerated, they're also quite useful. "These are urban legends that serve a purpose. You're building a discipline of fiscal responsibility for everybody," says Garnick. With 60,000 dedicated cost cutters on staff, Wipro shaves expenses in thousands of tiny ways, day in and day out. Employees I spoke to embraced the philosophy. "It's a frugal culture. Premji travels coach, so we follow him," says Wipro consultant Satish Hariharan. "There's a business purpose. We pass the savings on to the customer."

There's some fundamental behavior modification going on here. Wipro's frugality doesn't have to be enforced aggressively by the spending police. Instead of the company relying on managers to assure discipline, employees do it themselves. "Wipro entrusts its employees," says Hariprasad Hegde, Wipro's vice president of operations support. "It's a good burden. It comes from within. That's the kind of sweet burden trust is."

At many Western firms, cost cutting typically comes only as a result of a crisis. Quarterly earnings fall short and suddenly there's a mad rush to fire people, freeze the travel budget, and cancel bonuses. While those are some of the quickest ways to cut costs, they can have serious longer-term effects on companies' abilities to serve customers and motivate employees. At Wipro, cost cutting is routine and continuous, which tends to head off crises and the need for hurtful reactions. Not only that: It's strategic. The senior executive group considers cost cutting as part of their annual strategic planning exercise; they come up with focus areas and savings targets at the beginning of each year. Every expense item is fair game. "Nothing is sacrosanct," says V. Balakrishnan, the former chief financial officer of Wipro Technologies.

Make Travel Management a Core Competency

Moving people around is a sizable expense for many companies, but for Wipro, it's huge. To make its global delivery model work, it dispatches thousands of employees to visit or work at clients' offices scattered all over the world. In fiscal year 2005–2006, it bought no fewer than 40,000 airplane tickets. Done wrong, travel could ruin the company, or at least wreck its profit margins. That's why Wipro has made managing travel one of its core competencies.

This discipline starts with a set of sound rules and policies that not only keep costs low but shape employees' behavior. Almost everybody flies coach. Only about 100 top executives are permitted to fly business class, and nobody flies first class. Routine travel arrangements are handled routinely, by rules. But if employees wait until the last minute to arrange travel, they have to get the okay from the senior managers. And they simply won't get it unless the trip is vital to customer satisfaction. This policy deters people from paying bloated fares. They also learn to plan ahead. But all of the attention to planning also sends a deeper message to employees: Consider alternatives to travel. Every Wipro office is equipped with video-conferencing equipment for conducting virtual meetings with far-flung coworkers. In addition, they can use Internet collaboration services and their PCs to give presentations and technology demonstrations to customers and prospects.

To maximize the potential for cost controls and savings, Wipro in 2003 decided to set up its own in-house travel agency. It wasn't enough to get corporate discounts from airlines and hotel chains. In addition, like any other registered travel agency, Wipro Travel Ltd. gets paid commissions by those same companies. "We get the discount on one end and the bonus on the other, says Sekar Sankaran, the travel manager who supervises a team of 19 people in Bangalore and three other Indian cities. Unlike outside travel agents, who tend to bend the rules if somebody pressures them, Wipro's own travel agents can't be pushed around. Sankaran figures that by operating its own travel agency, the company saves 20 to 35 percent in travel expenses per year. Another advantage: The operation provides a test bed for Wipro's software programmers to write for travel-related clients.

The system is highly automated. When employees plan a trip within India, they use the Travel page on Channel W, the employee portal on the company's Web site. They fill out an electronic form with information about themselves and their trip, and then they select from a database of preapproved airlines, flights, and times. The form is sent to their supervisor, who immediately approves or turns thumbs down on the trip. If the trip and itinerary are approved, the travel bureau issues an e-ticket.

International travel is a little more complicated. Once employees fill out their electronic forms and submit them, travel counselors use a software program that analyzes the trips and fares available from their preferred airlines. They help the employees choose the least expensive acceptable flight. For both domestic and international trips, employees make lodging arrangements on the hotel chains' own Web sites, using Wipro discount codes. Once all the arrangements are made, the travel office compiles the details and sends electronic itineraries to the employees by e-mail.

The rules are clearly spelled out on Channel W. Each employee has a grade level, and each grade has spending limits for hotels, meals, and other expenses. Most employees, for instance, are supposed to use mass transportation. They can use a taxi only if they're transporting a customer. The company doesn't compromise on the quality of the airlines or the scheduling of flights, however. Employees aren't required to take flights if they include more than two transfers, and they don't have to put up with long layovers.

The travel office demands more than basic across-the-board corporate discounts from airlines. Because of Wipro's high volume of travel, it's able to get deeper discounts on some of its highly traveled routes. In addition, Sankaran and his crew negotiate five to seven pricing levels within economy class with each international carrier, depending largely on how heavily booked a particular flight is. Sankaran figures he saves $300 to $400 per ticket this way.

Wipro does another unusual thing. It actually operates its own guest houses for traveling employees on each of its campuses in India, plus a small one in London. These are buildings with double and single rooms; all told, they have 550 of them. They're nothing fancy: a bed, a desk, an Internet connection. Most don't even have a telephone—to discourage expensive international calling, employees say. But the rooms are clean and comfortable. The cost to Wipro is one-third that of a traditional hotel room.

Facilities: Design from the Inside Out

With 50,000 employees in India alone, Wipro isn't just a major software company, it's a major real estate developer. It's constantly building new campuses either in cities where it already operates or in additional cities where there isn't yet such fierce competition for fresh college graduates. As of March 2006, it had 6.5 million square feet of office space in India and was planning on adding 1.4 million square feet in the next fiscal year. In Bangalore's Electronics City alone, the company houses 15,000 employees—a number that is expected to reach nearly 20,000 in 2007. The company plans and designs its own campuses. With each new generation of expansion, it rethinks the way it does things, redesigning from the inside out. The goal is to achieve comfort for employees and utility for the company, while at the same time eliminating waste.

Designing from the inside out means these aren't general purpose buildings. They're designed specifically for the work Wipro's employees perform: software programming, hardware engineering, and business process management. The optimal work space for programmers is individual cubicles; for business process agents, it's long tables almost like factory production lines. First, the size and layout of the individual work space is carefully thought out. Then Wipro's planners consider the need for conference rooms, labs for hardware engineers, cafeterias, and bathrooms. There's no waste. As of early 2006, the new buildings coming online allotted just 110 square feet of total space per employee. Through redesign and other efficiencies, the company achieved a 17 percent office space productivity gain in fiscal 2005. It followed with a more modest 10 percent gain in fiscal 2006, which was hampered mainly by rising steel prices.

Just because Wipro continually cuts costs out of construction doesn't mean it does things on the cheap. Its buildings are first class: comfortable, safe, and attractive. The company operates its own fitness centers and runs exercise and yoga classes. Employees are charged about $1 per month to participate, just so they value the program. Also, the company is willing to spend money to save money. For instance, in 2004 it began replacing traditional boxy PC monitors with more expensive flat-panel screens. The move saved on electricity, gave employees in existing buildings more room to maneuver, and made it possible to shrink the cubicles slightly in new buildings. With so many cubicles going up, every square foot counts, and the incremental savings add up. "We'll spend extra if there's value in it," says Hegde, the facilities boss.

Once a building is up, the quest for economies doesn't stop. If anything, it intensifies. In 2001, the company did a detailed analysis of food waste in its cafeterias. The tally: 85 grams (almost 3 ounces) of waste per person per day. That seemed excessive, so it began sensitizing employees by setting up a procedure for them to scrape their leftovers into bins when they finished a meal. The company measured waste weekly and published updates. "When you publish the numbers, you make people conscious. Maybe tomorrow they won't take such a big helping," says Hegde.

The tactic worked. The latest tally was just 45 grams (about 1.6 ounces). To make sure even that measly amount didn't actually go to waste, Wipro began a composting program. It uses the compost to fertilize trees and shrubs on its grounds. The company later analyzed the cost of using paper towels in bathrooms and discovered that air dryers would be cheaper and more sanitary—it made the switch.

While Wipro seems to have facilities management down to a science in India, it needs to spruce up some of its international offices. These are typically rented spaces, and sometimes, because of concerns over economies, they're in second-rate locations or their decor and amenities are substandard, according to staffers. That's a negative for recruiting and retaining employees, but just as significantly, it can create a poor impression on clients or prospects. It's something the company is conscious of and working to fix.

Where Cost Cutting and Conservation Meet

At Wipro, there's a natural synergy between saving money and conserving natural resources. They are two of the company's core values. You can see the overlap most clearly in the way Wipro handles water. In 2003, Premji and his executive team recognized that potable water was becoming a scarce resource, and they set out to do something about it. Premji himself set the ambitious goal of reducing Wipro's water consumption per employee by 60 percent. The first step was putting in meters and publishing consumption metrics. The next: recycling. The company began using recycled water for its grounds and for flushing toilets. Within one year, from May 2003 to May 2004, the savings were huge: 58 percent. Next: a water harvesting program. The company installed systems in its Bangalore campuses for capturing and storing rainwater. In 2005, it captured rainfall during just a part of the monsoon and harvested 12,000 kiloliters (3,170,132 gallons) of water. At that rate, the system will produce 45 days of water for those facilities per year. Now it's replicating the system at all of its Indian campuses.

The company is increasingly taking conservation into account when it designs new buildings. Its new software development center in Gurgoan, near Delhi, in late 2005 was recognized for its energy conservation features by being named one of just 10 platinum-rated buildings worldwide by the U.S. Green Building Council. The features include motion sensors for dimmable lighting and a battery charging facility for electric vehicles.

Conservation not only saves money directly and is good for the environment, but it also sends the message to employees to persist in conservation in everything they do. "This is how we do business. It's not complicated," says Hegde. "You ask questions. Is there waste? If there is, how do you cut it out? Then you ask yourself what is the value in every single thing you pay for."

Manage Costs While Gaining Value

Wipro employees are acutely aware of the need to trim costs, and they work diligently at it. But at this point, much of the low-hanging fruit has already been harvested. Making additional gains requires creative thinking. The essential question is: How do you turn a cost into a savings—and better yet, a source of long-term value? This is one of Wipro's most crucial skills as an organization.

The company's technique for handling overseas employees shows how expert it has become at spotting opportunities for saving money and adding value. About 20 percent of its employees are outside India. In addition to salespeople and its small team of IT consultants (who typically live in the countries where they work), Wipro also employs thousands of software programmers, program managers, and IT services people in or near its customers' offices. In order to be competitive on price and service quality, it must put just the right people in front of customers—and no more.

This requires nimble planning and management of people in the field. The company tracks the status of work on projects daily and maintains forecasts of upcoming work. Using this data, it then does weekly analyses to determine which employees it needs overseas and where it needs them, matching up its supply of overseas labor with demand. A key metric in the IT services business is the utilization rate. That's how much of the labor that's available is actively engaged in client projects. Wipro's on-site utilization rate is typically 97 to 98 percent. It compares quite favorably to a utilization rate of about 65 percent for Western IT services outfits. Wipro accomplishes this tight budgeting of talent by keeping employees back in India who aren't immediately required overseas. "We keep the entire bench offshore. We can quickly fly them to the United States or Europe when they're needed," says Balakrishnan.

And when staffers are called back to India to await another overseas assignment, they don't sit on their hands. Instead, if there isn't work for them to do in the home offices, they're placed in training programs. The tech industry is constantly changing, and engineers need to constantly refresh their knowledge to keep pace. So as long as they're not needed immediately, why not upgrade their skills? Programmers who are temporarily on the bench also upgrade their knowledge about the business dynamics of particular industries, or learn foreign languages. In this way, an expense is translated into an opportunity to create future value.

You see case after case where Wipro spends very little and Western IT services companies spend a lot. Consider marketing. For starters, outside of India Wipro does not spend a dime on advertising its brand or services on television or in print media. It figures that its target market is the top 1,000 corporations in the world, and it really only needs to communicate with about 6,000 people—so paying for advertising that reaches millions of people makes little sense. "It would cost millions to do basic brand advertising in the United States during a year. That's a large chunk of the budget. We feel we can come up with better ways to spend the money," says Jessie Paul, the company's chief marketing officer.

Rather than traditional advertising, Wipro focuses on being recognized as a thought leader within its industry. It coproduces informational Web sites and Web seminars in conjunction with business publications and university research programs. It also sponsors industry conferences, where its leaders participate as speakers and panelists. This kind of marketing works for Wipro. It's carefully targeted, and it's much cheaper than advertising.

Know When to Spend

In a few cases, Wipro spends where some of its competitors cut corners. These exceptions are usually related to staff improvement. Training is one. During the services industry downturn of 2001 and 2002, rather than cutting back on training, the company actually increased the budget to fund its new talent development programs. It doesn't scrimp when it comes to tapping expensive external expertise either. The company uses McKinsey & Company consultants to provide strategy or planning advice and to conduct seminars for its leaders. It engages the world's top management gurus. In 2004, for instance, the company paid C. K. Prahalad, the noted author and management professor at the University of Michigan, to conduct a three-day leadership program in Bangalore.

Team building is another area where Wipro is willing to loosen the purse strings. The company arranges two- and three-day group bonding programs for managers at facilities outside Bangalore run by former Indian military officers. It also encourages managers to conduct off-site meetings and retreats for their staffs. These aren't extravagant affairs at expensive golf and spa resorts, but they achieve some of the same goals: boosting morale, strengthening bonds between colleagues, and encouraging free thinking.

Here's a typical Wipro retreat: In late 2005, marketing chief Paul treated her staff of 20 to a weekend at Devbagh, a tiny island off the coast of India. They learned rock climbing on a 40-foot cliff, played a cricket match, and went dolphin watching. But it was boat rides on a nearby river that provided the catharsis that leaders hope for in situations like this. Four at a time, young Wipro marketers outfitted with life vests climbed into rubber boats. Since few Indians know how to swim, this by itself was a leap of faith. Then, out on the river, they all agreed to have the boats capsize, trusting in each other and their life vests. In India's risk-averse culture, this is a big step. "At Wipro, this isn't considered a frill," says Paul. "We cut corners when we can, but it's not on the important stuff."

There's no easy magic formula here. Wipro's ability to run fast on a tight budget is based on fundamental values that infuse the organization from top to bottom. Leaders lead by example. Employees not only police their own spending, but they also continuously look for ways to get more value for money. Rules and processes are set in place to systematically gain and lock in savings. There's little friction, and there's a big payoff in profit margins.

10

BUILD A FOUNDATION OF VETERANS, BUT REFRESH YOUR TEAM WITH OUTSIDERS

Pop quiz: What do IBM, General Electric, and Microsoft have in common? Besides the fact that they have been successful over a long span of years, one common thread is that many of their executives have spent all or most of their careers working in that one place. These blue chip companies have strong cultures where certain types of people thrive—and stick to it. The same is true for Wipro. It obviously hasn't achieved the success of these giants of capitalism, but its ability to nurture and develop its own stable of executives has been a key factor in its success so far, and it provides a strong foundation for its future growth.

Wipro has also benefited from infusions of fresh blood. The most important addition: Vivek Paul, who came to Wipro in 1999 from GE and helped to give it the discipline and ambition to take on the world's tech giants. Another important add was Rich Garnick, who taught Wipro a new way to sell its services to large American corporations. With their departures in 2005, Wipro lost some of its diversity. Now it plans on recruiting a new crop of outsiders to help it achieve the next level of globalization.

Cultivate a Sense of History

Back in 1996, when Subroto Bagchi had been running Wipro's global hardware engineering operations for a couple of years, he

went to his boss, Ashok Soota, then vice chairman of the technology group, and told him he was restless. He wanted to try something
new. When Soota asked him to describe the kind of job he was after,
Bagchi said he wanted to work on a problem that kept Soota and
Premji awake at night. A few months later, Bagchi got a call from
Premji's office. The two met, and the chairman asked Bagchi to
become the corporate executive in charge of quality, binding
together all of the company's disparate businesses and turning it into
a world-class quality organization. Bagchi thought it over. He was a
bit intimidated. He had no experience in the area. He asked: Why
not hire a quality expert for the job? Premji's answer was that "he
said he wanted someone with a 'sense of history,'" recalls Bagchi,
who is now chief operating officer for MindTree Consulting.

If you look at Wipro's executive and management ranks, you'll see
a whole shelf of history books. While it's typical for senior executives at other Indian tech firms to be long timers, the theme is even
more pronounced at Wipro. About 85 percent of Wipro's most
senior 300 managers grew up within the company. For several people in Premji's inner circle, Wipro was their first employer out of
university, and they have worked there for 20 to 25 years. These guys
were on the ground floor when the tech business was started, and
they stayed with the organization as it emerged from backwater
upstart to global contender. Among the company's battle-tested veterans are Sudip Banerjee, head of Enterprise Solutions; G. K.
Prasanna, head of the infrastructure services group; Ramesh Emani,
head of Product Engineering Solutions; A. L. Rao, the chief operating officer; and Divakaran Mangalath, the chief technology officer. Premji says he's proud that so many people have stayed with
Wipro for so long. "We select superior people, train them well, and
give them responsibility at an early age. They stand out," he says.

The academic credentials among Wipro's executives are also quite
impressive. Premji was forced to drop out of college, but that's not
typical of the people clustered around him. Take Sudip Nandy, the
chief strategy officer. He grew up in the hinterlands of eastern India
but was one of 150 high school seniors nationally to win a govern-

ment science talent scholarship. He was schooled at some of India's elite universities, receiving a Bachelor of Science (B.S.) degree in physics from the Indian Institute of Technology, a B.S. degree in electronics from the Indian Institute of Science, and a Master of Business Administration (MBA) degree from the Indian Institute of Management.

Wipro doesn't put people with fancy degrees straight into corporate jobs. They have to learn the business first. After Nandy arrived at Wipro in 1983, he held a series of computer sales jobs in eastern India, then supervised sales in the network systems division in Bangalore, later headed product engineering sales and marketing in the United States, then supervised marketing for a chip design subsidiary in Silicon Valley, and still later managed European sales. Finally, he became chief strategy officer in 2004.

While so many of the company's top managers are veterans, others who climbed through the ranks later moved on. There was a wave of departures in the late 1990s, as seasoned executives responded to the siren call of the dot-coms. In addition, after Paul took over the tech group, he pushed a handful of people out. Lower in the ranks, there's a natural selection process. Not everybody is built to handle the stress and long hours required to succeed at Wipro, where a typical manager's week stretches to 65 or 70 hours and Premji is known to wake people with weekend phone calls and pepper them with questions about their businesses.

Why do the veterans stay so long? "There's a self-selecting mechanism. After five years, if people are still here, they're likely to be here forever," says Banerjee, president of Enterprise Solutions. "It's the combination of learning and opportunities to lead. That's what you stay for."

How to Create a Zero-Politics Culture

Wipro's management culture, of course, is a reflection of the personality of the company's leader. In addition to shaping the values of the entire organization, Premji established two core principles

that are instrumental in forging the character of his leadership
team. The first one is quite rare among Indian family-controlled
companies: The chairman is not king. While Premji owns a controlling stake in the company, he shares authority and responsibility with his lieutenants. He plays a major role in shaping the
company's values, vision, and strategy, but these are essentially group
activities. The second key management principle: Open and honest disagreements are not just tolerated but required. Premji believes
in a zero-politics culture. "I set the example by tone and practice,"
he says. "The openness with which we run the company brings
politics to the surface. A person can't outsmart the system. Things
can't be hidden."

Indeed, with Premji, there are no secrets. If somebody meets with
him or e-mails him and tells him something of importance, everybody who needs to know about it will know the next morning or
within a couple of days. He doesn't keep anything to himself, his
lieutenants say. As a result, people don't feel comfortable giving him
gossip. Also, whenever an important decision has to be made, Premji
will not make it without talking to all the stakeholders who are positively or negatively affected.

All of this creates an environment where backstabbing, self-
dealing, playing favorites, lying, and kissing up to the boss don't
work. Many of the tactics that occupy so much of the time and
energies of American executives simply aren't tolerated. When managers hired from the outside try Machiavellian maneuvers, either
they don't stay long or they quickly learn to change the way they
operate. "There are absolutely no politics. It has been like that from
the beginning," says A. L. Rao. Former executives, including Paul,
confirm that very little internal politicking goes on.

One way an organization can minimize politics is by being very
careful about who it allows in. Premji has a strong voice in recruiting and choosing key people who are hired from the outside. He
wants to make sure these people will be a cultural fit before he
brings them in. He interviews a lot of the management recruits.
These aren't perfunctory affairs either. He spends hours with peo-

ple, encouraging free-flowing conversations, finding out how they think and operate, and exploring their values. Suresh Senapaty, the CFO, recalls that when he interviewed with Premji for a job as an internal auditor in 1980, the meeting lasted from 2 p.m. to 7 p.m. "It was as if he was trying to extract everything I had in my mind. He gave me enough time to think and talk. It became the reason I wanted to work for Wipro. I felt I could think and work innovatively." Rich Garnick had a similar experience in 2000.

Premji mentors his executives throughout their Wipro careers. As chairman, he has more than a dozen executives reporting to him. They say he does a good job of giving them room to make their own decisions but he also knows their businesses well enough that he can ask them smart questions and give them good advice. He has an impressive capacity for recalling details of conversations. "You have a review and then meet a week later; he remembers right where you left off," says Rao.

The boss doesn't play favorites. This starts with his family. While he has two sons, neither of them works in the company. The older one, Rishad, who got an MBA from Harvard, is a management consultant for Bain & Company in London. The younger son, Tariq, works in the family investment company. Premji made it clear to them from an early age that there would be no place for them in Wipro. No other relatives work there either. He decided on a strict no-nepotism policy from the very beginning, figuring it would help him recruit and retain talented people.

It sends a signal to his executives and staffers that people will succeed or fail at Wipro based on their merits. Also, on a practical level, it means that when Premji retires from actively running the company, something he expects to do in five years or so, neither of his sons will succeed him. That gives his top executives a shot at running the show, which is a strong motivator for people to give their best to the organization and to stay around to see how things work out. "I have told them that in all probability we will hire from within. We'll look at their performance and give preference to a person who has helped build the company," says Premji.

Wipro management meetings aren't polite affairs. Premji encourages people to disagree with one another and to express their true opinions. "I never before had this degree of freedom of expression. He's actively building a culture of dissent. It's one of the reasons that he gets good people and people stay with him," says Anurag Behar, managing director for Wipro Infrastructure Engineering. Behar joined Wipro in 2002 from General Electric, which has a reputation for letting people speak their minds. But Behar insists that at Wipro the trait is even more pronounced. "Irrespective of what level you're on, you're expected to have a view of your own and also to express it and defend it. That's not true at GE," he says.

During the company's strategic planning sessions in late 2005, after Paul left, there were frank disagreements and long debates. How to approach China was one: Several of the executives favored staffing up aggressively and marketing to homegrown Chinese corporations, not just the multinationals. But in the end, the group decided on a go-slow strategy for the time being. "Sometimes it gets really hot. But at the end of the day we make the right call," says Suresh Vaswani, head of Wipro Infotech. "There are dissents. But once a decision is made, we all get behind it."

One more point about openness. Premji doesn't just encourage his lieutenants to debate one another; he insists that they debate him as well—or even take him to task for his decisions or actions. "The man takes frontal criticism, and it's celebrated. You can openly disagree with him," says Bagchi, the former Wipro executive.

An episode from the mid-1990s shows how tolerant Premji is of disagreement, even when it gets very personal. At the time, Bagchi was in charge of the company's quality initiatives, but Premji had asked him to also handle major office building projects in Bangalore and Hyderabad. When Bagchi was slow to get something done, Premji called him at his home one afternoon when Bagchi was having tea with his mother. Bagchi resented Premji piling more responsibilities on his plate. "I said, 'I'm corporate vice president of mission quality, and what do I have to do with real estate?' I told him, 'Don't expect me to do your clerical jobs for you!' I actually screamed at him over the phone," Bagchi recalls. Bagchi's mother was appalled that he would speak to the chairman that way, and after the call ended, she lectured him about showing proper respect to one's boss.

The maternal tongue lashing made Bagchi worry that he might have crossed the line. Would Premji be furious with him? Yet a couple of hours later, after he had returned to the office and he ran into Premji in the hallway, the chairman didn't even mention the episode. He spoke to Bagchi about something else. By Premji's rules of conduct, Bagchi's reaction had been okay. Bagchi was supposed to tell him exactly what he felt. "He would tell us, 'My job is to push you. When you reach your limit, you need to push back,'" recalls Bagchi.

Familiarity Breeds Teamwork

Over the years, Premji has cooked up and refined a unique management recipe. Most of his managers have an intimate knowledge of the company and of each other stretching over many years. They're required to discuss and debate all the issues with one another and Premji. And they have a thoroughly matrixed organization where people can't succeed on their own. The people who run the industry verticals need to collaborate closely with the people who run the service practice groups, the sales leaders, the HR planners and trainers, and the quality leaders. This assures that teamwork isn't something that is tacked on. It's woven into the organization.

At Wipro, familiarity doesn't breed contempt; it fosters a willingness to help and be helped. These siblinglike relationships at the office, combined often with social ties outside the office, bind people together. "In this situation, having a long-term relationship helps. The person you want help from might have worked for you before, you know them well, and you do family things together," says Sudip Banerjee, president of the Enterprise Solutions business unit. "Sometimes you'll have sharp differences. But if you have a family get-together scheduled for two weeks ahead, you can't hold your differences for long."

The executives' ease with one another makes it possible to make decisions quickly when necessary. For example, in 2000, at the time of the dot-com boom, a handful of managers came up with the idea of starting an e-procurement marketplace, like CommerceOne and FreeMarkets in the United States. These were electronic exchanges where buyers and sellers matched up supplies and demands for materials, components, and products—and the exchange operator took a transaction fee. The business model was hot at the time, and if Wipro wanted to get first-mover advantage in India, it had to move quickly. Because the managers understood their company's capabilities and trusted one another, they decided after only a short discussion to green-light the project. A small team drew on resources from all over the company. They went from concept to an operating business in just six months. And that included writing the business plan, getting approval, assembling a team, writing the software, and putting in place alliances with other companies.

Knowing when to quit is another Wipro knack. The executive group constantly monitors the progress of initiatives to see if they are panning out. The leaders are very patient if it looks like a long-term investment will eventually pay off. In other cases, the group decides to back out. An example is Wipro's foray into running an Internet service provider (ISP) business—like AOL, MSN, and EarthLink. It launched its ISP in 1999, but within three years, it became obvious Wipro didn't have much value to add to this business by leveraging its software and computer management skills. Also, ISP margins couldn't match those for software development or product engineering. So while this was a good business for others, it wasn't strategic for Wipro—so the company got out. It quickly handed off its customers to other ISPs and folded the employees back into its other businesses.

Every new business venture that's proposed at Wipro has to pass through a gauntlet of skepticism. The aim is to avoid big costly mistakes. This culls out the flimsiest ideas early. And it forces people with good ideas not only to back them up with loads of facts and a sharp rationale but, often, to test concepts in small pilot projects. In

2004, for instance, a group of people in the company's technology infrastructure outsourcing business started pressing for an expansion of the strategy. They wanted to add to the portfolio of services and, for the first time, commit Wipro's own capital to buying computers and networking gear from its clients, the way EDS and IBM did. They saw this as a necessary step for getting into the big leagues of infrastructure outsourcing. Rather than being in a more limited market where Wipro could collect $10 million a year from a major client, it could aim for $50 to $75 million.

Straight off, they met resistance from members of the IT Strategy Council. The concern was about committing Wipro's own capital to these deals. Anand Sankaran, who was pushing the proposal, says that if he hadn't been working with this group for 15 years, he might have thrown in the towel immediately. "If I was an outsider joining the company, I would have probably given up, with that kind of resistance. But I knew the DNA. I knew that there was a set of people who would challenge it, but in an open organization, every idea is open for debate," he says, adding that these discussions rarely get personal. "Nobody is trying to shoot a person. They're questioning an idea."

Instead of giving up, Sankaran and his colleagues came back with a stronger proposal. They would test out the new strategy in India first before attempting to take it global. And rather than always using its own capital to buy clients' computing assets, Wipro would in some cases form alliances with banks to finance the deals. The banks would take the credit risk and Wipro would take the performance risk. The strategy council approved the project, and Sankaran got the job of making it work. He was so successful in India that in early 2006 he began expanding the strategy to the United States and Europe.

This culture of debate has worked well for Wipro. The company enters a lot of new businesses, but it rarely suffers a major defeat. Aggressive people in the middle and even lower ranks feel empowered to propose new ideas. Yet, at the same time, they know that they won't get approval unless they have done their homework. "It's not rash decision making, but calculated risks are encouraged," says

Sankaran. "Managers who have spent time at Wipro are willing to put their foot forward and try something different."

Rotate Jobs to Rejuvenate Your Managers

While many of Wipro's top managers have been there for many years, they rarely stay in one spot for long. Instead, most of them change jobs every few years, often switching back and forth between line management, corporate functions, sales, and quality. It's a rotation that refreshes. It prevents narrowing and hardening of executives' attitudes about what's possible. Take the career of Selvan Dorairaj, the vice president for talent transformation and staffing. Before taking that job in 2002, he previously ran a business unit within the financial services vertical for two years, spearheaded the Six Sigma quality initiative before that, and earlier ran a regional software distribution operation for northern India. "The rotation gives you a very holistic view of the organization. It also gives you the rounded training and the confidence to take on any situation," Dorairaj says. It also creates synergies between corporate and business-line people. Dorairaj's experiences in line management and quality were what inspired him to lead a huge talent transformation initiative once he took on the training role.

Rotating through jobs also gives executives knowledge they can use to handle their new assignments better. Laxman Badiga, Wipro's chief information officer, was formerly in human resources. The company has a database of employees that it uses to organize and manage project teams. But the database doesn't have features that make it easy to forecast changes in demand four or six months in the future. That shortcoming sometimes results in delays in projects getting started or in slower-than-expected progress. Laxman is working on improvements to the project management system that make it possible to match upcoming project demands with the availability of talent—and proactively train people to meet future demand. He's able to deeply understand what's required in this software application because of his understanding, gained through his previous jobs, of how the existing personnel management systems work.

Another benefit of the Wipro's job rotation practice is that it shakes people out of their routines. After managers in any company have been doing the same job for five or six years, they tend to become complacent. When they shift to a new job, they get a burst of adrenaline. "When you move, you're stimulated, and you're more productive," says Dorairaj, the training leader.

Replenish Your Leadership Team with New Blood

Since the late 1990s, Wipro has hired from the outside both to get specific skills and to refresh the organization. From GE or the Wipro GE Medical Systems joint venture, Premji hired Vivek Paul, P. R. Chandrasekar, who now manages the U.S. and European organizations, and T. K. Kurien, head of BPO. Rich Garnick had been running a Boston wireless networking start-up. Sanjay Joshi, the co-CEO of consulting, came from Infosys; and Timothy Matlack, the other consulting chief, came through the acquisition of American Management Systems. While Premji hires people whom he expects to share his values, he isn't looking for a bunch of yes-men. He wants to be challenged and he wants his lieutenants to be challenged, as well. Bagchi recalls that on his last day at Wipro, in 2000, Premji asked him to stay. "I told him that we were very different people. He told me, '*That* is why we should work together.'"

Paul arrived after Ashok Soota had run the tech business for 15 years. People respected Soota, who left in 1999 to cofound MindTree Consulting, but looking back, they say Paul gave the organization a shakeup that was long overdue. When Paul arrived, he had worked in GE for four years and GE's joint venture with Wipro for six years. He also had put in several years as a Bain & Company management consultant. So he had broad management expertise, knowledge of GE's world-class processes, and more than a passing knowledge of Wipro. In fact, during his last couple of years running the joint venture, he had served on Wipro's corporate marketing council.

When he took on the global technology job, Paul spent 100 days looking and listening. Rather than firing a bunch of leaders almost immediately, which would have been the GE way, he decided to move more gradually. He also felt it was premature to come out with some grand new strategy. "I said we don't even deserve a vision until we achieve a new level of operating efficiencies," he says. He spent the next half year identifying what he felt were the correct metrics to measure progress and coming up with process improvements that would improve those metrics. When he felt the company was on firm ground, he and his executive team laid out the aggressive growth goals that gave Wiproites a target to aim at for the next four years.

Rich Garnick came on at a time when Wipro's U.S. sales were bogged down in the wake of the September 11, 2001, terror attacks. Also at the time, there were no non-Indians in the executive ranks. "Premji hired me to drive change. He made that clear," says Garnick, who had been CEO of a wireless networking start-up, Global Digital Media. Garnick started off as head of American software services sales, but within six months he was promoted to run all of the North American operations. "I found my karma there," says Garnick, who left in mid-2005 to run North American operations for Keane Inc., a Boston-based tech services outfit.

When he arrived, Garnick had found that the business model was sound but the sales tactics were less than optimal. "They were selling Wipro like it was a body shop, rather than selling the solutions and value they could bring to clients," Garnick recalls. So he focused on marketing solutions to customers, rather than just responding when they sent out requests for proposals. He also pitched Wipro's services to decision makers higher in the clients' organizations. And he personally trained Wipro salespeople in how to prepare sales strategies, how to make their pitch, and how to negotiate terms. The salesforce was almost 100 percent Indian at the time. A number of Americans had quit. They were frustrated, Garnick says, with the fact that so much decision making had been done in India. "I came in at a high-enough level that I had clout to get things done," Garnick says.

Paul and Garnick came in at the top of their organizations, so they didn't face some of the challenges that midlevel managers do when they arrive. For these others, Wipro's strong culture is like a foreign language that they have to learn before they can truly fit in. "It takes some time. It's not easy to get everybody comfortable with you, and you with them," says V. Balakrishnan, a former CFO for the global technology business. He had previously worked at Wipro GE Medical Systems, where the GE culture predominated, before he arrived at Wipro in 1996. It took him two to three years to find his place. One thing he discovered was that Wipro is full of paradoxes. "You have to have a strong will and at the same time be very humble," he says. "Being flashy and aggressive isn't appreciated here."

Balakrishnan learned this lesson in an embarrassing way. Early on, he was the general manager of finance for the computers and peripherals division in India. At one management meeting, the head of the peripherals unit had committed to very aggressive sales gains. But when the quarter ended, his unit missed the target, and worse yet, he had not given the other managers any warning that bad news was coming. So at the next management meeting, Balakrishnan dressed him down. This was the GE style. Balakrishnan was stunned when, rather than joining in, the boss reproached *him*. "He told me 'That's not the way we do things at Wipro,'" Balakrishnan recalls. "You're supposed to be factual and not emotional. The point I made was right, but the way I did it was wrong."

Jessie Paul faced a double barrier when she took over as chief marketing officer in mid-2005. Not only was she an outsider from rival Infosys, but she was heading up a function for which some of Wipro's engineering-oriented executives had low regard. Paul's main task was to get the top executives to appreciate the value of communicating regularly with industry analysts and journalists. Since brand advertising was a no-go, she felt the most effective way to introduce the company to prospective customers and shape opinion was through these influencers. She hired a consulting firm, Knowledge Capital Group, to conduct training programs on how to talk to industry and stock analysts—one for the top corporate executives and others for midmanagers. Then she arranged for half the executives to travel to Boston in February 2006 for a full day of presentations with America's key tech industry analysts. These are the people that corporations count on to tell them which service providers they should use. It was the first time Wipro had ever done that sort of briefing. To help raise Wipro's profile as a thought leader, Paul also arranged for Premji to attend the World Economic Forum annual meeting in Davos, Switzerland, just before the analysts' meeting. Paul won cooperation from executives for her program through persistence and persuasion. "They're fairly open-minded," she says. "If you can explain why something should be done, they'll do it."

She also got help from some members of the inner circle. Girish Paranjpe, head of financial solutions, and Pratik Kumar, head of HR, were always ready to lend a sympathetic ear when Paul needed to blow off steam. Suresh Senapaty and T. K. Kurien gave her advice about how to present her ideas to the executive group.

Know When to Follow the Rules and When to Break Them

It's clear that Wipro's tight-knit culture is open to new people and new ideas, but it's also clear that the company could use another infusion of outsiders with bold initiatives. Several former executives told me that Wipro needs to be more ambitious and less averse to taking risks. "Because of the way the company has been built, people who sought nonlinear rewards have gone elsewhere. The remaining people are great at executing and delivering," says Vivek Paul. "That's a good match with the current business model. But, if there's a turn in the road, they might miss it."

It's not that people with an entrepreneurial spirit aren't welcomed at Wipro; but at its size and with its culture, it's just not the kind of place where a classic entrepreneur feels a rush of excitement. Raman Roy, the founder of Spectramind, stayed with Wipro for three years after the merger before resigning in June 2005 to go off and launch a new start-up. "In a large corporation like Wipro, you don't get the elbow room to do what you want to do," he says. "When you come up with a new idea, you want the flexibility to experiment. You don't want to spend a lot of time making presentations about the idea."

Breakthrough innovation comes from breaking rules, and that's a challenge for Wipro, too. This is an organization whose success, for the most part, has been based on following rules to the letter. That's the path to improving quality in software development and business process management. Wipro needs to operate with a split personality, to be a stickler for rules in much of what it does and a rebel in others. That's tough. One former executive said Wipro's advances in pure technology are competent but uninspired. They're too incremental to turn the company into a tech leader. "It's not real innovation," he says.

Some of Wipro's leaders believe these critiques are overly harsh. Senapaty points out that Wipro was the first of the Indian tech outfits to enter Europe and Japan. "We're risk takers," he insists. Anand Sankaran, head of the Total Outsourcing unit, believes that the dynamism of the tech industry and the impatience of Wipro's young up-and-comers have kept its leaders from becoming complacent. "As the younger people come in, they're enterprising. They want to do things faster and better. That keeps the managers on their toes," he says.

Yet even Premji agrees that Wipro has some remodeling work to do. He acknowledges that the company must recruit from the outside to avoid becoming inbred. It needs more non-Indian executives and board members. "We're going to drive that now," he says. At the same time, he launched the Quantum Innovation initiative, aimed at making game-changing technology discoveries. So the boss is shaking his team up. We'll see over the next few years if the changes he's making now will power the company to the $5 billion revenue mark, and then on to $10 billion.

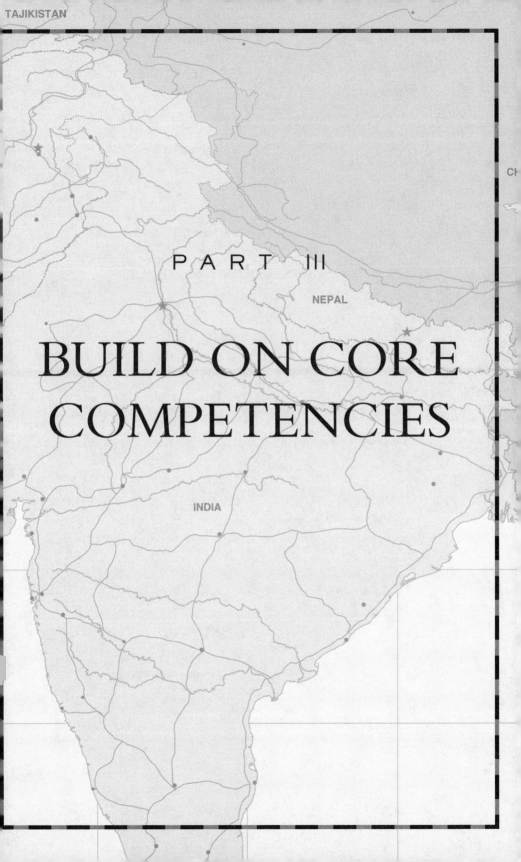

PART III

BUILD ON CORE COMPETENCIES

11

MEASURE EVERYTHING CONSTANTLY

Constant improvement is one of Wipro's mantras, but it would be a hollow rallying cry if the company didn't back it up by constant measurement of its progress as well. This effort comes naturally. After all, most of the employees in its tech business were trained as engineers, more comfortable handling calculators and spreadsheets than they are making speeches and sales pitches. Wipro benchmarks its practices and performance against those of the top companies in the world and, especially, against its competitors. It keeps an internal scorecard of key operational metrics, including quality, financial performance, and efficiency, and it sets ambitious goals for improvement of each. Within the software services groups, Wipro's managers track and measure every step of the development process, both to keep projects on course and to spot ways to improve the development process itself. As you might expect, personnel evaluations are rigorous. In the dog-eat-dog tech services business, a company can't afford to give itself any slack, and Wipro doesn't.

Living by Numbers

In the early days after Premji arrived back in India to take over a failing cooking oil operation, the company's most basic operation—assessing and buying peanuts—was handled through intuition. Buyers would handle and bite nuts to help them guess the oil content level and to come up with a price they'd pay the farmer.

Premji changed that practice straight off. He made people use rudimentary measuring tools. Facts replaced intuition as one of Wipro's core competencies. A short while later, Premji began measuring his managers' performance by the numbers, comparing one against another and using the results to motivate them. This was the foundation of the metrics-obsessed Wipro of today.

Wipro's executives don't believe performance metrics can be completely effective unless you tell a large number of people about them. So it publishes a tremendous amount of data internally in reports for managers and on its various Web sites for mass internal consumption. That includes everything from details of quarterly earnings reports to the amount of food wasted in the cafeterias. The company also believes in telling investors exactly what's going on inside—positive or negative. In 1984, Wipro was the first company in India to break out its earnings by business segment. That didn't become a regulatory requirement in the country until 2003. These practices provide practical information that employees can use to improve their performance and investors can use to make better investment decisions. Not only that, but these practices send a bigger message loud and clear: This is an honest and credible company. In the era of corporate malfeasance at the likes of Enron, Adelphia, and WorldCom, that's a valuable message.

To be useful, metrics need to be placed in a framework where they're evaluated rigorously and in context. Wipro does this religiously. Think of any of the most popular business performance methodologies of the past 20 years, and you can bet that Wipro is using it—or at least has checked it out. Typically, the company will study a popular method and then modify it to fit the Wipro culture and business model. These methods include scorecarding for financial performance, benchmarking for business practices, "agile" metrics for operational performance, customer satisfaction surveys, and for personnel evaluations, both 360-degree feedback and a management-by-objective assessment.

These aren't separate islands of data and analysis. Wipro integrates data and goals from one metrics framework into another, so efforts to achieve one goal help accomplish others. This integration aligns the efforts and goals of everyone in the company, from Premji all the way down to support agents in the company's tech help desk operations.

The company's elaborate personnel assessment process, for instance, is woven in tightly with its business scorecarding system. It's a cascading process. Every December, Wipro's top executives prepare their strategic plan for the next three years, and that flows, in February and March, into creating a detailed operating plan for the next fiscal year. Those annual plans include business scorecards for the corporation and the various business units—specific goals such as revenue growth rates, operating margin improvements, new market entries, and mergers. The annual personal goal-setting process incorporates goals and metrics from the scorecards. For senior executives, many of their personal goals are drawn directly from the scorecards set up for the corporation or the business unit they run. For lower-level business managers and functional managers, the goals are more job- and function-specific. For example, a sales manager will have to improve customer satisfaction ratings, a software programming manager will target coding error rates, and a finance manager will have to improve accounts receivable numbers.

Wipro's performance metrics systems don't just measure how people are performing; they also set goals for improvements. These goals aren't easily achievable either. They're designed to force people out of their comfort zones and make them think differently and do things differently. In Wipro's own technology department, for instance, the ongoing goal is to find 20 percent in cost savings per year by reducing the acquisition costs of computers, software, and services—and by improving the efficiency of delivering tech services. Since Wipro is growing rapidly, that doesn't mean the IT budget goes down 20 percent per year. It means the IT budget is expected to become 20 percent more efficient each year. To be able to achieve that scale of savings, the IT managers have to know every detail of their costs and to understand the alternatives. For example, they constantly monitor their overseas phone calling volumes and destinations and then negotiate with their long-distance telephone service providers to get better rates.

While planning exercises shape the goals and metrics for the organization, feedback from the organization also shapes the plans and goals. It's a virtuous circle. You can see this clearly in the way Wipro's functional departments such as finance and HR operate. They see themselves as internal services for the business units, so they come up with ways of measuring how they're performing for those internal customers. The finance departments, for instance, conduct annual internal customer satisfaction surveys. They typically do so late in the fiscal year, in February or March. Finance managers then analyze the results and propose changes in the one-year operational plan.

One of the challenges at Wipro is maintaining an intense focus on day-to-day performance metrics without losing sight of the company's loftier goals. While profit margin is clearly a key measure of the company's health, Wipro believes in sacrificing margins to some extent in order to promote revenue growth. It also believes in focusing primarily on long-term goals rather than the next quarterly results. Many companies profess to be long-term oriented but don't follow through. Wipro does. That's partly because it can. The fact that Premji owns 81 percent of the company means that Wipro can resist pressure from investors to maximize current returns at the expense of long-term consequences.

Another challenge for Wipro is tempering its tendency to engage in self-criticism. With all those metrics floating around, it's easy for managers to fall into a pattern of beating themselves up for not meeting or exceeding the aggressive expectations their bosses have laid out for them. The trick is to find the proper balance. "There's a thin line between cynicism and self-criticism that's healthy," says BPO head T. K. Kurien. "Cynicism saps the organization. You have to watch out for it. There are times when we get into the cynical mode. If somebody else did something better, we beat ourselves up too often."

Compare Yourself to the Best

Wipro's benchmarking process took hold as a result of its joint venture with GE to build and sell medical equipment in India. This was in the early 1990s, when India was opening itself to the world after a decade and a half of self-imposed isolation. In GE, for the first time, Wipro came face-to-face with one of the most respected companies in the world. It was an opportunity to compare, learn, and adopt some of GE's best practices. Since then, Wipro has been benchmarking itself against other companies in all sorts of categories, everything from internal audit procedures to salesforce practices and software coding defect rates. "We have a huge amount of humility. We want to learn what's best in class. So we constantly benchmark ourselves against other companies, and even other people," says Girish Paranjpe, president of the Financial Solutions business unit.

Every Wipro business unit and corporate department does its own benchmarking. Most companies keep a veil of secrecy around their internal processes, so it's often difficult to get details and performance numbers. But consultancies that specialize in various business functions conduct best-practices benchmarking surveys and publish the results—without identifying the companies that participate. Wipro participates in some of those studies and compares its results to averages and top performers. In addition, it does some of its own research either by closely studying financial performance numbers published by leading companies or by directly approaching people within companies it doesn't compete with and simply asking them for help. Ishwar Hemrajani, Wipro's chief risk officer and chief ombudsman, talked to people at IBM, American Express, and India's Tata Motors when he was designing the ombudsman program. "We keep asking how they do it. How can we learn?" says Hemrajani.

When operational problems emerge, Wipro's managers use internal benchmarking as a sharp tool to hasten change. In mid-2005, for instance, the BPO unit was afflicted with high turnover rates and flagging productivity. Kurien, the BPO boss, looked through the portfolio of data available to him and decided the key benchmark he needed to track was revenue per employee. When he started the exercise, in September 2005, the overall revenue-per-employee number for his business unit was not nearly good enough. He told his segment managers to start charting their performance by this benchmark, and to do the analysis right down to the level of a line manager handling a single process for a single customer. All managers were given a revenue-per-employee target they had to meet. If their unit's performance fell under the target, they were told by their bosses to fix things within a certain amount of time. If they failed to do so, they'd have their employee headcount reduced to a level where they achieved the revenue-per-employee goal. That forced them to scramble to come up with productivity improvements.

Wipro is just as aggressive when it compares itself to its Indian rivals. For example, Wipro studies rival TCS to learn its tricks. TCS is known as an extremely efficient organization, which makes it possible to price very competitively. For instance, in 2003, Wipro was paying U.S. and U.K. law firms as much as $500 a pop to process work visas. If it sent 2,000 Indian employees overseas during a year, that effort would cost the company $1 million. TCS, Wipro learned, was saving money by doing a lot of that work internally. So Wipro trained its own staff to handle the applications. Only when a case was very complex did Wipro kick it out to a law firm to handle.

The company also studies its Western competitors. Those firms have been in the tech services business much longer, and they're particularly good at off-loading administrative tasks from their salespeople so those highly compensated people can concentrate on selling. Like its Western rivals, Wipro pays most of the incentive pay due to salespeople only after the contracted services have been delivered and the customer pays the bill. In 2004, the company realized that salespeople were spending too much time chasing after customers to make sure they were paying their bills on time rather than focusing, as they should have been, on making new sales pitches. It looked at how the Western firms handled such things, and it discovered that they relied on clerks to stay on top of the bills. So

Wipro set up a special accounts receivable collection center in Mumbai. The salespeople were worried that the clerks would be too aggressive with their customers and alienate them, so the company trained the clerks to be diplomatic—persistent but not obnoxious.

In the end, the Wipro solution was even better than the methods it copied from its competitors. By locating the service center in India rather than in the United States or Europe, it saved a bundle on salaries. "It was offshore, so it was cheaper. We saved twice," says Sudip Nandy, the chief strategy officer and former head of sales for Europe.

The other top Indian tech services firms are also obsessed with benchmarking. TCS has established a set of internal standards called the Tata Excellence Model, which is based on America's Malcolm Baldrige National Quality Award. TCS looks for companies that are particularly good at specific things and sees how it stacks up against them. They include IBM, Dell, Accenture, GE, Cisco Systems, and others. "Unless you have a culture where you're going to look and compare yourself with the best, how can you tell how you're doing?" says TCS chief executive S. "Ram" Ramadorai, "You can't just look at yourself and say, 'I did better today than yesterday.'"

Link Strategic Goals to Daily Performance

In 1992, when management gurus Robert S. Kaplan and David Norton introduced a management system called Balanced Score-card, they set off a quiet revolution inside corporate executive suites that is only now coming to a high boil. The idea was to create score-cards that lay out the strategic and operational goals of a company, measure performance, and link performance directly to executive compensation. In some cases, Wipro has adopted and customized the best management concepts and practices, but when it comes to scorecarding, Premji and his crew were way out ahead of the game. They didn't call what they did a Balanced Scorecard, but that's what it is. Starting in the mid-1970s, Premji began using a management system he called Goals and Objectives. Back then, there were four elements: financial, people, quality and operational performance, and customers. The company set goals each year for these categories, measured them monthly, and tied them to compensation.

These days, Wipro's Goals and Objectives system is even more elaborate. Now there are six categories: quality, financial, people, innovation, business development, and a sixth one that is chosen by each business unit. Categories come and go as new priorities arise. Innovation, for instance, was added in 2001. A typical financial metric: The company's goal is to grow a minimum of 1.25 times as fast as the Indian software services industry as a whole. The metrics used to measure performance in each category gradually morph. For instance, in the quality area, one of the earlier measures was how many Six Sigma quality projects had been initiated and completed. Later, as the company became more competent with Six Sigma, it demanded more of itself. It created an "engagement index," which tracks the number of available people who are working on Six Sigma projects, and an "effectiveness index" that measures the payoff from such projects. "The purpose is to raise the bar as we start improving," says V. Balakrishnan, the former CFO for Wipro Technologies.

Each March the scorecards are set up as part of the annual planning exercise. The goals are established at the corporate level, and those same goals and the measurements cascade down to the strategic business units, to vertical business units and practices, and to sub-verticals and subpractices. The finance departments of each business prepare progress reports every month, and the reports are distributed in a management information system to Premji and all the top managers in addition to business unit managers. Each business head reviews the reports with his or her subordinates.

Any deviation from the plan is flagged in the system for Premji to see. When he spots something that's amiss, he calls in the business leader to find out what's the matter, and the leader comes up with an action plan to fix things. That way, problems don't linger for months before something is done about them. Premji also has detailed quarterly scorecard reviews with the business units. Every business head is evaluated based on how well his or her unit performs against the scorecard goals. The leaders don't get rewarded for standing still or jogging at a slow pace.

In addition to the Goals and Objectives exercise, Wipro's tech unit has a grueling exercise all its own. Think of it as scorecarding squared. This is a little something Vivek Paul invented to sharpen performance and improve operating margins. The system tracks eight crucial parameters that the company believes are key to improving margins. It's a formula. Through deep analysis of how the tech services businesses work, the company understands the levers it has that can be used to improve performance. Here are the parameters:

1. The average monthly billing rates for labor in India and overseas
2. The ratio of work being done in Bangalore compared to other Indian cities where costs are lower
3. The percentage of employees who are working for clients at any given time
4. The ratio of work that is done in low-cost countries
5. The average experience levels of team members working on a particular project
6. Productivity on fixed-price projects
7. The average number of hours billed per day for each programmer
8. The length of duty for each engineer stationed overseas

The business managers and their bosses put these metrics under the microscope. If something's out of line, they take action. For instance, one of the few perks of working at Wipro is that Indian employees who excel stand a good chance of eventually getting an overseas assignment. It's an advantage Wipro has over Accenture and IBM, who hire Indians in India because they want them to stay there. But to keep top employees happy, Wipro has to keep the overseas rotation flowing. If a business unit begins to have a large number of overseas employees who have 24 and 36 months under their belts, alarms start going off. It's time to pull back some of the long-timers and give other people a chance to expand their horizons.

Track Processes to Achieve Improvements

As you might expect, Wipro uses technology heavily to define and automate its operations and to track its performance. It has a well-defined core process for software development and maintenance called Veloci-Q. The steps in the process are spelled out in a project management software application. Whenever a new service engagement is begun, it's logged into the system by program managers. They map out the project and set goals for the group and individual assignments for employees. Employees are automatically notified by mail when they get a new assignment. Programmers fill out daily progress reports in an online tracking system called the Agile Integrated Metrics Scorecard, or AIMS. In earlier days, to cull information out of the system, managers used simple automation tools based on spreadsheet technology. But that was too time consuming, so in 2001, they came up with a highly automated way of tracking progress, called the integrated process automation tool, or iPAT.

This is a powerful management tool. Managers can look at a report on the progress of an entire project, and if they see a troubling trend, they can drill down into the data to find the causes of the problem. They can quickly spot if the problems originated with a particular programming team, or, even, a particular employee who has fallen behind and is a bottleneck. Without iPAT, it might take managers a month or more to find out that there's a problem, and longer still to figure out what the cause is. With the tool, they can spot problems immediately and take corrective action. They track 42 metrics, including such things as the defect ratios. So quality problems, not just deadline problems, surface immediately.

Not only are Wipro's managers able to track progress in real time, but the iPAT data is also delivered to customers in monthly reports via the Internet. The information is available within the first few days after the end of the month. That assures clients that they're in touch with work that is being done for them, which is often a worry for companies that outsource vital tasks to others. It makes it impossible for Wipro to cover up problems. Everything is laid out for everybody to see.

The iPAT program has paid off big time. Not only has it resulted in improved customer satisfaction survey responses, but it also has improved the accuracy of billing invoices. The system has also increased the staff utilization rate and improved the accuracy of revenue recognition in quarterly reports. Perhaps most importantly, it has brought about a cultural change to the engineering groups. Suddenly, project management was driven by *data,* not the gut feelings of program and project managers. It takes a lot of the guesswork out of developing software.

People Evaluations: The Wipro Tuning Fork

Every mature corporation takes personnel evaluations seriously, but for Wipro, evaluations are a core competency. Employees always know what their goals and priorities should be. They know how they're doing relative to their goals and their peers. And they know what they have to do to perform better. Wipro's people performance measures are ever present. They are referred to throughout the year, not just on the one day when employees sit down with their supervisor to discuss their annual evaluation. Often, when HR boss Pratik Kumar meets one on one with a manager from anywhere in the organization, he puts on the desk before him the person's annual performance review and the 360-degree review, which includes input from supervisors, colleagues, and staff. That way, Kumar enters the conversation with a deep knowledge of the person with whom he's talking—without a long preliminary discussion—and can give advice and instructions tailored for the person and the situation. Is Wipro a tightly managed organization? That would be an understatement.

Let Managers Know What Everybody Thinks of Them

For Western companies, 360-degree feedback evaluations became all the rage in the late 1990s. Wipro had been doing them since the mid-1990s. Unlike at some American companies, all Wipro managers are required to participate. Nobody's shielded. In addition, technology architects and presales consultants who prepare proposals for customers are also roped in. That's because they often work in quasi-management roles. All told, about 20 percent of the workforce gets feedback, and most employees participate in the exercises, since subordinates complete reports on their bosses.

This isn't something people dash off in a few spare minutes. The process begins in January and the appraisals are finished in March, just before the end of the fiscal year. Managers are reviewed by their supervisors, peers, and subordinates. They're rated on how they perform in eight leadership categories: customer orientation, strategic thinking, self-confidence, global thinking and acting, commitment to excellence, making aggressive commitments, building future leaders, and working in teams.

When the reviews are compiled, managers get a detailed report. They see the responses to questions about their performance, and on a series of bar graphs, they see how they rate in these categories on a scale of 1 to 5, compared to the average and the top 25 percent among their peers, as rated by supervisors, peers, and direct reports. Then there's a breakdown of aspects of each category, and, once again, they see their ratings by supervisors, peers, and subordinates. They rate themselves so they can see if there's a gap between their perception of themselves and how others see them. They also see how their ratings have increased or decreased since the previous year.

To show how detailed these evaluations are, here are the items in the "commitment to excellence" category:

- Constantly benchmarks with the best in the industry and develops similar relevant capabilities within Wipro.

- Encourages continuous improvement in quality of products, services, and processes.

- Encourages innovative solutions with team for sustained competitive advantage.

- Drives Wipro's quality journey.

• Demands the highest quality output and stretches team members to deliver on high expectations.

In addition, there are some open-ended questions:

• What should the leader continue to do?

• What should the leader start doing?

• What should the leader stop doing?

Once managers receive the results of their feedbacks, they are not left to fend for themselves. The HR department conducts four-hour workshops to help them understand the results of their report and respond to it. With the help of HR advisors, managers come up with an action plan, which might include improvements in knowledge, skill, attitude, and behavior. The HR people also help them prioritize by balancing the ease with which an improvement can be made with the importance of the improvement. The idea is to make noticeable improvements quickly. Managers show their action plans to their supervisors and subordinates, partly so these people can see that their feedback is being taken seriously.

This review process can be painful for managers, but they say it's extremely valuable. "The feedback is very genuine. You can see what people in the organization expect of you. It forms the basis of our leadership plan," says Anand Sankaran, vice president of Total Outsourcing Services. A few years ago, when he was running managed services for India and the Asia-Pacific region, he got feedback from subordinates that he wasn't doing enough to get their ideas and include them in decision making. After that, he made sure to invite three of the people who reported to him to participate when he began working on a new business plan. From then on, his subordinates felt they were respected, and he got some good ideas he might not have thought of on his own.

The feedback gives managers practical information about their behavior and helps in making improvements, but the way the review process is handled also sends a vital message to the entire organization: We're all in this together.

Give Employees Detailed Guidance

Wipro takes performance evaluations more seriously than do most organizations. That's partly because so many of its employees are hired right out of college. They're young, impressionable, and inexperienced. That means the company has a rare opportunity to shape their personalities, work habits, and ways of thinking. It's good for Wipro. The company gets more effective employees out of the deal. But it also provides significant benefits for the employees. Whether they work at Wipro for the rest of their careers or seek opportunities elsewhere, they start with a solid grounding.

All employees participate in an elaborate performance appraisal system. The system has four elements: goals, competencies, potential, and how critical the employee is to the company. The process begins in January, when employees sit down with their managers and set goals for the year. At that time, the employee and manager identify which 8 or 10 of the company's 24 employee competencies are most important for somebody with that particular employee's role in the company. Assessments of the previous year's performance are completed in March, resulting in a Capability Maturity Rating, or CMR, which is a numerical expression of how well they did in the four elements. Everybody is rated on a four-point scale within each element and is then given an overall numerical rating, with 1 standing for "outstanding," 2 for "exceeds expectations," 3 for "meets expectations," and 4 for "does not meet expectations." Employees are benchmarked against their peers and placed in a percentile ranking. Those percentiles are mapped to annual pay increases.

Employees say the performance appraisal system is fair and very useful. They like the fact that they begin the process by suggesting their own goals and that they get guidance from managers. While much of the goal setting and evaluating is done on computer, there are plenty of opportunities for employees and their supervisors to meet face-to-face. Most supervisors seem to take this responsibility seriously. "I speak openly to my supervisor about my aspirations," says Rudra Pratap, a third-year tech support analyst. "We have crafted objectives for my future. He keeps asking me about my career path and how I'm approaching things. He uses his own experiences with Wipro to help me."

While performance evaluations weigh heavily on promotion decisions, they're not the only factors. Wipro structures its workforce like a pyramid and tries to avoid getting a "bulge" in the middle of the pyramid as a result of promoting too many people. For starters, so-called threshold competencies are identified for each promotional level. Employees who hope to be promoted must prove themselves in advance by doing the job at the next level for a year before they are formally promoted. "We don't just promote people on the assumption that they might do a good job. We see them do it first," says Rajesh Sahay, a general manager in the HR department. The next step is a review of each potential promotion by a combination of business unit and HR leaders. They take into consideration how many promotions they can do and still avoid the "bulge," plus assess what categories of low- and midlevel managers are in demand. Any candidate who doesn't land a promotion is given a detailed report on what he or she needs to do to improve to get one the next time.

Wipro doesn't often fire people. The exception is when somebody violates an ethics policy. For the bottom 10 percent who simply don't measure up to the company's high standards, there's a rigorous process for trying to help them to improve. These employees get feedback from their supervisors on what they need to do differently, and they are given a detailed performance improvement plan. They are monitored closely. After a period of time, if they still can't pass muster, they are advised that Wipro is not the right place for them. People get the message, and they find jobs elsewhere. Fortunately for them, having Wipro on their résumé makes it relatively easy to find jobs at other companies.

All of this measuring keeps managers and employees alike focused on the company's top priorities. Anybody whose mind tends to wander or who likes to take long lunch breaks won't succeed there. The result is a high-performance culture and an organization that often does things right the first time, and when it doesn't, it learns and improves and performs better the second time around.

12

PLAN THREE YEARS AHEAD TO PREPARE FOR RAPID GROWTH

B ack in the go-go days of the 1990s, Masayoshi Son, head of Japan's Softbank Corporation, used to say he had a 100-year plan for his company. That was probably overdoing it. But there's no question that long-term planning has been a key factor in Wipro's success. The company works hard at it. Wipro has a planning rhythm designed to incorporate its values, its vision of its future, strategy, and operational planning. It conducts a corporate values exercise once or twice a decade. That's followed by a visioning exercise. The executive team does formal strategic planning annually on a rolling three-year basis, and then annual operational planning every March. One initiative flows into the next, creating strong links that connect the company's core values, how it plans for the future, and how it operates day by day.

Consider Strategy a Core Business Process

Because Wipro's fiscal year ends in March, executives begin their strategic planning cycle in October and November of the previous year. The process starts with Premji, Chief Strategy Officer Sudip Nandy, and the company's top executives meeting regularly to talk over the competitive landscape, Wipro's opportunities, and its challenges. Over a period of two months, they map out strategies and goals for the next three years. The exercise is typically wrapped up by the end of the year, and results are presented to the board of directors in mid-January. Once the board approves it, each of the business unit heads goes back to his or her division and works up a detailed plan for meeting the revenue and profit growth goals laid out for the division for the next 12 months. In the plans, leaders spell out the targets for the division, quarter by quarter, for growth in revenues, operating margin improvements, and growth in staffing. These plans are typically approved by Premji in March.

While having a three-year rolling strategic planning process would be a plus for any company, it's absolutely necessary for Wipro. Growing as fast as it does, the company can't wait until new contracts are signed to start building the infrastructure of people and buildings and technology to handle the work. So it has to anticipate demand and build out in advance of it. That's a tricky balance. If it underestimates, it won't be able to bid on some contracts or meet the needs of its customers. If it overestimates, it will have employees sitting around without enough to do. So even the three-year planning process is a rigorous, metrics-heavy exercise.

Wipro adopted this strategic planning system in 2001 with guidance from McKinsey & Company consultants. The idea is that the system is supposed to be remodeled when need be to meet the changing needs of the company. Nandy, who had formerly run sales in Europe, took over as chief strategy officer in late 2004, but he didn't start tinkering with the strategic planning processes until 2005, in the wake of Vivek Paul's departure as head of the global technology business. In late 2005, after Paul left, Wipro undertook a much more intensive process of self-evaluation and planning. Still, the core structure remains the same.

Here's Nandy's definition of how Wipro differentiates its approaches to three-year strategy planning and one-year operational planning:

Strategic Planning	Operational Planning
Start with a clean slate	Identify strengths and weaknesses
Explore the market	Build on strengths; eliminate weakness
Discover customer values	Focus on competition
Create customer propositions	Build operational efficiencies
Seek to invest	Focus on cost effectiveness
Dare to be different	Seek to be the best
Goal: sustained business success	Goal: sustained management success
We will decide what to do	We will decide how to do it

While Wipro is farsighted, it's not the champion of long-term planning among the Indian tech services leaders. That distinction belongs to Infosys. It has one- and three-year planning cycles, and most of its strategic initiatives are designed to create their full effects within one to three years. Yet Infosys also has a five-year planning process. The goal is to come up with an assessment of the truly long-term prospects for factors such as wage inflation, market growth, and adding new capabilities that allow it to climb the industry food chain and provide ever-more-sophisticated services. This process has helped Infosys achieve the highest operating margins among the major services companies worldwide—typically above 30 percent. Wipro also looks out five years, but it's for the purpose of visioning and setting stretch goals rather than conducting a detailed planning exercise.

Set Audacious Goals to Inspire Bold Strategies

Premji is a great believer in getting people together for intensive reflection and discussion far from the day-to-day pressures of business. He encourages his managers to hold off-site meetings regularly. When he feels that the whole corporation—or big chunks of it—need a fire lit under them, he'll conduct what he calls visioning exercises. "It's a simple principle. You ask yourself what you want the company to look like in five years," he says. Wipro takes stock of all the basics: size, profitability, direction, and respect in the community. Then it maps its own capabilities and aspirations against forecasts for its industry and macroeconomic trends. "Then we set a goal, and it becomes a turbocharge for senior management," Premji says.

The company's visioning exercise in 2000 shows how it's done. The summer of 2000 was a moment of irrational exuberance in the global software industry. Not only had tech stocks in general shot through the ceiling, but demand was extremely strong for corporate software and tech services. Paul, who had been hired a year earlier from GE to improve the operational performance of Wipro's global technology business, had been rewarded with a string of strong quarterly financial results. Wipro's global technology revenues had grown by 70 percent for the 1999–2000 fiscal year. For Paul's next act, he wanted to accelerate growth. He and Premji decided it was an opportune time for the leaders of the global technology business to step back and see how big they could dream.

Paul planned on getting the team to set an ambitious sales target at the conclusion of the exercise. It was partly about inspiring people and partly about getting them to do the things that would be necessary to make all that growth possible. "You have to plan for success as much as you plan for failure," Paul says. "I asked, 'What if our dreams come true? Do we have the management talent to manage it and the ability to do all the hiring and training?'"

The visioning exercise was held that July in a resort on the outskirts of Bangalore. For three days, about 50 senior managers were sequestered there day and night. They included corporate officers in additional to the tech business management team. The all-day talk sessions were guided by Sumantra Ghoshal, a professor of strategy and international management at London Business School. Premji and Paul participated, but they didn't control things. The idea was to let people express themselves freely and not feel they were being pushed one way or another by the big bosses. During the first two days, Ghoshal led the managers through a series of exercises aimed at sizing up Wipro's capabilities and its potential.

The third day was the biggie. It was time to set a growth goal. The team was spread out at a handful of tables in a large conference room, with each table holding its own discussion. At Paul's table, a small group began taking stock. "Everybody was feeling good, and we wanted to wrap it up," recalls Girish Paranjpe, who was CFO of the global tech unit at the time. They wanted to select a goal that was both audacious and catchy. Quickly they came up with both a revenue target and a slogan: "4 in 4." Wipro's global tech business, which had $240 million in sales the previous fiscal year, would aim to grow to $4 billion in four years. The company was just about to list on the New York Stock Exchange, and it would have the currency to make acquisitions overseas. So for the first time, it would be able to grow through acquisition. They figured it was possible they could hit the $4 billion target through a combination of rapid organic growth and aggressive mergers and acquisitions (M&A)—about half and half. Audacious? Sure. But Paul wanted a number that would be very hard to achieve and would demand the best effort from everybody in the company. "The purpose of the vision wasn't to set a budget. It was to lay out a range of what was possible. It was to wake everybody up to the possibility," says Paul.

It was time to take the 4-in-4 proposal to the entire group. At first, many people in the room were skeptical. The M&A piece was the most worrisome. Wipro had never done acquisitions. It didn't have the skills to size up potential merger partners, cut deals, and integrate the acquired companies. So when Ghoshal first asked people to raise their hands if they thought the company could hit the target, only about half responded. Gradually, after hours of discussion, almost everybody came around. There was just one lone holdout: Sudip Banerjee. "I said, 'It's unrealistic. Why do it?'" he recalls. No matter what anybody said, he couldn't be swayed. Says Paranjpe,

"He said he just didn't believe it. He was very forceful. He stood his ground in front of everybody. He was very courageous."

He was also very right. Within a matter of months after the vote, the U.S. economy slipped into a slump from which it didn't fully recover until 2003. Demand leveled off rather than accelerating. Wipro took a few stabs at acquisitions, but it soon decided to be cautious and avoid big risks. So in the end, the global technology businesses revenues fell far short of $4 billion in fiscal 2004. Instead, they hit $900 million. That was very impressive growth by any normal standard, but nowhere near the ambitious target. Looking back, most Wipro executives don't regret setting such a lofty goal. "I don't think it was a mistake to do it," says Paranjpe. "If you don't set ambitious goals, you don't have the motivation to take a stab at it."

The company's next visioning exercise was less of a stretch. As part of their big strategic planning journey of late 2005 and early 2006, the top executives mapped out a new vision for the company: Within three years it would be among the top 10 information technology services companies in the world, as measured by revenues. At the time Wipro ranked sixteenth. They also set an ambitious revenue target but didn't make it public. "It would become a benchmark for investors, and that's too dangerous," says Premji.

Three-Year Plans: Take the Blinkers Off

The year 2000 was a turning point for Wipro. After the global technology business leaders held their visioning exercise, they went on to establish a bold, new long-term strategy they hoped would accelerate growth. The strategy was to create a more comprehensive services portfolio than Wipro's Indian competitors and, at the same time, to deepen expertise and capabilities for delivering services to companies in specific industries. Wipro executed well on that strategy. It organized around industries, and it developed strong industry-specific packages of software and services. It built consulting and infrastructure outsourcing businesses, and it expanded into business process outsourcing through its acquisition of Spectramind, the Indian leader of the call center industry.

Yet Wipro's performance wasn't good enough. In 2005, archrival Infosys was growing a bit faster than Wipro and had achieved richer profit margins. You might ask, "What's all the angst about?" After all, Wipro's revenue and profit growth was better than those of its Western competitors and most of its Indian peers. But Premji simply wasn't satisfied. He knew they could do better. So when Paul gave the word in the summer of 2005 that he was leaving, Premji decided to take the company by the lapels and give it a shake. He took over day-to-day management of the tech business and reorganized the executive staff. Then, simultaneously, he revamped the company's values (see Chapter 5), kicked off a new innovation initiative (more on that in Chapter 13), reshaped the company's quality programs (more in Chapter 14), and launched a major strategy overhaul.

Premji's take on things was that for several years, in spite of Paul's fast-growth mantra, the company had actually underinvested in growth. It had focused sharply on quarterly results and on efficiencies and not enough on innovation and market expansion. Instead, he believed Wipro should invest in expanding its salesforce, in marketing, and in innovation. At the same time, the company would temporarily accept having lower profit margins than Infosys. "We're willing to think more boldly. We're willing to commit more up front, take more risks," Premji says. "You'll see results two or three years from today. We will be successful at this, and you'll find us a much stronger company than we are today."

Out of that planning process came Wipro's new three-year strategy. The *über*goal was to transform the company from a large Indian player to a large global player. The team defined 10 growth-driving themes aimed at achieving that goal. They included four "growth engines" and six "enablers."

Here are the growth engines:

1. *Organic growth in global technology.* Increased penetration in the top 100 accounts. Investments in high-growth markets. Addition of new verticals. Creation of packaged solutions in BPO.
2. *Organic growth in India and the Middle East.* Penetration of key accounts with all service lines. Focus on networking within the computer hardware business and consulting in services.
3. *Game-changing initiatives.* Within the salesforce, creation of a separate team to focus on large deals. Continued incubation of new services. Expansion of strategic alliances.
4. *Strategic acquisitions.* Making of acquisitions to improve the capabilities of vertical business units and service lines. Creation of a full-time position of "integration officer" for each transaction.

The following are the growth enablers:

1. *Building the right capability and leadership.* Creation of a new cadre of leaders at all levels. Improvements in the new-hire induction process. Better vertical industry expertise.
2. *New delivery paradigms.* Reduction in the manual labor elements of services. Leveraging of "lean" techniques to increase productivity. Enhanced multilingual capabilities.
3. *Performance management.* Designing compensation programs that reward growth. Development of a real-time software dashboard to track service delivery performance.
4. *Innovation:* Building a strong innovation brand. Addition to the current incremental innovation model with a program for encouraging "quantum innovation."
5. *Consulting.* Turning consulting into a high-growth business. Use of consulting to penetrate accounts and to win client reengineering deals. Attracting talent to Wipro through the consulting organization.
6. *Branding.* Aiming to be number one in rankings of employers, customer satisfaction, and corporate governance. Cultivation of a reputation as a thought leader among analysts and clients.

One element of the strategy that Wipro didn't talk about much externally was actually very crucial. The company likes slogans, and this initiative got one too. It's GROW. That stands for **GR**ow with **O**ne **W**ipro. Already, Wipro was one of the most comprehensive tech service providers in the world. The next big step would be to synthesize its capabilities, bringing the power of all of those services together. Rather than being seen as a useful provider of bits and pieces of service to its customers, it would be seen as a strategic partner capable of handling large swaths of their operations.

Here's a scenario that shows what's different about the new strategy: Today, for a large bank's mortgage department, Wipro might have separate contracts to provide custom software development, a desktop computing help desk, and mortgage application processing. In the future, under the GROW strategy, it would take care of the entire mortgage process. That would include software application management, computer management, help desk, and business process outsourcing. Rather than just selling the pieces, Wipro would manage the whole process. And rather than charging by each part of the process, it would be paid based on the value it brings the client, perhaps in so many dollars per mortgage processed. Simply put by Nandy: "We have decided to integrate the company before the customer."

The idea was to pursue this strategy in some of the more mature vertical industry businesses, including manufacturing, telecommunications, retail, banking, and insurance. Other verticals, such as health care, would continue to focus on improving their domain expertise and the depth of their services. In the vertical business units where the new strategy was to take hold, Wipro reorganized to put people in charge of coming up with holistic packages of services for customers and for coordinating with the whole array of service units to get it done.

The timing for this expansive strategy was good. About $100 billion worth of large outsourcing contracts were coming up for renewal worldwide in 2006 and 2007, according to outsourcing industry consultant TPI. Almost all of these contracts had been controlled by Western outsourcers such as EDS, IBM, and Accenture.

But Wipro had a global footprint and a comprehensive set of services. And now, with this strategy of taking over and transforming whole segments of a client's business, it had a compelling sales pitch that could help pry some of those massive contracts away from the incumbents. "The basic theme is we're trying to grow faster and globalize more," says Premji. "We're trying to be a one-stop partner to our customers. We want to add more value and innovation to the whole process."

Rethink Strategy Step by Step

This planning exercise was quite a departure from the past. For starters, it began in midsummer rather than in October. And rather than relying on each of the business unit heads to kick things off with their broad strategic goals, the management team went through the process of fundamentally rethinking strategy. Premji cranked up the planning process in July by enlisting Nandy and Paranjpe to run it. They gathered market data and did detailed comparisons of their processes and performance with that of their peers. They held meetings about every two weeks. The feeling was that Wipro's process and quality expertise were superior, but that it wasn't as good as TCS at managing costs or as Infosys at marketing. "There was a sense we could do better with our strengths. We're a very left-brain company—very number and process driven," says Nandy. "We have a very good engine, but we don't yet have a great car."

Some of the early gatherings were raucous. There was finger-pointing about who was to blame for the company's disappointments and lively debates about what should be done to set it on a better track. Things didn't jell easily. The executives had to tear apart the old strategy before they could come up with a new one. In October 2005, about halfway through the process Nandy said the team had a long way to go before it would reach consensus. "Right now, if you asked each person separately about what our strategy is, you'd get a different answer. But in three months' time you'll have one answer from everybody," he predicted.

As part of the process of stripping down to the basics, the group invited lower-ranking people to get involved in the discussions. Typically, these three-year strategic planning exercises are handled almost exclusively at the senior management level. But this time they sought input from the heads of subvertical business units. Within the retail vertical, for instance, there are consumer packaged goods and distribution subverticals. The management team probed for hidden opportunities. What growth potential did the managers of these subverticals see? What acquisitions could springboard them into new markets? No idea was too radical. They even entertained business plans that would have most of the staff overseas rather than in India.

By late December, Premji and his lieutenants had a proposal in hand. They did some polishing. Then on January 17, Premji presented the plan to the board of directors at a meeting in Bangalore that lasted from 8:30 a.m. to 6 p.m. There was a lot of discussion, but no real disagreement. The board endorsed the plan enthusiastically.

It was time for the grand rollout. In the past, Wipro might not have made much of its new strategy externally. But part of the strategy is to be seen as a thought leader and to market itself more aggressively to industry and stock analysts. So a lot of planning went into how to present the shift to create the greatest impact. The company conducted briefings with Indian stock analysts in Mumbai on January 25, with U.S. tech industry analysts in Boston on February 6, and with Wall Street analysts in New York on February 8. Premji rang the closing bell in the New York Stock Exchange on February 8, which got attention from Indian and international media.

Communicating with the staff was just as important. After Vivek Paul left in mid-2005, the Indian press was full of reports speculating that Wipro had lost its way and would be left behind by the competition. Morale was wobbly. It was important to tell both the management team and staff that the company was on the march. So from January 21 to 24, Premji conducted off-site events for the executive management team in the clubhouse of Palm Meadows, a residential community near Bangalore's airport. There were briefings on the strategy and workshops on cross-business-unit collaboration and innovation. A one-day version of the program was held for the company's top 300 managers on February 20. They were encouraged to raise questions and make suggestions. This event served as both the introduction of the three-year plan and the launch of the annual planning exercise.

Wipro's 60,000 employees had a lot to digest in early 2006. Within a matter of weeks, they learned about the new values, the new vision, the Wipro Way quality program, the new innovation program, and the strategic plan. In the wake of Vivek Paul's departure, Premji had sent a strong signal that management had plenty of fresh ideas and Wipro was on the move.

Tap Employees for Their Strategy Ideas

As part of his resculpting of the company, Premji invited employees to suggest ways to boost performance. Under a new program called Growth Accelerator, he earmarked about $15 million of the company's $800 million cash hoard to be used to finance special projects over the next 12 months. It was like an internal venture capital program. He sent a companywide e-mail that solicited proposals for new business ventures, and they came flooding in—more than 75 in all—from all of the business units, service lines, and geographies. By early 2006, the company's IT Strategy Council, which includes Premji and six others, had funded 16 of the proposals. "We were getting genuine entrepreneurial ideas," says Nandy.

One of the most promising proposals was an aggressive expansion of the company's fledgling computer and network security practice. Wipro had about 60 people working in security services at the time, with annual revenues of about $22 million. The hope was that by adding technology to the company's already existing network operations centers and hiring high-skilled security experts in the United States and Europe, the business could grow to $100 million within a few years. The proposal came from Prasenjit Saha, the general manager of the security practice. "My vision was to turn it into a truly global practice, and I saw this as my chance to make it happen," Saha says.

Ever since Saha started up the practice in 1999, security from intruders and viruses had been a top concern of corporate chief information officers. Over the years, Saha and his team had created an extensive portfolio of services and software modules to help clients with every aspect of their security strategies. At any given time, about 45 percent of Saha's staff was working on-site with U.S. or European clients, though they were all home based in India. As a result, contact with customers was inconsistent. The business had been growing by about 45 to 50 percent per year, but Saha thought he could accelerate that rate to perhaps 75 percent. His plan was to hire 60 to 70 local people to be high-end security consultants in both the United States and Europe. He also proposed establishing an ambitious security technology training program for Indian employees and creating extensive go-to-market alliances with other security technology suppliers, including American giants such as Cisco, Symantec, and CA.

Saha had to pass through a rigorous approval process. He wrote up a business plan, supported it with metrics, and submitted it to Premji and the IT Strategy Council. One potential hang-up was the fact that he wanted to hire so many people overseas, which meant considerable expense. Wipro would voluntarily give up some of its usual labor arbitrage advantage. But he found that it wasn't a show-stopper for the council. "The main encouragement we're getting from management is to come out with innovative solutions. Now we're being more bold with our investments," Saha says. In fact, the council opened its wallet and committed to spend $15 to $20 million over a period of 18 months on the project.

Results from the Growth Accelerator program weren't expected for one or two years. Still, Premji had enough faith in it as a growth stimulus that he decided to make it a formal annual process separate from the strategic planning exercise. The new program was expected to run every quarter, at least, and perhaps more frequently. Now, Wipro had a grassroots business venturing process to stand alongside its grassroots innovation program (more about that in Chapter 13).

The year that Vivek Paul left turned out to be a watershed for Wipro, but not in the ways that skeptics thought. Rather than stumble, the company's management team pulled together and came up with the boldest set of initiatives to come from the company since 2000. As a result of taking that journey, the company also modified its three-year strategic planning process. It would be more of a deep-thinking exercise than in the past, by challenging assumptions and the unwritten rules for doing things. And it would have more input from the lower ranks. In a sense, Wipro put its own mark on the planning process. Now it was less an invention of McKinsey & Company and more, well, Wiprolike.

13

INVENT NEW THINGS EVERY DAY, OR ELSE

Most info tech companies focus on a handful of technologies and markets. Not Wipro. In order to serve 500 customers worldwide, it has gained expertise in a broad range of technologies. And while tech services companies of the past didn't have to do much innovating, that's changing fast. It's vital for them come up with new technologies and ways of doing things so they can distinguish themselves from the competition. Wipro innovates in three ways: technology, service solutions, and business processes. So far, most of its innovations have been incremental. But in 2006 it launched a Quantum Innovation initiative aimed at producing breakthroughs that boost revenues in a big way.

From Body Shop to Brain Shop

In the early days of Indian outsourcing, the typical jobs were modernizing software programs that had been in use for decades or doing the routine coding on new programs. The corporate customers wrote specification sheets that described in detail what they wanted done, and the Indian "body shops" followed those instructions to the letter. There wasn't much creativity in that. It was all about doing ordinary programming tasks more cheaply. Wipro and its peers still perform a lot of that kind of work, but to differentiate themselves from the Indian also-rans and to take on the top Western services firms, they have been rapidly adding new technology and process excellence capabilities.

In effect, they're redefining innovation. Typically, people associate it with breakthroughs in core software, computer, and semiconductor technologies. But these days the top global tech services companies in the West and India are defining a new innovation paradigm that's commonly called *services science*. It's a combination of technologies, business knowledge, business process expertise, and prepackaged services that help their clients transform the way they do business. Already, Wipro is recognized as a leader in business process excellence. That's the ability to do brainwork most efficiently and with the highest quality. Now the company is determined to excel across the board.

Wipro began to get serious about innovation in 2000. It was part of Vivek Paul's growth acceleration drive. Programmers and engineers in the company's business units were producing day-to-day advances in quality, process excellence, and technology, but in an effort to goose things along, the company set up two programs designed to encourage creativity and to free innovators from their normal duties. One, the Innovation Initiative, is a grassroots effort aimed at soliciting ideas from the Wipro staff. Anybody from a programmer to a senior vice president can submit suggestions via the company Web site or e-mail to an Innovation Council, chaired by Chief Technology Officer Divakaran Mangalath. It's like an internal venture capital fund. The council reviews proposals, allocates funds, and sets up project teams, which often include the person who had the original idea. The other route is more top-down. Executives in each of the vertical industry business units spot emerging technologies that they believe will be vital for their clients in the not-too-distant future and work with Mangalath to establish Centers of Excellence in those areas. Sometimes these centers focus on creating services for particular industries; others have uses across a broad array of industries.

The company has developed well-defined processes for capturing ideas, evaluating them, incubating them, and turning them into services. Innovation is part of every employee's performance evaluation, and it's included on every senior manager's business performance scorecard. Premji reviews all innovation metrics quarterly.

Still, at the end of fiscal 2006, in March 2006, only about 5 percent of Wipro's revenues came directly from these two pipelines. It wasn't nearly good enough. "Most of our innovation projects are built around ideas, not breakthrough insights," observes Mangalath. He points to one Center of Excellence, which focuses on grid computing—technologies used to hook together hundreds or even thousands of small computers to create a virtual supercomputer. "In the future, we have to not just come up with ideas like how to use grid computing, we have to come up with core insights like those that gave birth to grid computing," he says.

The new Quantum Innovation program is aimed at producing breakthrough insights. Like the original Innovation Initiative, it's an internal venture capital program, but this time, top management identifies targets that are synchronized with its three-year strategic plans. Funding is served up in bigger pieces, but to get money, projects must have the potential to accelerate growth significantly. "The objective of Quantum Innovation is to make bigger bets," says Premji. "We want to look beyond this year to horizon two and horizon three. We want to take revenue from innovation from 5 percent to 10 percent in a three-year period."

At the same time, Premji and his lieutenants decided to create innovation facilities that would stand apart from the normal software development offices. The idea was to make a visible show of innovation, so people involved in the projects would feel special and the entire staff would understand how important it is to the company's future. The plan was to set aside a special 500-seat lab in Bangalore and smaller satellite labs near other Wipro offices. Wipro's labs aren't an attempt to match the basic research capabilities of major corporate facilities such as IBM Research. It doesn't have the money or need for that. Still, the goal is to set innovators off in a zone of their own where they have the time and permission to invent.

Technology Innovation

Much of Wipro's technology innovation happens in its Product Engineering Solutions group. Its engineers do design jobs for companies on everything from telecommunications devices to TV set-top boxes and MP3 players. They design chips and circuit boards, develop software to control devices, and do industrial design. The company's chip design service is something the other Indian software services giants can't match. Rather than designing each product from the ground up for clients, Wipro over the years has created fundamental design components, which are its own intellectual property, that serve as building blocks for clients' products. In such cases, Wipro sells not just the engineering services but licenses the intellectual property as well.

One example is Wipro's wireless networking technology. This can be used, for instance, to connect a digital camera to a PC to download photographs. The company understood that wireless networking would play a major role in connecting consumer devices to one another and PCs, so it invested in developing technology that it incorporates into specialized microprocessors for clients. It started licensing the technology in 2003 and has so far lined up 10 customers. "We believe that this is a big wave that will last 10 to 15 years," says Ramesh Emani, president of Wipro's Product Engineering Solutions group. Wipro can use that basic intellectual property repeatedly on behalf of clients and keep updating it as new uses and technology standards emerge. So this investment could pay off over and over again.

Wipro is applying for patents for the wireless technology, but, typically, when it invents something, the patents go to its clients. It encourages engineers to look for patentable ideas that emerge out of their work. If clients apply for patents based on that, the Wipro engineers file invention disclosures, and if the patents are awarded, they get their names on them. While neither Wipro nor the engineers share ownership of the intellectual property, the engineers get incentive pay, and Wipro gets grateful customers.

Solution Innovation

One of Wipro's biggest opportunities for innovation is in solutions. No traditional software company has all of the programs necessary to handle every aspect of information security or supply chain management or customer relationship management for every potential customer. What often ends up happening is that corporations pick what they consider to be the best applications, cafeteria style, from a wide variety of programs and then hire services companies to weave them all together. To make this picking and weaving process easier, Wipro has developed a large number of solutions that include software, services, and methods for getting things done.

One highlight is a family of solutions Wipro built to address one of the most important software technologies in corporations today, something called *service-oriented architectures* (SOA). Under SOA, modular pieces of software are written using industry standard rules. This practice makes it easy to combine many of them, like so many building blocks, to create powerful new applications. Many corporations have begun building applications this way. Wipro spotted the opportunity early and created a sizable business around it. Wipro engineers not only created a technology framework that can be used for any client, but they precooked about a dozen solutions for specific industries, including retailing and insurance. So far, Wipro has done more than 120 SOA projects, including 10 very large ones.

Solutions are particularly attractive to Wipro because they elevate the company's importance to it clients. In these engagements, it's not just doing routine coding on applications the clients themselves designed. With its solutions, Wipro takes large, complex problems off clients' hands. And because a major part of the labor is done offshore and much of the coding is prepackaged, Wipro can offer these solutions at costs significantly lower than if all the work was done by the client and starting from scratch.

Even better, by offering services like this, Wipro can position itself as a trusted advisor to clients. In the enterprise security realm, for instance, the company has built up expertise in data security and regulatory compliance, and it offers what it calls an end-to-end security solution. It not only develops security programs for clients and mixes and matches off-the-shelf applications built by others, but it also manages clients' security systems once they are in place and advises clients on all aspects of their security strategy. That last part is key. It's a true consulting capability, and it puts Wipro on the map alongside the world's elite tech services outfits, including IBM and Accenture. In a little more than two years from its 2003 start, Wipro had done risk management projects for nearly 50 customers.

Process Innovation

Wipro embarked on its process-excellence journey in the early 1990s when it began adopting international standards for use in software development and engineering project management. The innovation part came when it took standards and techniques such as ISO [International Organization for Standardization] 9000 and Six Sigma that were intended for manufacturing and adapted them to software. Wipro constantly tinkers with processes to squeeze out extra efficiencies. Or it rips apart an existing process to replace it with a better one. Over the years, the value of process excellence has penetrated into everything the company does. The goal of constantly striving for excellence is a deeply held conviction, almost a religion.

Process innovation happens in all sorts of places, some you might not expect, including sales. When Sangita Singh left her post as chief marketing officer and took over as senior vice president of the Enterprise Application Services (EAS) business unit in early 2005, it was a small colony in Wipro's rapidly expanding global technology empire. The business installs complex run-the-business applications from software makers SAP and Oracle. Singh wanted to increase her penetration into large accounts, so she decided to create a new process for identifying and going after prospects. "Innovation isn't necessarily about building a new application. It's about always trying to see how you can drive rapid growth. And it's about building new tools and components that can be reused," says Singh.

The process Singh and her team have developed, Proactive Demand Generation, has turned up the heat under the EAS business. The process is based on a lead-generating process Singh created while she was chief marketing officer. Step one is to identify new prospects by tapping the expertise of Wipro's salesforce and project managers within the vertical industry business units. A digital "account map" is created for each prospect, including the names of decision makers, a history of the company's interactions with Wipro, and a profile of the technology it uses. Step two is to target decision makers and choose the best way to approach them. Step three is engagement, sending technical white papers or using telesales or Web seminars to get the attention of decision makers. Once prospects show interest, the leads, complete with a database of pertinent information, are handed off to the sales team.

Through this process, Singh and the EAS team have aided the company's relatively small salesforce by identifying and qualifying leads and giving salespeople all the information they need before they approach a customer with a customized sales pitch. Each step is thoroughly researched, analyzed, and mapped out.

In just two quarters, the process delivered promising results: EAS quadrupled the number of target accounts, approached 100 companies individually, and conducted Web seminars that roped in more than 300 prospects. In the quarter before Singh took the job, the unit grew by just 3 percent sequentially. The Proactive Demand Generation project helped boost growth to 10 percent quarter-on-quarter, though Singh stresses that she still has a way to go to achieve her target. "If you have rigor in a process, results happen. It's just a matter of time," says Singh.

Wipro not only uses process innovations to tune up its own business, but it does the same for its clients. This is particularly important in its outsourcing engagements, where it takes charge of accounting, bill paying, travel expensing, and the like. In the early, simpler days, outsourcers typically took over processes that their clients already had in place, even if they had obvious flaws. They used offshore labor and scale to reduce costs and prices. Over time, the top outsourcers began offering to transform the clients' processes to make them more efficient. It's commonly called business transformation outsourcing. In some cases, Wipro convinces several clients to adopt the same set of processes, the so-called shared services model. That gives Wipro and its customers huge economies of scale. Other tech services outfits are moving in the same direction. Business transformation outsourcing is about improving efficiency *and* the customer experience.

In many cases, this kind of innovation is even more important to Wipro than the technological kind. T. K. Kurien, head of Wipro's BPO unit, explains: "With technology innovation, the up-front costs are significant, and a lot of the projects won't pay off. With process innovation, the cost of creating new processes isn't high, and they're less likely to fail, but the business payoff can be high."

Still, Kurien believes Wipro can bring the most value to its BPO clients when it combines business process excellence with technical innovation. An engagement with a U.S. PC maker in 2006 shows how this is done. The project started after V. Anand Kumar, Kurien's general manager of business planning, visited a technical help desk crew in Kolkata (formerly Calcutta) that was providing Level 1 technical support for the PC maker. Level 1 call-center agents handle the initial calls from customers who have problems with their PCs. Kumar's mission was to improve the working environment for employees, and the discussion quickly turned to frustrations with the customer service process. Sashwati Dasgupta, an agent who had been working there for six months, shocked Kumar by telling him that the average initial call took 28 minutes to resolve. That compared to an 18-minute average for another Wipro BPO client. The difference was partly because agents in Kolkata had to search through 12 different knowledge management programs to diagnose and fix problems. There were just six at the other call center. Another glitch: The script of questions agents were required to follow was not ordered properly. In some cases they'd ask a long string of questions before discovering that the customer should have been immediately routed to a different call center. This process was a prime candidate for transformation.

A small Wipro team spent the next few weeks preparing a proposal to totally revamp the PC maker's help desk operations. It included a revised script, a better knowledge management system, and the ability to shift some customers to self-help Web sites. The team also developed a technology package to automate the process; they tapped into software programs that had already been built by others and wrapped them together into a unified system. The technology made it possible, with a push of a button, to download diagnostic software to the customer's PC, run automated tests, and fix a set of common problems, all without agent involvement. Within three weeks, Kumar presented the proof of concept to the client and got approval to develop a formal proposal.

Kurien and Kumar saw this as potentially a watershed event for the BPO business. It was an opportunity to transform the help desk operations of a major customer and reposition Wipro as an innovator rather than a commodity provider of help desk services. "Hard work is fine, but we have to move from labor arbitrage to doing things smarter," says Kumar. "If we can do this successfully, it will differentiate us from the rest of our Indian competitors."

The top three Indian tech outsourcers all push aggressively in these three types of innovation. While in many ways their approaches are similar, right now TCS stands out for its creativity. It is teaming with academic scientists in India and the United States to come up with practical applications for scientific breakthroughs. For instance, TCS hooked up with the Indian Institute of Science to develop a new heart monitoring device. Patients download the results onto a PC, and their results can be e-mailed to their doctors for review. TCS has also forged links with venture capital firms to spot start-ups with cutting-edge technologies. That way it's able to get the jump on competitors in bringing those new technologies to market as part of its service solutions. So it's a seesaw battle between Wipro and its rivals. They keep each other hopping.

Centers of Excellence

In Wipro's Centers of Excellence, the company explores the whole range of existing and emerging technologies and figures out how to apply them to the IT and BPO services. As of early 2006, the company had 40 such centers that employed about 250 engineers and programmers. Their topics ranged from grid computing and wireless communications to consumer and automotive electronics. They follow a four-step process called 4A. Here's how it works:

- *Awareness.* Set goals, select team, and create a project road map.

- *Assimilation.* Understand the technology and how it applies to particular industries. Create prototype services. Publish white papers to establish thought leadership.

- *Application.* Develop a sales kit. Conduct Web seminars that demonstrate the services. Form alliances with technology providers.

- *Advancement.* Assist the salesforce in making pitches. Once sales are made, improve software and service modules for use in future engagements.

Typically a Center of Excellence has a life span of 12 to 18 months. It takes that long to develop a new practice, get it established with customers, and hand it off to the business units. Wipro is constantly spotting and establishing new Centers of Excellence even while it's phasing out mature ones.

Some Centers of Excellence keep chugging along year after year. The technologies keep morphing. In those cases, the center may produce one practice after another. A prime example is the SOA Center of Excellence, mentioned earlier in this chapter. The SOA Center of Excellence was launched in 2000 by Krishnakumar Menon, one of the first engineers at Wipro to recognize the importance of emerging Web services technology standards called Extensible Markup Language (XML) and Simple Object Access Protocol (SOAP). They make it possible for the computing systems within a single company, or those owned by different companies, to share information with each other without manual human intervention. These technologies are the foundation of SOA, which allows programmers to create large, complex applications out of many pre-built and loosely coupled components. Web services and SOA enable something the tech industry's visionaries call "frictionless commerce."

Menon assembled a team of 10 engineers and picked a target. It was a subset of Web services used to enable electronic commerce between businesses. The group built pilot projects and had a flurry of engagements with clients, but demand dropped off when delays in creating industry standards slowed adoption by corporations. Menon refocused his group and began developing a set of SOA services that could be used by corporations to rebuild the applications within their walls. Demand was strong, and his bosses created an official Wipro SOA practice and put him in charge of it. He now runs a 500-person team. Embedded within the practice is the 35-person SOA Center of Excellence, which gets funding from the chief technology officer's budget and incubates new services for the SOA practice. "Every year I see a lot of ideas coming up. It just multiplies," says Menon.

The expertise that the Centers of Excellence develop isn't confined to the practices that spin out of them. That knowledge is spread like wind-borne seeds throughout the entire organization. Engineers in the centers train people in other practices to use their technologies and services. They train the presales people in the vertical business units, helping them prepare proposals for clients that show off Wipro's ability to handle cutting-edge technologies. They also help the HR department create classes for any programmers or engineers who want to upgrade their knowledge.

And that's not all. The Center of Excellence Program, together with the Innovation Initiative, helps Wipro hold on to highly talented people like Menon. At another Indian tech company where Menon worked, employees were not empowered to innovate or to incubate businesses. Engineers simply took orders. If they had a great idea and wanted to try it out, they had to leave the company. Not so at Wipro. "The Centers of Excellence allow people to be entrepreneurs without taking the risk and quitting to form a start-up," he says. "There's a lot of freedom here. You can make things happen."

The Innovation Initiative

Consider the milieu when Wipro launched its initial Innovation Initiative. The dot-com craze was in full fury. New tech companies were popping up by the dozens in India and the United States. In comparison, Wipro's routine work seemed rather drab. At the same time, the huge upswelling of demand for programming brought on by the Y2K glitch was tailing off. The company needed innovation, both to give it a next act with clients and to hold onto its brightest stars. The Innovation Initiative was conceived as a mini–Silicon Valley experiment. The Innovation Council, made up of Mangalath, two other technologists, and four "champions" from vertical business units, serves as a captive venture capital firm. "We have two goals," says Mangalath. "The ideas that are coming in must deliver growth for our businesses. The second goal is to create an innovation culture in the people who participate."

People with ideas submit them to the Innovation Council, which meets once a month. The council approves about a half-dozen proposals per quarter and has 40 to 50 projects running at any given time. The focus here is on technology with high intellectual property content, solutions for particular business functions (say, order-management automation), and technology platforms upon which solutions are built. Mangalath adopted a product development method that was being used by Unilever and adapted it to Wipro's needs. There are three stages, each of them followed by a review, or gate. Here's how it works:

- *Idea Generation:* Ideas are collected from employees, Centers of Excellence, customers, partners, and academics. The ideas are focused, evaluated, and if they're approved, pass through the Entry Gate.

- *Idea Incubation:* A core team is formed to understand the market potential, prepare a prototype, and write a business plan. If the plan is approved, the project passes through the Commitment Gate.

- *Successful Execution:* The Innovation Council funds the project teams, marketing, and sales support. The idea is taken through the regular product development process, including beta testing and, after the final review, launch.

The projects have the feel of start-up companies. Typically they're made up of small teams, from 5 to 40 people. If the person who suggests the idea has the appropriate experience, he or she becomes the leader. If not, somebody else is drafted. Premji lavishes attention on the participants, inviting them to lunch in small groups. The entire team gets a stake in the success of the project. They split 3 percent of the sales over the first 18 months and 1 percent of the sales during the subsequent 12 months. After the new services are launched, they remain independent until they're considered mature, about two years, and then are attached to practices or vertical business groups and have to fend for themselves. Only about 10 percent get into the incubation stage. Of those, about 70 percent eventually produce services.

One of the commercial successes is Wipro's Flow-briX workflow software. It's being used by clients across a handful of industries, including telecommunications, financial services, and publishing, and it produces about $4 million in annual revenues. Its creator is Anurag Seth, who is now the general manager for solution delivery for the company's Technology, Media, Travel, and Logistics vertical. He now leads a team of 2,500 programmers at delivery centers in Bangalore, Chennai, and Hyderabad. He also oversees the Flow-briX solution, with its 35 programmers. Back in 2000, when Seth was a sales executive, he was recruited by Mangalath to help him shape and launch the Innovation Initiative. They worked on it for eight months, and then he launched it in 2001 with Seth as one of the initial project leaders.

That was the beginning of a bumpy journey for Seth, and it shows the challenges a tech services firm faces when it sets out to become a technology innovator. At first, Seth and his initial team of five people didn't even have an idea. All they had was a topic. They were supposed to establish a foothold in the e-commerce and content management areas. They began by talking to sales account managers to find out what customers were asking for. They gathered, collated, and looked for patterns. Finally, after three months, they settled upon a project: building a workflow management solution for publishing companies to handle everything from document creation and editing to layout and printing. Seth set out to form alliances with software makers who sold products for each stage of publishing, but they turned him away. Wipro didn't have enough knowledge of the publishing industry to become a player. So that idea was a dead end. Seth learned a lesson that Wipro executives were learning all over the world as they tried to expand their footprint beyond routine coding: without specific industry expertise, they wouldn't get high-value contracts.

Fortunately for Seth, there were plenty of other uses of workflow technology. He happened to have lunch with the chief technology officer of a large financial services firm who said he was in the market for workflow software for the company's HR department. "He wanted to use my workflow product, and I didn't even have the core technology yet," recalls Seth, who put 25 engineers on the project and had a rough prototype ready in three months. But when he contacted the CTO again, the officer was on the verge of buying software from another company. Seth begged for a chance to make his case, and in three more weeks, his team had whipped the prototype into good-enough shape that the CTO bought it.

The next hurdle: Wipro was a services company, yet Flow-briX was a software product. That could cause friction with the software makers with whom Wipro allied in the marketplace. Plus, customers could become confused. They were accustomed to buying services from Wipro, not products. Seth's answer was to build the product in modules. Customers could pick some or all of the pieces. Other software makers' products could be included in a Wipro solution, which it would deliver to customers as a service. That way, Seth avoided conflict with his partners and confusion among potential clients. He sold $10 million of business process management services directly or indirectly enabled by Flow-briX in fiscal 2006, and he hopes to double that number the following year.

While Seth and Mangalath consider Flow-briX a success, they have only qualified praise for the Innovation Initiative. Originally, when they conceived the program, they hoped it would deliver breakthrough innovations that would lay the foundation for sizable businesses. Instead, it produced several dozen modest innovations and small businesses. "In 2000, we talked about breakthroughs, but the organization wasn't ready," says Seth. "Now, I think we're ready."

Quantum Innovation

If Wipro is to grow rapidly to become a $5 billion company, it will require breakthrough innovations in technology, solutions, and business processes. The goal of the Quantum Innovation initiative was to set up perhaps four "mission" projects in the first year that are capable of producing $40 million to $50 million businesses over the next half decade.

The management team kicked off the process by scoping out sizable projects that could deliver revenue growth on that scale. Some of the concepts call for creating brand-new business models, a new kind of innovation for Wipro. One idea under consideration: application outsourcing. Right now, Wipro writes software applications for clients and, often, continues to maintain and improve them over a number of years. The new idea is to manage the computers and foundation software that the applications run on. Clients would pay Wipro based on the amount of data or transaction processing it provides for them. This would require Wipro to set up secure networks and to own or lease data centers. There would be big investments up front, but, later, potentially large and steady streams of annuity-style income.

Wipro hired an Indian innovation consulting firm, Erehwon, to help it scope out and produce quantum innovations. The first stage for Erehwon, called "gravity analysis," was to perform in-depth interviews with about 35 senior executives to get their assessments of Wipro's innovation capabilities. Then, on January 20, 2006, the consultants presented their findings to the executive team. There were no surprises. The existing programs were delivering incremental innovation. They should be kept and improved. But the organization needed to come up with new processes aimed at enabling larger-scale innovations. Rather than focusing on ideas that would bolster individual vertical businesses, the company needed to identify projects that could have major impact across its business lines. "Quantum Innovation starts with figuring out what you want to be. It's about your aspirations, not an idea about a technology," says Mangalath.

By mid-2006, the IT Management Council had selected five broad target areas. One example: studying the company's talent pipeline and coming up with better processes for preparing employees for the newest technologies and business challenges. Mangalath chose five "champions" to lead the incubation teams and about 20 top people to work with them. Erehwon consultants guided the programmers and engineers through a series of workshops designed to help them think more creatively and plan more successfully. The teams' task is to develop specific proposals and return to the IT Management Council for approval and funding.

The idea is to launch a handful of projects, and then, each year, launch a few more. If the Quantum Innovation process works, Wipro will become an innovation factory.

14

ADOPT THE BEST IDEAS,
THEN MAKE YOUR OWN WAY

When it comes to making a commitment to quality and operational excellence, Wipro ranks right up there with the global leaders. The company began its focus on quality and process improvements in the mid-1990s to gain credibility with Western corporate customers. Year by year, it adopted the world's best business practices and adapted them to software, hardware engineering, and business process outsourcing. It was among the first Indian companies to use Six Sigma for quality and lean techniques for operational improvements. Those skills are key competitive weapons against Indian rivals and the West's top tech services outfits. Now Wipro has combined the lessons it learned from others with its own innovations and codified them as the Wipro Way.

Wipro's Software Factory

There's a strong temptation to use the term "factory" when describing how Wipro operates. Just like the world's top manufacturers, Wipro has mastered the science of organizing processes and people to perform complicated tasks with a high level of quality and efficiency. What started off as an effort to take advantage of India's high IQs and low wages has now morphed into something quite different. "We have created an efficiency machine," says Sambuddha Deb, the company's chief quality officer and head of operational excellence.

The company combines quality and operational excellence for good reasons. It discovered a decade ago that the things an organization does to improve quality also improve productivity and profitability. If quality is assured early in a process, there's less rework. And if a process is simplified and streamlined, there are fewer places where mistakes can be made.

Everywhere you look, Wipro's dedication to quality is clear. For starters, it's a top priority for Premji. Deb reports directly to him, and when business leaders present their business performance scorecards to Premji for quarterly reviews, quality metrics make up one-third of their slides—and they're the first ones he sees. That assures that even if the businesses have outstanding revenue and profit results, quality literally comes first.

As quality leader, Deb is relentless. He has been involved in quality on and off since the early 1990s, so he's intimately familiar with each of the disciplines Wipro has put in place to produce incremental gains. He oversees an employee Web site that's packed with information, including the latest case studies on Six Sigma and lean. His organization reviews the results of all customer satisfaction surveys to spot places where improvements in quality or efficiency could help gain customer loyalty. Each business unit has to fulfill a quota of Six Sigma and lean projects in a year. And they have to show results.

Wipro's quality leaders are like religious evangelists. While Deb's staff is relatively small, just 225 people, they organize activities in the business groups that make sure quality stays on top of the mind. Quality managers from different business groups meet regularly to compare experiences and techniques. Quality is high on the agenda each month, when each business group holds meetings of 50 or so top project managers. And once a quarter, when Wipro holds a tech forum—a show-and-tell of new things that are going on in the company—Deb and his crew highlight their latest projects and successes.

Special status is conferred on people who get involved in quality projects. They get awards and accolades, and it figures in their performance evaluations. So it's no wonder that so many employees participate. More than 15,000 of them have been trained in Six Sigma. Of those, more than 200 are certified black belts, experts in Six Sigma techniques, and 10 are master black belts. In addition, Wipro has 600 Project Management Institute–certified consultants—people trained in project management skills established by that institute in Pennsylvania.

Each of the disciplines Wipro has adopted addresses different aspects of quality and operational excellence. ISO 9000 is the basic framework for project management and documentation. The company complies with the Software Engineering Institute's Capability Maturity Model (CMM) standards as the basis of its core software development processes, and uses the institute's People Capability Maturity Model (PCMM) standard for training and managing programmers. Six Sigma is aimed at reducing the number of mistakes and reducing the time it takes to complete a task. Lean (which, as I have written, is derived from the Toyota Production System) is all about improving business processes or solving problems as they arise.

Wrap it all together and you have the underpinnings of the company's core software development process: Veloci-Q. This process is too detailed to go into in a non-software-development book, but here are the basic steps: (1) project initiation, (2) requirement study and project plan, (3) high-level design, (4) low-level design and test design, (5) coding and test-case development, (6) system testing, and (7) release.

Wipro's focus on quality and operational excellence has produced outstanding results over the past decade. Its field error rate (the measure of defects found once software is in use) declined by 85 percent between 1995 and 2001, and that level of improvement has held steady since. During the same 1995 to 2001 time span, the company's adherence to schedule in customer engagements improved from 60 percent to 91 percent. Productivity has also improved dramatically. Based on an index of 100 in 1995, it has increased step by step to 178 in 2000 and 267 in 2005, the company says. Compared to the tech services industry as a whole, Wipro has achieved a 37 percent higher productivity rate, a lower defect rate, and a 15 percent higher on-time project completion rate. (Ninety-one percent of its projects are completed on time, while the industry average is 76 percent, says a 2004 META Group market research report.)

You can clearly see the cumulative effect of Wipro's operational disciplines on its profitability. While the company's revenues grew at a steady pace through most of the late 1990s, profitability was low. That changed in fiscal year 2000, after Vivek Paul came in to run the global technology business and enforced new rigor in the company's business processes. The following table bears that out.

Fiscal Year	Revenues ($M)	Net Income ($M)
1981	63.74	1.23
1982	83.97	3.02
1983	62.43	2.68
1984	64.55	2.59
1985	66.00	2.35
1986	85.12	3.29
1987	114.48	4.35
1988	152.13	3.58
1989	114.66	2.40
1990	169.39	5.00
1991	191.74	5.82
1992	137.21	4.04
1993	165.91	5.06
1994	201.62	8.35
1995	292.40	16.21
1996	402.50	18.91
1997	430.22	18.44
1998	444.22	25.42
1999	417.22	37.18
2000	522.98	76.38
2001	654.07	137.42
2002	685.50	172.35
2003	901.51	178.35
2004	1,346.38	230.23
2005	1,892.49	373.35
2006	2,385.50	455.71

Source: Wipro

The Wipro Way

There comes a point in every outstanding company's life cycle when it knows what it is and it's very good at what it does. That's a mature organization. While Wipro is still a continuously changing company in a dynamic business environment, 2005 marked a watershed year. Premji and his executive team decided it was time to spell out for employees, investors, customers, and partners what Wipro is about and how it operates: the Wipro Way.

There's a long tradition in business of self-defining exercises like this. Ever since David Packard and William Hewlett, founders of the Hewlett-Packard Company, laid out the HP Way in 1957, companies have sought to create such distinctive corporate cultures that if somebody simply says the "HP Way" or the "GE Way" or the "Toyota Way" everybody knows what it means. When this book went to press, Wipro was still in the process of formalizing the Wipro Way and communicating about it, so it was unclear if the label would carry weight outside the company's walls. However, inside Wipro, the leaders had defined their culture and were beginning to teach it—Bible-like—to employees. "The main vision is to build a culture of excellence in the organization," says Deb. "We're mature and we're setting our own direction."

The Wipro Way, in part, is a set of objectives. First, in keeping with the company's predilection for metrics, there are three of those. It aims to have the best operating margin growth in the IT services industry, the best Net Promoter Score (in which you subtract the percentage of customers who would not recommend you from the percentage who would), and the highest productivity in a set of critical business processes. Also, the company wants to build a culture of excellence across all of its business units and functional groups. That is to be achieved through constant improvement, focus on customer satisfaction, putting people with the right skills in the right place, and experimentation.

These goals are achieved through a framework that brings together all of the things the company does that produce high-quality services. "We're distilling everything we have learned in 15 years about quality and business process excellence," Deb says. Here are the elements of the framework:

- *Strategy.* Plan for world-class performance. Execute robustly. Establish reviews and controls. Manage change and risks.

- *Customer-centricity.* Understand customer needs. Move from the role of contractor to being a partner in the customer's success.

- *Process excellence.* Create well-defined and efficient work processes. Align them with functional support systems like recruitment, training, and finance.

- *People management.* Put people with the right skills in the right places in the organization. Align HR practices with business needs. Engage employees in continuous improvement of the organization's capabilities.

- *Personal change.* Focus on customers. Adapt to changes. Be proactive to anticipate problems and develop relevant skills.

The Wipro Way is part distillation of the wisdom of others and part Wipro's own invention. "This wraps it all together," says Premji. "We're developing cross-synergies, so it's not a matter of 1 plus 1 equal 2. It's 1 plus 1 equal more than 3."

Deb and his organization were given the task of infusing a deep understanding of the Wipro Way into the organization. The major task was preparing guidebooks that laid out the details for current employees and new hires. Deb's plan, at press time, was to create role-oriented booklets aimed at people at different levels in the organization.

But he didn't wait for the guidebooks to be published before he began evangelizing the company's new creed. He started with project managers. These people are really the company's backbone. They manage engagements with clients. Deb felt that the project managers were well schooled in procedures and policies, but he saw the Wipro Way as an opportunity to reshape their consciousness. "Now we're moving to a way of life," he says. "It's getting people to understand things deeply enough that even if a rule or policy isn't written down, they know what to do in every situation."

The exercise began with a series of workshops. First, Deb and his crew gathered information. How did the project managers use the company's written procedures and policies in their day-to-day jobs? The second step was migrating the managers from work by rote to work by understanding. He used three techniques: teaching the tenets of the Wipro Way and getting people to use them in their day-to-day jobs, setting up an incentive system to reward people who live and breathe the Way, and enlisting senior managers as exemplars.

Deb is under no illusion that cultivating the Wipro Way throughout the organization will be quick or easy. "This is very early stages. It will take years and years," he says. "It's an ambition we have set for ourselves, and we are staking our reputations on it."

Learn from the Masters

In the American tech industry, there's a syndrome called "not invented here" that has held a number of companies back. (Digital Equipment Corporation is one example frequently cited.) It's an idea that executives and engineers get that they should create everything themselves, whether it's technology or a way of doing things, rather than learn from others. Premji never caught that disease. Ever since he ventured into the unfamiliar realm of information technology in 1980, he has believed—and preached—that Wipro needs to spot and adopt the best business practices in the world. It's one of the reasons he formed Wipro GE Medical Systems, the joint venture with General Electric in India to produce medical equipment. "It was a good company to learn from," he says. From GE, Wipro picked up the discipline of strategic planning and adopted the practice of performing internal audits. Also, it was GE's embrace of Six Sigma that made Wipro take a look at it.

From the beginning, Wipro has seen its quest for quality and operational excellence as a journey. It has adopted the best ideas from the best companies or standards organizations, adapted them to software, melded them with its own best ideas, and come up with its own recipe for excellence. The same is true of its chief Indian rivals, Infosys and TCS. Wipro's Deb has noticed that with each new quality or efficiency initiative, the company achieves step improvements over a period of one to three years. Then gains level off, and it's time for a new initiative.

When Wipro began establishing offshore delivery of software services in the early 1990s, it was a fly-by-the-seat-of-the-pants affair. Bhanu Murthy, now the senior vice president in charge of the Retail, Consumer Packaged Goods, and Distribution vertical, remembers those crazy days. He set up one of first delivery centers in Bangalore for an American customer. He had to think about everything: people, buildings, computers, phone connections, processes. He looked to the International Organization for Standardization (ISO) for guidance. While the ISO 9000 standard had laid out quality management principles in general, it didn't have anything to offer specifically for software development. So Murthy set up a software process engineering group to study ISO guidelines and software development processes that had been used at other companies and come up with a basic process for Wipro. In some cases, Murthy would run into a problem and ask the group to go off and find the answer. In others, the project managers came up with solutions on their own.

Out of this exercise came a project managers' notebook—a three-hole binder—that each manager could add to easily as the organization developed and became more sophisticated. If something didn't pan out, they could rip out the pages and throw them away. Over the years, those binders evolved into role-based rulebooks that Wipro's project managers, quality managers, and account managers follow to do their daily jobs.

The next step on Wipro's journey would see it emerge as one of the top software quality organizations in the world. Help came from a surprising source: the United States. In the late 1980s, Carnegie Mellon University's Software Engineering Institute had established a set of software programming standards for the U.S. Department of Defense. They had been adopted by a handful of defense contractors but no software companies. Watts S. Humphrey, SEI's director at the time, traveled to India in the early 1990s to give lectures about Capability Maturity Modeling, or CMM, the institute's quality framework. Humphrey has been called the W. Edwards Deming of software. Deming was the quality guru who went to Japan after World War II and taught manufacturing principles to the Japanese that helped them build world-beating auto and consumer electronics industries. Led by Wipro and other pioneers, the Indians adopted each new version of the CMM standards just as soon as they came out. "They came on board and turned on fast," says Humphrey.

For Wipro and its Indian peers, CMM was the equivalent of the Good Housekeeping Seal of Approval. "In the global marketplace for services, brand was so important. In the absence of an Indian brand, you had to have a differentiator that was significant. Our first move was CMM," says Premji. In fact, with A. L. Rao, then the chief technology officer, leading the charge, the company went to school on CMM. Wipro was certified in 1997 with CMM Level 3, meaning it had documented processes for developing software and low defect rates, and it had demonstrated that it was a "learning organization" capable of improving its processes. It achieved CMM Level 5, the top CMM level, in 1998, PCMM (People Capability Maturity Model) Level 5, which governs the management of people, in 2001, and in 2002, it was the world's first company to achieve Level 5 for CMMI (Capability Maturity Model Integration) version 1.1, which governs high-level management of software projects. The letters and numbers become dizzying, but the message was simple: This company is serious about quality and operational excellence. "This became our calling card. Wipro represented quality as well as low cost. We could get appointments with prospects," recalls Sudip Banerjee, president of the Enterprise Solutions business.

Even before Wipro mastered CMM, it started eyeing Six Sigma. Premji began pushing it in 1997. The two disciplines served different purposes. CMM was about putting sound policies and structures in place and managing them well. Six Sigma was about spotting problems, analyzing them with sophisticated mathematical tools, and fixing them. The company hired Motorola University to do the Six Sigma training.

But it took a while to adapt Six Sigma to Wipro's businesses. Software programming is different from manufacturing in significant ways. No two projects are the same, so processes can't be 100 percent repeatable, which is one of the basic rules of Six Sigma. Some of the company's business leaders didn't believe it was a good fit, Deb says, and they just went through the motions rather than going at it aggressively. "We stumbled. Nobody had tried this before. But Premji was insistent, and we kept at it," Deb says. Wipro had to create its own tools for investigating and analyzing problems. As a result, it wasn't until 2002 that it had Six Sigma firmly established in all of its business units.

Here's an example of how Wipro uses Six Sigma: In mid-2005, the company wanted to figure out why its operating margins were lower than those of rival Infosys. One cause, it discovered through a Six Sigma project, was that the average experience level of employees in individual projects for clients was higher than it needed to be to get the job done. The company used a Six Sigma analysis tool, Taguchi Design, to figure out an optimum mix of experience levels on its project teams. It concluded that the optimal mix was 25 to 30 percent for those with zero to two years of experience, 30 to 45 percent for those with two to four years' experience, and less than 30 percent for those with more than four years of experience. At the time, the average was higher than five years. The Six Sigma team recommended increasing the percentage of people with two to four years of experience on teams and reducing the percentage of people with four to six years. Top management instructed the business units to reduce the proportion of senior people on teams by 10 percent by March 2006.

At Wipro, good is never good enough. In 2003, the company didn't make gains in field error rates and schedule adherence, though productivity continued to improve. Deb decided it was time to look for "the next new thing" that could produce another generation of improvements in operational performance. "We had to shake things up and get people to reexamine how they were doing things," says Deb. "When you launch a big initiative, it gets everybody excited."

He shopped around for months and finally focused in on lean. Deb saw how effectively Toyota had used its manufacturing excellence to gain ground on GM. He was drawn to lean because, unlike Six Sigma, which was handled by relatively few people and was statistically oriented, lean could involve every Wipro employee and a project could start with something as simple as having a good, commonsense idea about how to do something differently. Still, the prospect of taking on yet another quality and efficiency discipline was daunting. Nobody had ever applied lean to software. And Deb couldn't find teachers. "We had to learn lean by doing it. That was the scary part," he says.

Wipro Goes the Toyota Way

In the summer of 2004, Deb, Premji, and a handful of other Wipro executives got a rare glimpse inside a Toyota assembly plant. As they toured the factory that produces Corollas in Bangalore, there were plenty of lessons to learn, but for Deb, one stands out. At one point, he began to take a shortcut when the safety path painted on the factory floor made a sharp turn. The Japanese manager walking behind him reached out, took his shoulders, and gently guided him back onto the path. The message: All the little rules count. "They had that sort of discipline. It's second nature to them," Deb says.

Within a matter of weeks, Deb decided to use Toyota as a model for overhauling Wipro's operations. His aim was to make software development and business process management as simple, smooth, and replicable as the way Corollas slipped off the Bangalore assembly line every few seconds. He asked for a meeting with Premji and the senior executive team, including Vivek Paul, who then ran the global tech business, and laid out his proposal. "They said, 'Prove it,'" Deb recalls. He decided to run a handful of pilot programs as proof of concept. He selected 10 project managers as his SWAT team, eight in the software businesses and two in BPO. The initial pilots were to run 30 to 90 days. Everything was queued up so the project would launch on August 16, 2004, the day after India's Independence Day. The date was significant for Deb. He saw lean as a major step forward for the country's tech industry.

The overarching goal of lean is to compress time from the receipt of an order to the receipt of payment. A lean process is set up like a factory assembly line, with tasks performed in the optimal order, often by different people. Activities are designed to be continuous, with no delays while people wait for somebody else to complete a task. Employees are expected to make suggestions, and they're empowered to stop the process if something has gone seriously wrong. Visual displays in the work area show employees how they're performing against goals and minimums. That way, if something goes out of whack, everybody can see it and solve the problem on the spot. Most important is the principle of *Kaizen,* or continuous improvement.

You can see how lean is a good fit with Wipro's culture. The two share the values of employee involvement, continuous improvement, and rigorous measurement. Yet, adapting lean proved to be tricky. In order to adhere to some of the lean principles, the leaders of the pilot projects would have to violate rules they had established as part of CMM. Was that okay? Deb urged them to stick with their current standard as much as possible and to deviate only with his permission.

When the three months were up, it was clear that lean was going to work for Wipro. Deb began the process of getting all of the business units to adopt it. They were quick on the uptake. By early 2006, more than 300 lean projects had been launched. But that was just scratching the surface. Deb figured that lean wouldn't reach maturity at Wipro until the company had completed 500 to 600 projects. Partly, the reason was because it took a long time to test things out and get experience. But partly, it was because adopting lean forced some fundamental changes in the way Wipro did things. Take software development. Up until that point, most of the testing had been done at the end of the process. Yet with lean, the idea was to test things continuously so flaws could be fixed immediately. "Earlier, we wrote, froze, tested. Now we write, test, find mistakes, learn, and don't repeat them," says Deb. At press time, Wipro was still working on modifications to Veloci-Q, its core software development process.

How Lean Reshaped Wipro's BPO

Today, Wipro's paperwork processing operations in Bangalore, Pune, and Chennai bear an uncanny resemblance to a Toyota plant. Day and night, thousands of eager young men and women line up at long rows of tables modeled on an assembly line. Signs hanging over each aisle describe what process is being handled there: accounts receivable, travel and entertainment, and so on. Just like in a Toyota factory, electronic displays mounted on the walls will shift from green to red if things bog down.

It's quite a change from the way Wipro formerly handled this type of work. The company's software programmers labor in cubicles, but that setup interrupted the flow for business process employees. So T. K. Kurien, president of the BPO unit, came up with the idea of positioning people side by side at long tables and running processes up the line, step by step. Wipro also adopted the Kaizen system of soliciting employee suggestions for incremental improvements, and Kurien required his managers to read *The Toyota Way,* a 2004 book by academic Jeffrey Liker that dissects Toyota's manufacturing management techniques. The company even did old-fashioned time-and-motion studies. One discovery: It took an average of nine minutes for employees to regain optimal performance after water and bathroom breaks. The water coolers were quickly moved closer to people's desks.

The initial response from employees to all this "was a roaring disaster," admits Kurien. Some staffers felt like cogs in a machine, and they dragged their heels. After hearing from his middle managers,

Kurien did a reboot. He set up classes to explain the concepts and show how the methods would make their lives easier.

Indeed, now Wipro's paperwork-handling operations run with factorylike efficiency. There are two shifts: 8:30 a.m. to 6 p.m. and 6 p.m. to 3 a.m. When each shift starts, the teams, which are organized by process categories, gather with their team leaders for 10 minutes to discuss the day's goals and divide up tasks accordingly. Then they scatter to their desks. During a tour of a BPO office in Bangalore, I followed the journey of a single invoice through accounts payable. The first stop was the "imaging" room, where C. Venkatesh fed documents into scanners and attached electronic copies to workflow software, which manages each step of the process. Then H. V. Shivaram typed data from the invoice into the accounting software program, M. Rassal checked the math, Srikanth Vittal Murthy posted the charges in the general ledger, D. S. Varadharajan authorized payment, and B. Ravi Sekhar arranged for a check to be cut. Finally, V. Karunakaran printed and mailed it. If the process had hit a bottleneck, a digital display on the wall would have turned red. That would have prompted managers to swarm the center of the room, confer, and fix the problem on the spot.

Kurien adopted lean at a difficult time. He was dealing with a high attrition rate and was shifting the mix from the heavy focus on call center work to more paperwork-handling jobs. As a result of all the tumult, revenue growth flattened out in the middle of the transitions, but it started to grow in late 2005, and profit margins were up significantly. He attributes a significant portion of that improvement to lean.

A Radical Shift for Software

There's an inherent inefficiency in the way most corporations handle software outsourcing. They leave it up to medium- or low-level info tech managers scattered across the globe to decide which software programming jobs to farm out to specialists like Wipro. Typically, each manager signs a series of one-off contracts with a handful of service providers. The corporations don't have standards for how programs should be written, so, later, if they want to tie one program to another one, they have to do extra work to create those links. Wipro has come up with a new way of handling this kind of work, called the "Factory Model," which could revolutionize the way corporations handle a huge chunk of their IT budgets.

It all started back in 2003, when N. S. Bala, then a 13-year Wipro veteran, was assigned to lead the company's manufacturing business unit. He had spent the previous nine years in the United States as a sales executive handling accounts in the Midwest, so he was intimately familiar with how large corporations handle software outsourcing, flaws and all. At the time, Wipro had about 900 programmers in the unit, which handled auto, aerospace, and high-tech manufacturing. (Now it's up to 2,400.) To familiarize himself with his new assignment, Bala studied the Toyota Production System (TPS), and visited a Suzuki factory in India that was using TPS. Then he learned that Deb was sizing up lean as a new discipline for Wipro, so, on his own, he started thinking about how lean could improve the way he dealt with manufacturers. Wipro had done well in manufacturing, and customers were willing to hand it more challenging assignments. So the time was ripe for Bala to try something radically different.

Now that he was back in India, he could see firsthand how the way corporations handled outsourcing contracts caused problems for Wipro. It had to treat each client IT manager who signed contracts almost as a separate customer. Each contract was a discrete piece of work. With each new deal, Wipro had to reinvent the wheel, building a team, selecting technology, completing the project, and disbanding the team. Nothing that it created could be applied to the next project. All of that starting and stopping was extremely inefficient.

In lean, he saw a possible solution. Toyota assembly lines are set up so they can handle orders from many different sources, they know in advance what's coming, and since they build different models using a limited number of chassis and basic components, they can shift from one model to the next without interrupting the flow on the assembly line. What if a corporation aggregated all of those separate contracts scattered all over the world and funneled them to a single software factory in India? It would be good for the corporation, because it could set standards that all of its IT managers would follow. All the software would be built in a prescribed way, and it would be easier to integrate the pieces together. Costs would go down because the new system would allow its supplier to operate more efficiently. The scheme would be good for Wipro, because it could get a larger volume of business from a single customer and could deliver a continuous flow of work. No more starting and stopping.

Bala started with General Motors. GM was a good choice because it had already begun funneling a lot of its programming jobs to Wipro. They came in from GM operations around the globe, plus from Saab, Opel, and other subsidiaries. Bala and his GM colleagues created a global demand management system that GM IT purchasers and Wipro service delivery managers share. All of the software projects are built using the same set of technology standards and components. Wipro teams are fed a continuous stream of projects. Progress on projects is logged continuously and can be monitored by people from both companies. And rather than waiting for a particular person to finish part of a project, a programmer who is finished with a task can tap into the system via his or her PC and find another task that needs to be done. Testing is done continuously, so problems can be spotted immediately and fixed quickly. "We call it the factory model, but we're not commoditizing the work. We're not micromanaging our employees. We're allowing people to pace themselves and look at the bigger picture," says Bala.

This is just the beginning for the factory model. Harvard Business School wrote a case on it in late 2005, which gives Wipro a lot of credibility. So far, in mature engagements, the system has increased efficiency by between 8 and 16 percent on average—and that's beyond the basic offshore delivery advantages. The system saves clients money. Wipro uses fewer people per contract, which, in many cases, means lower fees for each contract. But because the company gets higher volumes of business from each customer, its revenues and profit margins improve. "We end up with a more sustained relationship with the customer," says Bala. "You gain their confidence. So it pays off in different ways." So far, Bala has three clients operating under the new system, and he's doing workshops for other clients to explain how it works.

Other Wipro business units have begun experimenting with the factory model. A half dozen engagements are underway, so far. "People are taking Bala's success stories and modifying them for their own industries," says Deb. Nearly 60 percent of the company's software business could be handled this way, so it could eventually have a major impact on revenue growth and profitability. Also, if this takes off, you can expect companies throughout the tech services industry to give it a try. A few years from now management gurus may be trumpeting a new model for running a tech services business: the Wipro Way.

15

BE OBSESSIVE ABOUT CUSTOMERS

Some of the top American software companies became notorious in the go-go 1990s for their hit-and-run sales tactics. They pursued customers with great ardor, but once the contract was signed and the check made out, that was the last the customers would see of their sales representatives for months on end. Traditional software companies sell licenses and are primarily paid up front, so they could get away with this kind of behavior—for a while, anyway. Wipro and the other tech services outfits can't do that. They provide service for months or years. They have to keep pleasing their customers week in and week out or they won't get paid. Rather than just resigning itself to being at the beck and call of customers, Wipro has turned customer service into a competitive advantage.

It's the Relationship, Stupid

On July 27, 2005, Mumbai, India's financial capital, was deluged with a record 37 inches of rain in a 24-hour period. More than 1,000 people died. In spite of massive flooding and chaos, Wipro employees throughout the city stayed on the job to help their clients. In one notable situation, a Wipro help desk team assigned to CRISIL, one of the country's leading credit rating agencies, worked practically around the clock to get the company back on its feet after three of its five offices within the city were knocked out.

Things were particularly dicey at a CRISIL office in the Solitaire Park complex. The basement flooded, soaking employees and swamping computer equipment. Wipro and CRISIL people rushed to help. They broke a wall to release flood waters, rescued terrified people, and then carried network routers and computer servers upstairs. The next day, since vehicles weren't able to move, the Wipro engineers hand-carried gear through the soggy city to another CRISIL office about one kilometer away. They set up networks and desktop computers in conference rooms so that about 100 people could work there temporarily.

CRISIL was amazed at how well the Wipro people handled the crisis. Not only did they save people and equipment, but they had basic operations working at the second office within 48 hours after the storm ended. Ramesh Kumar, the Wipro program manager, worked every day until the people and equipment were back in action at the Solitaire Park office on August 19. "They went into the water for us," says Thaseen Sayed, the technology manager for CRISIL in Mumbai. "It showed us that no matter what happened, they'd be there for us."

That's a point of pride for Wipro executives. Suresh Vaswani, president of Wipro Infotech, which handles the Indian market, says he got more than 40 commendation letters from customers after the Mumbai floods. "When it comes to customer delivery, we don't look at the contract. We look at what needs to be done. If there is a crisis, we solve it," he says.

A lot of companies talk a good game about customer service, but Wipro actually lives it. The company is organized to understand its customers' needs, serve them well, and respond quickly if something goes wrong. "It's really a no-brainer," says Sambuddha Deb, the chief quality officer. "People talk about how difficult it is to acquire a customer and how easy it is to lose one. It makes a lot of sense to concentrate on keeping them. This is the source of Wipro's long-term competitive edge."

One-on-one relationships between Wipro managers and their customers are vital for gaining trust and dealing with problems when they occur. Premji himself spends a great deal of time meeting with customers. He takes four overseas trips a year, and typically he meets with several client executives on each trip. At some other companies, the chief executive is also the chief salesperson, flying in to schmooze the top executives at a client just before they award a large contract. Not Premji. "I'm not there to visit them to close deals," he says. "I have team members whose job it is to do that. My priority is to build a senior-level relationship and trust, and see if they're satisfied." After Premji meets with customers, he doesn't keep what was said to himself. Within 48 hours, and often within 24, he e-mails full reports to everybody who has a stake in the outcome.

To keep in sync with clients, Wipro also conducts reviews with their leaders on a quarterly basis. Typically, one of the meetings will be at the customer's headquarters, and the next will be in Bangalore or another Indian city where the customer's tasks are handled. When the meetings are held in India, Wipro executives and salespeople who are responsible for the accounts show their guests the offices where their work is done and introduce them to the people who are their virtual employees. The clients help select employees for merit prizes and then participate in the award ceremonies. "There's a serious business agenda, but we also want them to have a feel-good visit," says Makarand Teje, sales vice president for banking, financial services, and insurance in the United States.

When a client complains, Wipro has a system for escalating the matter up through the sales and management ranks, and if need be, all the way to Premji. If it's a big deal, there's no waiting around for the chain of command to click in. Premji gets involved immediately. "When there are problems, managers come out of the woodwork to figure out what's wrong," says Mikelle Fisher, a Wipro consultant in the United States. "They'll start making phone calls from India. They're asking, 'Why did this happen? How can we fix this?'"

Sometimes Wipro's commitment to customer satisfaction is sorely tested. There are situations where something goes awry and it's not Wipro's fault, or both sides seem to deserve some of the blame. Ramesh Emani, president of the Product Engineering Solutions group, recalls a 2005 near disaster that shows how far Wipro will go to satisfy a client. The company had been hired to design a product from scratch. (It wouldn't identify the customer or the product.) The project was supposed to take a year to complete, but it took more than two, due to problems on both sides. Some Wipro executives didn't believe they were contractually obligated to finish the project, but after some internal debate, Premji insisted that they stick with it.

Ultimately, Wipro's engineers delivered the product, and the customer was pleased with the results. "We lost some money, but I think we won the trust of the customer, and that may mean more business in the future," says Emani. "But it's more than business. It's about a relationship. And it's about our reputation."

Make Customer Care the Foundation of Your Company

Wipro's obsession with customer care got its start with Ashok Soota. He had run both the domestic and global tech businesses before he left to cofound MindTree Consulting in 1999. Soota made a practice of calling on all types of customers, even small businesses. He'd never refuse a call from a customer at any time of day or night, current Wipro executives say. Even if the caller had bought just a single PC, Soota would still take the call. "That spirit remains in the organization," says Girish Paranjpe, president of the Financial Solutions business unit.

Satisfaction surveys are the second leg of Wipro's customer care strategy. The company started doing surveys almost immediately after it got into the tech services business. As soon as a Wipro team finished a project for a client, it would solicit detailed feedback from the person who managed the engagement from the client end. Later, it added a second survey. That one's an annual exercise, performed online, that goes to top decision makers such as vice presidents of IT, chief information officers, and even chief executives. That way Wipro hears from people with financial responsibility and finds out if the projects paid off for them.

To encourage a high response rate, Wipro keeps both surveys short, to about 20 questions. Clients are asked to rate Wipro on a scale of 1 to 5, with 5 being the highest. Results of the surveys of project managers have been very strong. These are the people who live down in the trenches with Wipro employees and know their work well. Those survey results rose steadily from an average of 3.85 in 2001 to 4.37 in 2005, with more than 90 percent of those surveyed rating Wipro above a 4. The results of the annual surveys are almost as good. They went from 3.85 in 2001 to 4.27 in 2003. Wipro's quality team wanted to make sure it was asking the right questions, so it had the Gallup Organization do an analysis that year. As a result, it reformulated the survey and asked some new questions to find out how loyal customers were and how they rated Wipro compared to its competitors. That brought the average ratings down to 3.96 in 2004 and 2005. The company isn't satisfied with its performance. It wants to bring up its score to at least 4.2.

Rather than using customer satisfaction metrics to aggrandize itself, Wipro uses them to make itself better. So in 2005 it adopted a new analysis tool introduced by management consultant Frederick F. Reichheld of Bain & Company. In a *Harvard Business Review* article, "The One Number You Need to Grow," Reichheld laid out his theory that what he called a "Net Promoter Score" was the most practical and useful measure of customer loyalty. In a survey, you ask customers how likely it is that they would recommend your company to a friend or colleague. You calculate your Net Promoter Score by subtracting the percentage of customers who are extremely unlikely to recommend you from the percentage who are extremely likely to do so. Wipro's Net Promoter Score in 2005 was 21 percent, compared to a median score in the United States of 16 percent. Right now, the top scoring companies achieve about 70 percent, so Wipro has a long way to go to get there.

Wipro's Net Promoter Score signals that while its customer satisfaction scores are high, it hasn't separated itself from the competition in the minds of many customers. "If we get the same score, we're not differentiated. That's cause for analysis and action. If our scores are worse, we jump out of our seats," says Alexis Samuel, general manager of the Software Engineering Process Group in the Office of Productivity.

Poor survey scores set off alarms up and down the organization. If an individual project survey results in a score of less than 3, the Wipro salesperson on the account or the service delivery people immediately call the client to find out what caused it. The rep draws in the service delivery manager in India, who conducts an investigation of the matter and comes up with an action plan for setting things right. Project managers have a lot riding on the outcome of the surveys. If their projects rate 2 or 3—or, heaven forbid, a 1—it counts against them when it comes time to do annual performance appraisals and pay raises. The results of the annual surveys are loaded into a Web-based computer program called the Annual CSAT Tool, where individual client scores can easily be broken out. With any score less than 4 in the United States (or a 3.5 in Japan and Europe, where executives tend to be tougher graders), senior managers get in touch with the customer and start the rehabilitation process.

Once Samuel and his colleagues get the results of the surveys, they slice and dice the data to look for patterns and draw lessons from them. For instance, in 2005 they did an analysis that broke down customer satisfaction by countries and regions. The U.S. satisfaction rating was a healthy 4.03, but Europe was significantly lower, at 3.68, and the level had dropped from the previous year. "We realized it wasn't just cultural. Something else was wrong," says Samuel. So the company set up a task force to investigate, which came up with an action plan for improving the situation in Europe. It included doing more Six Sigma and lean projects, and introducing software dashboards—visible on PCs to both Wipro people and the clients—that tracked the performance and progress of projects. At the same time, the company revamped its software coding standards to improve the quality of programming in Java and .NET, two of the more popular programming technologies.

Samuel and the quality crew break out detailed customer satisfaction results for each business line and even for individual customers. Each business has a Quality Improvement Council that meets once a month to review its ratings, typically cramming 60 to 70 people into a meeting room. The councils include business managers, project managers, technical managers, and the heads of the delivery groups. Every summer each business unit comes up with its annual quality action plan. In 2005, to help vertical businesses whose ratings were lower than average, the company created a new role, the strategic account manager, or SAM—a senior person with good technical and communications skills who works closely with dissatisfied clients to set things right.

One of the surprising findings that came out of this ongoing analysis of scores was that if Wipro's performance fell even slightly, customers noticed it. That was true even if the performance was within the norms the company laid out for its people. "The thing we learned is that we not only have to achieve our high goals, but we have to continuously improve," says Samuel.

Wipro reviews its customer relationships with all of the intensity that it audits financial reports. When the company gets serious complaints, Samuel's group conducts three- or four-day investigations to gather the facts. "We're like the FBI," he says. The quality team writes up a report that details what went wrong and recommends what needs to be done to fix things. Wipro managers talk over the recommendations with their clients, and both sides agree on an action plan. In addition to those investigations, the quality team conducts ongoing routine audits of 30 percent of all the projects, and an external auditor reviews about 60 projects per year.

One complaint that Wipro hears repeatedly from customers is that its employees are actually too obliging. That's right. They don't like to tell a customer no. They're reluctant to admit that a goal the customer has set for them is unreasonable or undoable. So they keep quiet and do their best, and sometimes they miss the target. "Some customers appreciate it, but others say, 'Please, tell your teams to say no if they can't do something,'" says Wipro's chief operating officer A. L. Rao. After hearing this critique a number of times, the company revised its training program for project managers. The new credo: Don't promise more than you can deliver.

How Wipro Turned Defeat to Victory at TUI

Here's a textbook case of how to win and keep a customer: It shows how the combination of relationship building and providing service that goes beyond the call of duty pays off for Wipro. The tale starts in 2003, just a few years after Germany's TUI (for *Touristik Union International*) AG, the world's largest travel company, was assembled through a series of acquisitions. Travel arranging is a low-margin business, and TUI was looking for ways to cut costs. It considered using Indian outfits for its call centers and some of its software development. It checked out several companies, including Wipro's BPO operation. TUI executives visited Wipro's call centers in India, but ultimately, they decided against outsourcing such operations. They were concerned about the logistics of serving European customers from halfway around the world.

Even more troubling for Wipro, TUI was dissatisfied with the way the negotiations had gone. Wipro seemed disorganized. Several Wipro executives got involved, and they told inconsistent stories about pricing and timing. "It felt big and hairy and risky," says Jim Mann, a Brit who is TUI's purchasing director and IT manager. "You're moving something a long way away. If it doesn't work, what the hell are you going to do?"

That was the first blow to Wipro's pride. The second came only months later when TUI passed it over and chose a small Indian software services rival, Sonata, to handle programming for its Web sites. TUI had discussed the contract with Wipro for months, but once again, it was put off by inconsistency in the way Wipro executives handled the discussions.

What came next surprised Mann. Premji asked for a meeting and flew to London, where Mann is based, to find out why Wipro had lost out and what it could do better. The two spoke for over an hour in Mann's office. "He came across as absolutely interested in what had gone wrong and what he could do to make it better," says Mann. "You hear people say things like this, and you don't believe it. But he was true to his word."

So Wipro got a third chance, and, this time, didn't blow it. TUI's multiyear technology management contract with another services company was coming to an end, and Mann picked Wipro to handle U.K. tech operations. Job responsibilities included manning a technical help desk and managing the company's security, servers, and networks. After six months of planning, the switchover came in November 2004. Not only did the handoff go without a hitch, but Mann was impressed that Wipro people spent so much time learning about TUI's business and its corporate culture so they could fit in. They also brought ideas to TUI about how it could run things better. "We benefit from their intellects," says Mann.

In fact, Wipro even suggested efficiency improvements that seemed contrary to its own interests. On several occasions, it suggested installing software that would reduce the number of Wipro employees required to complete a task. It also came up with the idea of consolidating services for four London offices into one. "Our philosophy is clear. We want to bring in value," says Vivek Sharma, Wipro's senior business development manager for the TUI account. "If you bring in value, you may have a short-term [negative] impact [on your billings]. But in the long view, you'll get benefits from that."

In the end, both companies made out. TUI has harvested a steady stream of productivity improvements. For instance, the average length of a help desk call dropped from 13 minutes to 6 minutes. Meanwhile, it has gradually handed more responsibilities to Wipro, including managing some operations in Germany. To get that contract, Wipro committed to training key technical people to speak German. In two years, Wipro's annual business with TUI went up by 60 percent. So TUI's overall tech management costs have gone down even as Wipro's revenues have increased. In early 2006, 60 Wipro employees were working for TUI in Chennai, and 20 sat on site in the United Kingdom and Germany. But those numbers seemed likely to grow rapidly. Mann is eyeing Wipro's new operations in Bucharest, Romania. "We're in every country in Europe, and we feel quite good about handing them more work in the future," he says.

Teach Your Customers Well

Once Wipro started gaining a strong reputation for operational excellence, some of its customers began asking for help with untangling their own operations. That's a nice spot to be in: Your customers so admire your way of doing things that they want to be like you. Over the past four years, Wipro has built a small but fast-growing business around quality and process consulting. "A lot of our customers had been with us for years. They saw us go from not so great, to good, to great," says Deb. "They wanted the same for themselves."

The consulting practice, which sits within Deb's organization, has handled more than 100 engagements and grew to be an $11 million business in fiscal 2006. The extra revenues are fine, but for Deb, it was even more important to establish Wipro as a trusted advisor. He figured that would help it get other advisory-type assignments, which pay better than routine programming. Also, he wanted to toughen up his quality experts. Within Wipro, quality is treated with reverence. Not so in a lot of other companies. He wanted his staff to learn to influence people who didn't want to be influenced.

This project didn't start off as a money maker. Premji had always encouraged Wiproites to share their expertise with clients as a routine part of doing business. And in many cases, when the company was hired to handle software development, the managers who launched the engagement would discover that their customers' development processes were not well organized. On their own, they'd call in Wipro quality experts to help them get things sorted out. If clients were inspired by Wipro's example and decided to launch a quality initiative, the Wipro people would help them get it going. But they discovered that, very often, these projects wouldn't pan out. The problem: Because customers weren't paying for service, they didn't take the projects seriously enough. So Wipro turned quality into a business so it would get the respect that was required to make sure the projects succeeded.

The key guy is Suraj Prakash, head of the consultancy practice. A 10-year Wipro veteran who formerly ran the corporate training programs, he was a one-man army for the first year. He would engage with clients and then pull in the people he needed from other Wipro units temporarily to help him out. By early 2006, the quality consulting group had grown to 140 full-timers, with 70 percent of its business in the United States and 30 percent in Europe. Wipro handles consulting just like everything else: There's always an offshore angle. In this case, more than half of the employees are based in India and fly to the United States or Europe only when they're needed for face-to-face consultations.

While the consulting practice started off by focusing on quality, it repositioned itself gradually. The new sweet spot: process excellence. In fact, the name changed in 2006 to Wipro Process Consulting. That's because clients' chief information officers are under intense pressure to manage IT better and cut costs. For them, quality is important, but secondary. Wipro sees the shift largely as a matter of semantics. It believes that process excellence and quality are two sides of the same coin.

Consulting engagements are pretty straightforward: Wipro teaches what it does. It has three practices. The core one is software development. Wipro helps clients use CMM and CMMI to improve their development process. It teaches them how to use Six Sigma and lean techniques to spot problems and continuously improve. An engagement starts with diagnostics, moves on to planning and training, and finishes with implementation and monitoring. The contracts last anywhere from three weeks to two years. If clients are willing to make major changes, they have the option of adopting Rapid-Q, a version of Wipro's Veloci-Q software development process. It's about 75 percent off the shelf and 25 percent customized to their particular needs. A second practice is teaching clients to manage their tech operations efficiently using the IT Infrastructure Library, or ITIL, a widely adopted set of best practices and benchmarks, which Wipro uses internally. The third practice is IT governance: managing and budgeting a portfolio of projects with the goal of doing more for less and getting results more predictably.

Even though Wipro is new to quality and process consulting, it has already taken on some high-profile assignments. At GM, for instance, it was one of two service providers (the other one, tech giant Hewlett-Packard) put in charge of handling the automaker's IT quality initiatives. This distinction highlights one of the things that has made the Wipro consultancy successful. Unlike some of its competitors, Wipro not only advises clients and helps them make a plan, but it also rolls up its sleeves and helps them manage the process. That's risky. "The challenge is to make quality improvements actually happen," says Prakash.

Wipro brings its measuring skills to bear in these engagements as well. In late 2005, when the tech managers of a major U.S. insurance client visited Bangalore for their annual status review, they confessed that they needed help in improving the effectiveness of their entire operation. Their systems for tracking software projects and other activities weren't up to snuff. When higher-ups questioned spending or asked why projects were behind schedule, they didn't have satisfactory answers. Wipro sent a team of four consultants to the client's headquarters to interview all of those involved and to assess what needed to be done to set things right. Within six weeks, they had all agreed on a new system for monitoring, measuring, and presenting all the critical pieces of information on software dashboards viewable on PCs. The system encompassed everything from budgeting and software development to staffing and maintenance of computers and networks. The dashboards were in place by midsummer. In essence, the consultants had distilled a decade of hard-won lessons into a six-month tutorial for their client.

These consulting assignments carry risks. They're high profile in the clients' organizations, and if they fail or don't produce outstanding results, it hurts Wipro's reputation. That could cost the company other business with the same customer. But that's the way it goes when you're committed to doing all that a customer expects of you and more. With many clients, Wipro's brand means quality and operational excellence. Those attributes will be crucial to its success as it attempts to differentiate itself from the competition. Without taking these kinds of customer satisfaction risks, there will be lesser rewards.

16

USE UP-TEMPO MANAGEMENT
TO BOOST PERFORMANCE

For the Indian tech services industry, speed truly is of the essence. To keep revenues growing rapidly, these companies have to do a lot of things right—and do them quickly. That effort includes landing new customers, launching new business lines, establishing new delivery centers in India and elsewhere around the world, hiring, training, erecting buildings, and fixing things when customers are dissatisfied. To accomplish all of this, Wipro's executives must deliberate and make good, fast decisions. The company makes time to ponder and debate the big strategic issues, but that means everything else must be handled with dispatch. And once a major strategic decision is made, Wiproites don't spend months getting organized. They get on with it.

Stay Nimble, Even When You Are a Global Giant

On June 30, 2005, just days after Vivek Paul told Azim Premji he was leaving Wipro, the chairman made a series of rapid-fire decisions. He would take command of the technology unit, meld it operationally with the domestic tech business, and so he wouldn't drown in operational details, he'd deal out some of Paul's duties to a handful of lieutenants. His key move was to choose A. L. Rao, who had previously run the telecommunications industry vertical, to be chief operating officer. When Premji offered Rao the job, he made it clear what the top priority would be: innovation. Rao had been a founding member of Wipro's info tech business in 1981 and was chief technology officer from 1996 to 1999, so Premji knew he had experience to lead this crucial initiative. "He said, 'Be bolder, and scale up innovation across the company,'" Rao recalls.

Rao barely had time to get comfortable with his new title and duties when Premji demanded a progress report. They met just two weeks after Rao took his new job. Premji peppered him with questions. How many projects did he plan on launching? How many people would be involved? What financial investments would be required? Rao had thought a lot about it, but hadn't launched anything yet. "I wanted to keep the heat up under him," says Premji. "It was a meeting to get him more actively moving forward."

There's a long tradition of decisive action at Wipro. Back in 1971, when it was still 100 percent focused on cooking oil, Premji created something he called Quick Management Inputs, or QMI. This was a special weekly meeting held every Monday morning to get a checkup on the company's vital signs. Premji didn't have e-mail, conference calls, or even direct telephone dialing in those days. He had to connect with his managers one after another between 9 a.m. and 11 a.m. Each regional manager would report sales and profits from the previous week, make a forecast for the coming week, and discuss problems or sales opportunities. During the calls, to kindle internal competition, Premji compared each manager's numbers to those of his or her colleagues. "It resulted in momentum on a weekly basis," he says. "I always emphasize the criticality of time, which is the most precious resource in an organization. You have to build momentum. You have to get a sense of urgency well dug in." Think of it as up-tempo management.

Quickness has mattered in business ever since the California Gold Rush, but the need for speed has become ever more acute. In the past few years, companies have come under increasing pressure to enter new businesses and bring new products to market quickly. That's caused by a number of factors, including international competition, pressure from investors to grow faster, and the convergence of the computer, consumer electronics, and media industries. Wipro is subject to all three of these influences. But it's also an enabler of speed to market for its clients. It helps them shed routine tasks so they can focus on what's more important, and it quickly creates new applications and products for them, often using ready-made technology components. To provide these services, it has to be able to go from zero to 60 as soon as it's called on by a customer. So speed must be built into the very fiber of the organization.

In many ways, this is a classic orchestration challenge. Wipro has 500 customers scattered around the world who are constantly launching or wrapping up mission-critical projects. Each one wants to be treated like it's Wipro's only customer, the top priority, so the company has to be extremely responsive but without being wasteful. At Wipro, almost everybody is a specialist, a part of a big puzzle that continuously has to be rebuilt on the fly. The people who can deal with this—and, better yet, manage it—are noticed and rise fast in the organization. "Our success is based on how quickly we do this. If you can't respond fast enough, you'll be left out of this business," says Sudip Banerjee, president of the Enterprise Solutions unit.

The ability to absorb information and act on it quickly has positive effects on a company's performance, but it also sends an important message: We know what we're doing. Premji does not tarry when he makes management moves. He has succession plans in place not just for himself but for all of his top executives. When people decide to leave, he already knows whom he wants to replace them. For instance, when Raman Roy, the founder of Spectramind, resigned in 2005, a year after Wipro bought the company, Premji immediately tapped T. K. Kurien to step in. "We don't leave leadership positions open. That would send the wrong message to the troops," says Girish Paranjpe, president of the Finance Solutions business unit. Kurien seems to have been an inspired choice. After he took over the troubled BPO unit in early 2005, he undertook a radical overhaul that resulted in a turnaround by the end of the year.

A spirit of experimentation pervades Wipro. The company is willing to try things, get them going fast, and if something doesn't work, quickly change course. Wiproites are cautioned against falling in love with their ideas and getting stuck on them. "We say, if it turns out to be a lousy idea, get out. Don't waste time," says Kurien. In June 2005, for instance, he concluded that he could deal with the BPO unit's ultrahigh attrition rates partly by hiring faster and requiring less training. The idea was that if BPO was going to be a revolving door, just run it that way. The strategy looked good on paper. Training costs and average salaries would be lower. But in the real world, within a matter of weeks, it became clear that it wouldn't work. Attrition went up by 10 percent, and customers grumbled. Kurien quickly returned to the strategy of trying to retain people. In fact, he went to the other extreme. He assigned special counselors to patrol the BPO offices and talk to the youthful employees—like school guidance counselors. It seemed to help. The BPO unit's attrition rate dropped by 22 percent two weeks after the new program began.

Kurien is not a patient man. His rule of thumb for experimentation is that if you come up with a new idea, you should get it launched within the same quarter. He typically gives a new tactic 30 days to work. "Sometimes the decision to exit is more important than the idea to jump in," he says.

The company's management matrix, linking service practices with vertical business units and sales organizations, allows it to respond quickly to opportunities and problems. In Chapter 15, I described how Suraj Prakash ran quality consulting as a one-person operation for its first year, drawing in talent from elsewhere in the organization when needed. That's typical. Theo Forbath, head of high-tech strategy consulting, has just 20 people in Boston and Mountain View, California, but he routinely taps into the regular consulting practice, market researchers in Bangalore, and others in the company to get studies for clients done quickly. On January 30, 2006, a client hired him to do a strategic study with a March 17 deadline. A few days later, the client asked Forbath to pick up the pace. They wanted the study on March 2. It was a scramble, but it was possible. Thanks to a virtual army of Wiproites that Forbath could use as reinforcements, he got the job done. Forbath used the company's TED Web, the database of employees and their skills, to find people who could help him out.

Wipro people are quick to send e-mails or pick up the phone to ask for help. That's especially true if something has gone wrong. "There's a culture of getting bad news early and good news late," says Forbath, who came to Wipro as part of its 2003 acquisition of Boston-based consultancy NerveWire Inc. In 2004, for instance, Wipro had a scare that concerned a marketing partnership with software giant Microsoft. During a quarterly review of the relationship, Microsoft executives raised questions about industry-specific service packages Wipro had built using Microsoft's .NET technologies. "It became a bit of a crisis," says Forbath. Wipro needed to show the Microsoft sales team something special, so it created a new sales program designed to stimulate demand for these services, which were packaged with Microsoft's server and programming technologies. The result, delivered in just one month, was a new sales process called ITBV, for IT Business Value. A Wipro team would approach prospective customers and offer to evaluate their current technology systems. They'd estimate the cost of upgrading their capabilities and put a business value on the gains. Then they'd make an offer they hoped the prospects couldn't refuse: They'd guarantee those results at a given price. ITBV helped kindle demand for Wipro's services and Microsoft's products, and it helped to raise Wipro's profile as a Microsoft marketing partner.

Customer emergencies require the quickest response from leaders. Typically, a Wipro manager will drop everything if a customer is unhappy. In mid-2005, for instance, Banerjee learned that a U.S. customer had a problem with the three Wipro people leading a seven-person project team. It was a matter of poor interpersonal chemistry. Banerjee knew he couldn't pull the three people off the project without causing chaos, so, within 24 hours, he decided to borrow two senior people from another American client's project and make them the leaders of the troubled one. He got news of the upset on a Thursday. On Friday he called the second client to get permission to temporarily reassign the employees and then told the unhappy client what he planned on doing. Over the weekend, he dispatched one employee from India and flew the two borrowed ones into the client's city. Banerjee had a conference call with all 10 employees on the Sunday afternoon in which he laid out how he wanted them to operate. The original seven team members would concentrate on the technical part of the project. The three new ones would handle communications with the customer. Then, on that Monday, he held a joint call with the client and the Wipro team. The story has a happy ending. The project was finished in two weeks, the client was pleased with the outcome, and the original team of seven went on as a group to its next assignment, says Banerjee.

The Flexible Leader

Vivek Paul was fortunate enough to have legendary GE chairman Jack Welch as one of his mentors. One of the most important management lessons he learned from Welch is that a chief executive has to continuously take fresh looks at the organization and the marketplace. "Jack told me that whenever he flew into New York from an international trip, he played a little game. He pretended that he had just been named chairman of GE. The old guy was a dud and had been thrown out. He asked himself what new things he would do," Paul says. It was thinking like this that prompted Paul to build up Wipro's software application implementation business, starting in 2002. During those years he would reorganize his executive staff three or four times a year. It wasn't about reshuffling the management deck for the sake of shaking things up. Each reorganization had a purpose, typically to launch a new business or add a new leadership function when a change was needed that spanned business units.

One thing Paul did to stay nimble was to separate his job into two types of activities. He calls it "playing at all altitudes." His main job was as a manager and decision maker, but he was also an individual contributor. That was his role when he visited customers to develop or maintain relationships and when he sized up technologies and strategies. To do these things well, he needed to develop his own expertise in technologies and market dynamics. The trick was to balance the two so he could make decisions quickly. "Taking a lot of time to make decisions can stall the CEO. Don't be afraid to move—and later make a correction," he says.

Paul was not afraid to admit mistakes. Wipro constantly has to size up new technologies, new geographic markets, and new business lines and decide in which ones to invest. Paul liked to pick one technology that seemed most likely to pan out and put most of the company's energies into that one. But he confesses that he wasn't always right. In 2001, for instance, he favored focusing on a certain wireless communications technology. Even though other executives with more technical expertise disagreed with him, he wouldn't change his mind. It turns out that he was wrong. The company had to make a quick midcourse correction. At the tech division's annual technology forum, Paul delivered a mea culpa. "I said I was wrong. I'm glad they fought me. I'm glad to reverse my position," he says.

One of Paul's key rules of leadership is not to decide on something if you don't have to. He believes that many leaders and organizations get into trouble because they commit to things unnecessarily. "Keep your options open as long as possible. If it's not important to make a decision, it's important not to make a decision," he says. The tech industry tends to move like a rushing herd. Some new, supposedly brilliant, idea pops up and everybody races to get involved. Wipro has a different approach. It believes in sizing up an opportunity quickly, perhaps placing a small bet, and being ready to ramp rapidly if and when demand picks up.

The question of when and how to enter China is a good example. The company first considered the move in 2001, but it put the decision off because there was very little interest from its customers. Later, it decided to make a placeholder and establish an office with a staff of 30; and later it opened a second office and expanded the staff to 60. As of early 2006, there still wasn't enough demand to sustain a major investment. Wipro was on top of things, ready to quickly scale up or scale back. Meanwhile, it wasn't spending money unnecessarily.

Organize for Speed

Wipro is an amazingly flat organization. Premji has 13 people reporting to him. (Paul had 19.) In order to operate effectively with such a flat organization chart, the company has to have clarity of roles, clarity of goals, and frequent structured reviews. Premji reviews business results on a monthly and quarterly basis. The quarterly ones are the most intensive. Each business unit team meets with him for part of a day. In addition, he meets with the IT Management Council (for operational matters) once a month and the IT Strategy Council (for strategic planning) at least once a quarter. To keep things moving at a crisp pace, Premji and his lieutenants try to avoid mixing the agenda of meetings. Strategy meetings are about strategy. Operational meetings are about day-to-day issues, goals, and problems. Each meeting should have a transactional purpose. Something is decided. That way, there's a payoff for attending.

Premji is no longer involved in QMI meetings, but the business units still use them as their weekly pacemakers. The president of a business unit (or his CFO) will hold a weekly meeting with his subordinates, and each of the vertical businesses and practices will typically hold its own QMI. For G. K. Prasanna, head of global infrastructure outsourcing, QMI is a "task-making" process. The goal is for people to head out of the meeting full of purpose with specific action items they're supposed to accomplish—often before the next weekly meeting. His QMIs take place on Monday afternoons in Bangalore. Since the outsourcing business is scattered across the globe, these meetings are conference calls linking people in a half dozen places, some of them just starting their workdays while others are finishing theirs. All of the people who report to Prasanna are on the phone, plus regional sales executives. They tick quickly through the usual agenda: sales figures, large contracts that are coming up for bid, customer satisfaction issues, quality issues. Plus, the participants are free to bring up anything that's bothering them.

Because the project-based customer satisfaction surveys come out only when a project is finished, the QMIs serve as an early warning system if something goes wrong. When an issue emerges, Prasanna puts one of the people on the QMI call in charge of resolving it and tells him or her to come back within a day or two with a plan. These can be serious matters. For instance, in late August 2005, during an otherwise routine QMI call, one regional sales manager said he was going to miss his quota because a large U.S. customer was unhappy. Wipro's engineers had not been able to meet their project milestones. Since the customer was a major one, Prasanna decided to take on this matter himself. He was on daily calls with Wipro account managers and twice-weekly teleconferences with the customer until the matter was resolved in mid-November. His boss, Suresh Vaswani, and Premji got involved as well. "All of Wipro was focused on a very tough problem," says Vaswani. Ultimately, the Wipro project manager was replaced, and there were other organizational changes on both the Wipro side and the customer side.

All sorts of action plans come out of these meetings. Often, problems are resolved in a matter of days. For others, it takes much longer. Prasanna once took personal charge of a large account for eight months. A recurrent issue is staffing: Sometimes Wipro simply doesn't have enough people with just the right skills for certain types of jobs. For a couple of years, for instance, there was a chronic shortage of database administrators. Hiring alone couldn't fix it. But a partial solution came out of one of Prasanna's QMI meetings. The idea was to set up a high-profile academy within Wipro's training unit, identify near-skilled people who were already in the organization, give them a quick dose of training, and then put them in entry-level database administrator jobs with senior people temporarily shadowing them.

Though Premji had been conducting QMI meetings since 1971, Paul brought a new rigor and an international scope to the exercise when he took over the global technology business in 1999. He was based in California, and at 7 a.m. sharp (which was early evening in Bangalore) he would connect via a conference call with the people who reported to him. Typically 8 to 15 people were on the calls, including sales managers, his functional executives, and representatives of the vertical businesses and service practices. The meetings lasted exactly 60 minutes. Paul's idea was to resolve as many issues as possible on the call rather than hand them out as action items to be closed later.

"A matrix can be powerful—or stall you. This meeting was set up to make sure it moved along," says Paul. To make sure everybody was prepared and fully grounded, he set up a reporting process. At the end of a week, each of his subordinates would write a wrap-up report and send it to him by e-mail on Mondays. He'd consolidate the reports, summarize them, add facts and observations of his own, and then send out a weekly report to all of them on Wednesdays.

While Paul is gone, his acolytes remain. Sangita Singh, whom he elevated from junior marketer to chief marketing officer, adopted his management techniques when she was promoted to senior vice president in charge of global Enterprise Application Services. She maintains a weekly e-mail reporting discipline in which she requires each employee to file a short report to his or her supervisor, and for each supervisor to file a report to her or his supervisor, on up to Singh herself. Employees are not supposed to spend a lot of time on this, just hit the highlights. For an organization that is spread globally, it's an effective technique for vacuuming up all of the vital information the leaders should know in a simple and repeatable way. She wants news on wins and losses, quality ratings, on-time performance, and training achievements. She gets about 15 reports on Mondays, reads through them, and on Tuesday evenings after 10 p.m., she writes up her own report and sends it to her people. "It creates a weekly rhythm," says Singh. Fridays are reserved for operational meetings. She gathers the heads of her seven practices (SAP, Oracle, etc.) and her HR and finance teams, and she hits hard on all of the key operational metrics: utilization rates, offshore labor versus onshore, and the rest.

Life at a Sprint

Wiproites are famous for keeping long work hours. I asked several people at different levels to describe how they work, and the answers

I got indicate that workdays include not just long days but a frenetic pace as well. Banerjee described a typical day: 8 a.m., 90 minutes of e-mailing; 9:30 to noon, one-on-one meetings with vertical business unit leaders and practice leaders; early afternoon, meetings with partners, customers, and analysts; 4 p.m., a second burst of e-mailing; 5 to 7 p.m., calls with sales executives around the globe; 7 p.m., take clients to dinner. This is a typical daily schedule for two weeks of the month. During the other two weeks he's on the road, and things get even crazier.

Makarand Teje, a sales executive in the United States, kept track of his daily activities for a week in late 2005 and sent me a detailed journal. Here's one day:

Monday, 28 November 2005

4:45 a.m.	Wake up and make coffee and check e-mails on the Blackberry simultaneously.
6:00 a.m.	Board taxi to get to Dallas-Fort Worth airport.
6:15 a.m.	Make couple of phone calls to check on the proposals due this week.
7:30 a.m.	Board flight for Chicago. Clear e-mails, review the presentation that is being prepared for a Tuesday morning meeting. We are pitching for a very strategic opportunity at one of the large insurance companies in Chicago.
10:10 a.m.	Drive the rental car to our Chicago office. On the way, I return the phone calls that I have had since morning as well as catch up with one of my team members who had just returned from his weeklong India visit. We go over travel planning to find out where he needs my presence for coming three weeks. I make some changes to suit his priorities.
11:00 a.m.	I meet seven of my team members who have assembled from various parts of the world and who have been closely working over last four weeks on this insurance case. They request another hour.

11:05 a.m.	Use this time to clear e-mails that I had noticed on my Blackberry but were worth second (or third) look.
12:00 p.m.	Over a lunch of take-out pizza, we spend four hours reviewing the 80-slide deck, slide by slide, by getting team's comments and balancing what could be client's expectations about the Tuesday meeting. Team requests about two hours to work on the suggestions and changes that are suggested, and I go into another office to start making some phone calls.
4:00 p.m.	I call back to one of my team members for a deal that is developing in an important service offering. I discover that we have serious competition from eight other players in this deal, and we need to really work hard and smart over next two weeks to be considered as a serious player in the ring. We sign off on couple of action items and decide to connect again in 24 hours.
6:00 p.m.	We do a second review of the presentation and feel comfortable about it. We close the presentations and send it off to our office printer for 15 color copies.
7:00 p.m.	We do a formal walk-through of the presentation, clarifying who is going to say what as well as rehearsing our answers to possible questions that we are likely to encounter in the meeting tomorrow.
9:00 p.m.	Fifteen sets of color decks are ready, we break into two teams. One team goes to Kinko's to get the color decks bound and second team heads out for dinner.
9:30 p.m.	While driving back in the direction of the hotel, team is feeling stressed and votes for a Greek restaurant next to the hotel for the dinner. We discuss the presentation and Wipro news over dinner.
10:40 p.m.	Check in at the hotel.
10:50 p.m.	Check e-mails and watch TV.
11:45 p.m.	Retire for the day.

This is a normal workday for a Wipro sales executive, Teje says. He's constantly on the move back and forth across the United States meeting with project teams, account managers, and clients. Every two to three months, he visits India for 10 days. "The old 8 to 5 workday is no more. Because of the Blackberry, everybody's life is 24 by 7," he says.

Anybody who competes with the Indians had better be willing to work just as hard, long, and fast as they do.

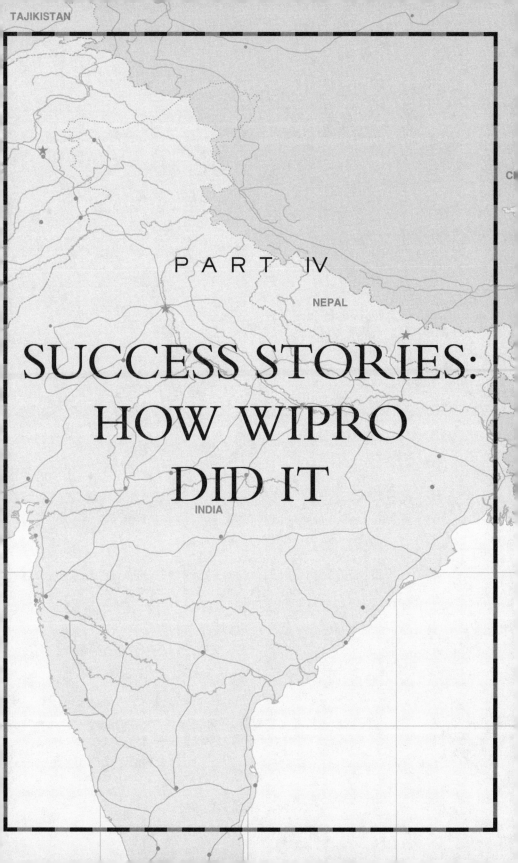

PART IV

SUCCESS STORIES: HOW WIPRO DID IT

17

HOW WIPRO SUPPORTS AVIVA'S GROWING INSURANCE EMPIRE

When Aviva plc, the largest insurance company in the United Kingdom, decided in 2003 to offshore some tech services, it started with a list of 27 potential service providers and, over a period of six months, whittled it down to two: Wipro and India's TCS. These sibling rivals got to divvy up a wide range of software programming jobs for Aviva's Norwich Union general insurance and life insurance businesses. In the beginning, Wipro's role was defined rather narrowly: Its engineers would serve primarily as extensions of Aviva's own programming teams. But over time, Wipro's responsibilities expanded, and so did the scope of its work. Today, it has about 700 engineers working for Aviva, both in the United Kingdom and in India.

For Wipro's info tech executives, the Aviva relationship has become an exemplar of how to engage with large customers. In the course of dealing with Aviva, Wipro created a formal approach to outsourcing that it calls the Engagement Maturity Model, or EMM. That's now a foundation for how the company explains its capabilities to customers and delivers software programming services. At each of four levels of engagement that make up the EMM, Wipro's responsibility—and its value to customers—rises. The story of the interactions between these two companies illustrates Wipro's journey from "body shop" to strategic partner to its customers.

Service Is the Sizzle, and Software Is the Steak

Wipro sells plenty of lightbulbs and bars of soap. Its hardware engineers design chips and all sorts of gizmos. But there's no doubt about what the company's core business is: delivering software services. In the early days, Wipro's engineers sat in their cubicles in Bangalore and repaired flaws or added new features to huge mainframe computer programs. That was a relatively simple activity. It required basic programming skills and process discipline. But over the years, Wipro's ambitions and its capabilities have grown dramatically.

Now, it's a soup-to-nuts IT service provider. On the front end, Wipro's consultants help customers scope out solutions to their computing problems or rethink the way they use technology to do business. Its software architects design programs and ways of fitting technologies together. Programmers don't just fix and enhance already existing programs; they write new ones from scratch. Other specialists install run-the-business applications made by the likes of SAP and Oracle. And Wipro people monitor and manage whole data centers and networks in the United States and Europe from remote locations in India.

The company's BPO division is getting plugged into the software business too. More and more, corporations understand that their business processes and their technology must be tuned to work better together. So they're outsourcing not just software programming but the business tasks associated with those programs, whether its taking orders, ordering supplies, or, in the case of an insurance company, underwriting policies. Wipro in 2006 hired 60 underwriters in Pune, India, to set up new accounts for a European insurance firm.

Wipro's array of software services is delivered by people spread across a wide swath of the company. The primary responsibilities lie within two of the strategic business units, Finance Solutions, which serves the banking and financial services industries, and Enterprise Solutions, which addresses everything else. Each of the strategic businesses has its own staff of programmers and service delivery managers in India—plus program managers and programmers who work in or near the customers' offices. To get additional services and expertise, they tap Wipro's Centers of Excellence and specialized software practices overseen by Chief Technology Officer Divakaran Mangalath. For instance, Wipro has 2,000 specialists focusing on data warehousing and business intelligence technologies, which are used to help with marketing and executive decision making. The Finance and Enterprise managers also bring in business consultants and people who specialize in installing software applications.

Those two strategic business units are sales powerhouses. Enterprise Solutions is the largest of Wipro's businesses, with 10,000 employees and $727 million in revenues in fiscal 2006, which represents 44 percent of the company's tech revenues. The industries it handles include retail, manufacturing, energy, health care, transportation, and the IT services part for the telecommunications industry. Finance Solutions is the feisty little brother. It addresses banking, insurance, and capital markets. When Girish Paranjpe took over as president in 2000, the unit had 1,000 employees and $50 million in revenues. In fiscal 2006, it had 5,800 employees and $405 million in revenues. It went from 12 percent to 22 percent of Wipro Technologies' overall revenues during the six-year period from 2000 to 2006.

Now the company is locked in fierce competition in the IT services marketplace. It's not just battling with its Indian brothers but with the large, established Western outfits, including Accenture and IBM. Wipro needs to aggressively add to its capabilities and efficiencies to keep up its momentum. "The competition is getting tougher, both with the Indians and with the global service providers," says Paranjpe. "We flew under the radar for 10 years, but we're in the big leagues now. The big players have woken up to the sense of our model, and they're emulating it. But they have to modify much more than we do. Customers have figured out that our way is best."

Where Technology and Business Meet

A key to Wipro's success will be its ability to deepen its knowledge of particular industries and its expertise in technologies that are particularly useful to them. When Vice President Soumitro Ghosh formed the insurance unit in 2001, his first hires and lateral transfers were technical people who had worked on insurance projects during their careers. He next began to hire people who worked in insurance companies, a blend of those with technology and business backgrounds. By 2006, he had more than 100 people who were essentially business consultants and 100 who had deep backgrounds in insurance industry technologies. On top of that, he had organized and focused his people on four practices: life insurance, property and casualty, brokerages, and reinsurance.

His next step was to go even deeper within those four specialties. His three targets were claims processing in the property and casualty business, and policy-owner servicing and new-business underwriting in the life insurance business. In early 2006, he got approval to work with Mangalath to establish new Centers of Excellence in these three areas, with 20 to 25 engineers in each of them.

At the same time, he shifted his go-to-market strategy. Account managers would continue to focus on a handful of large accounts, attempting to get them to buy a wider array of Wipro services, including business process outsourcing. The goal was to have several accounts that were worth $30 million to $50 million a year. Meanwhile, a new organization was focusing on selling to brand-new accounts. "We don't mix hunting and farming now. A special DNA is needed to get new accounts," Ghosh says.

A special DNA is required to satisfy existing customers too. Many of Wipro's employees seem to have been bestowed with a couple of extra strands of that stuff at birth.

How Wipro Teams with Aviva

Aviva was a relative latecomer to offshoring, but when it finally made its move, in 2002, it did so decisively. As the world's fifth-largest insurance company, Aviva is a sprawling organization with 30 million customers and 60,000 employees worldwide. So there are potentially huge economies to be had by moving work to low-cost countries. It chose India because outsourcing was a mature discipline there, and because, if jobs needed to be moved to other low-cost countries in the future, it trusted the Indian services companies to be able to handle that too. Aviva started outsourcing customer service call centers in 2003 and IT in 2004. By the end of 2004, it had 3,700 people in India, most of them in call centers. Already by early 2005, Aviva was calling its strategy a success. "We have delivered on our planned cost savings," said Ganesh Balasubramanian, the company's director of IT outsourcing, in a Web seminar put on by Wipro.

While Aviva moved aggressively, it didn't rush blindly into anything. The process of deciding how to handle IT offshoring and selecting two service providers took more than six months. Before engaging with potential suppliers, Aviva did its homework. It closely analyzed its own IT technologies and processes. The idea was to identify which of them could be done offshore or at least managed from India. It turned out that almost everything the company did was suitable for offshoring to some extent. The planning team then spelled out its strategy, made the business case, and won the approval of Aviva's top executives.

Aviva views information technology as one of its core competencies, so rather than giving up that expertise and control over IT, it decided on what it calls a "co-sourcing" model. The aim was to augment its homegrown talent with Indian managers and engineers. Also, by working with Indian tech companies that had mature IT process disciplines, Aviva hoped to learn from them and transform its internal tech organization. "We wanted to extend and grow our capability, not replace it," said Balasubramanian. "It's a partnering rather than a contracting approach."

The process of winnowing from 27 potential suppliers to 2 was painstaking as well. After sizing up the capabilities of all of those suppliers, Aviva short-listed four outfits that had broad arrays of services. Aviva's planning group explained to them in great detail the company's offshoring strategy and IT processes. It created a series of scenarios and asked each contestant to describe how it would respond to Aviva's demands. It also considered the "soft factors," said Balasubramanian: "We wanted to make sure we have a good fit of values and cultures." The company decided to choose two suppliers so it could tap a larger pool of talent and play one off against the other to get the best prices. In the end, Aviva picked Wipro and TCS because it thought they would be the best fit with its co-sourcing strategy. Aviva signed a memorandum of understanding with Wipro in 2003 and a contract in 2004. Because the insurer had spent so much time educating Wipro about its business, work began almost immediately.

Months before, Aviva had begun preparing its own employees for the shift. A key goal was getting buy-in from both its business and IT managers. That effort entailed sending Aviva delegations on multiple trips to India so people could see firsthand how things are done and learn to trust the Indians to do things right. But the company didn't ignore its rank-and-file IT employees either. The planning team conducted "road shows" to Aviva offices in the United Kingdom, where it explained how offshoring would work and would affect people's jobs. They even made a short documentary video about Wipro and showed it to employees. They wanted those who wouldn't lose their jobs as a result of offshoring to see the faces and hear the voices of the people with whom they would be working.

It took a lot of up-front planning to make the co-sourcing strategy actually work in day-to-day operations. There were two Aviva subsidiaries involved: the Norwich Union Life and Norwich Union General Insurance (the property and casualty insurance division). The idea was that in each IT function that was outsourced, half of the employees would work for Aviva and half would work for the outsourcing outfits, and initially, at least, half of the outsourced jobs would go to Wipro and the other half to TCS. Employees of the two Indian companies weren't commingled, however. Aviva identified the strengths of each supplier and dealt out the pieces to each that best fit their expertise. The life insurance business segmented the jobs by process: underwriting, claims processing, and so on. The property and casualty unit segmented by lines of business: personal, commercial, and so on. In addition, Aviva had some horizontal software that addressed both business units. It handed e-commerce and data warehousing to Wipro and testing services to TCS.

To handle the Aviva work, Wipro set up offices in Pune and Bangalore. Wipro keeps the engineers who are assigned to its different customers separate from one another, for privacy and security reasons. If the customer engagement is big enough, they might occupy a whole building. But more often, the work is done in a section of a building. Initially, most of the work Wipro did for Aviva was very basic. When Aviva needed programming done, Wipro would assign a team of engineers to the task, which would be overseen by Aviva's IT managers.

But Wipro aimed to play a more important role. Through its efforts to sell Aviva on that idea, in late 2004 and early 2005, it came up with its Engagement Maturity Model, or EMM. The core concept was to give Wipro more control over managing projects and its own people. As a result, it would be able to tap more of its own expertise and perform more of the work in low-cost India. "We felt like we could deliver a lot more value this way," says Rajiv H. K., Wipro's global program manager for the Aviva account. Here are the basics of EMM:

- *Level 1: Demand Supply.* Wipro's engineers are tapped to augment a client's own engineering teams, using the client's software development processes.

- *Level 2: Co-sourcing.* The overall management of software development remains with the client, but specific projects are handed to Wipro to manage from beginning to end.

- *Level 3: Managed Services.* Wipro is in charge, from start to finish, of a wide swath of software development and/or IT services such as desktop computing, data centers, and networks. It uses its own process discipline, Veloci-Q, for managing software development.

- *Level 4: Own/Challenge/Consult.* Wipro business consultants and technology architects engage with the client in discussions of business challenges and growth opportunities. Wipro proposes technology solutions that include a mix of services from the first three levels. In some cases, Wipro program managers actually supervise clients' employees.

Gradually, with the EMM as its guide, Wipro upgraded the sophistication of the services it provided for Aviva. A bit of analysis the company did in early 2006 shows how dramatically things changed over a relatively short time. The amount of Wipro's work for Aviva that was in the Level 1 category dropped from 52 percent in March 2005 to 9 percent in January 2006. During the same period, Level 2 work rose from 38 percent to 51 percent; Level 3 work rose from 8 percent to 33 percent; and Level 4 rose from 2 percent to 7 percent. The shift also changed the geographic makeup of where the work was done. Level 1 and Level 4 work are largely done on site. The shift to Level 2, Level 3, and Level 4 resulted in an overall ratio of offshore to on-site work of 60 percent to 40 percent in early 2006. The offshore component was a little lower than what is typical for Wipro. But, in this case, because more Level 4 work was being added, it wasn't a weakness. It signaled that Wipro's desire to be used as a strategic advisor was gaining traction.

One of the first Level 4 jobs Wipro did for Aviva was help it remodel its e-commerce strategy. Aviva had grown partly through a series of acquisitions, and as a result, it had a mix of different e-commerce technologies running its customer-facing Web sites. The company wanted to consolidate on a single technology framework, and it called on Wipro to guide it through the process of picking the optimal one. Wipro has deep expertise in e-commerce and no particular axe to grind, so it could mediate between the various factions at Aviva who favored one technology or another. Over a period of two months, Wipro consultants and technology architects interviewed Aviva business and technology leaders and made a recommendation which was ultimately approved by the company's chief information officer. As a follow-on, Wipro got a Level 3 assignment: designing and building the new framework.

The next step in the expanding relationship came when Aviva decided to hand over to Wipro responsibility for managing not just software but whole computing systems. It began by outsourcing remote management of the computers at RAC plc, a roadside assistance company it acquired for $2 billion in 2005. Wipro opened its new management center for RAC in Pune in March 2006. Thirty-five people monitored and managed RAC computers and networks located in the United Kingdom, plus they provided help desk support for RAC's desktop computer users. Wipro arranged with a service company in the United Kingdom to provide on-site repair services. Infrastructure management is a strategic growth area for Wipro because, of necessity, those kinds of services weave it tightly into the client's organization, assuring stable, long-lasting revenue flows. Rather than charging hourly rates for engineers, it charges a fixed price for services and is obliged to meet service-level guarantees. This way of doing business is several steps up from the body shop.

The EMM model works for both Wipro and Aviva. Now, Wipro's Finance Solutions unit introduces it to all of its major customers and to prospective clients. In addition, the Enterprise unit has adopted it. "We educate our customers about the benefits, and we make sure our delivery teams have all the capabilities they need," says Ghosh. "As we move higher in the model, the customer gets more value from us and we get higher rates."

All the effort Wipro has put into cultivating Aviva has paid off handsomely. As of early 2006, it had about 700 people working on the account, up from 270 at the end of 2004. That made Aviva one of the largest of Wipro's 15 insurance customers.

One of the keys to making the relationship work is the governance system the two companies have put in place. Aviva established an office in Pune called Aviva Offshore Services (AOS), which coordinates activities with its outsourcing partners in India, both for software services and business process outsourcing. Wipro has assigned two people to manage the Aviva relationship, Rajiv H. K., who is in charge of delivery of services in India, and Ajoy Menon, the client relationship manager in the United Kingdom. There is no traditional sales manager. "That's one of the things that's different about this account," says Rajiv H. K. "We don't believe a pure sales guy can play the best role. It's better to have solution-focused people running the engagement." The two Wipro managers keep in constant touch with Aviva's people in Pune and with the business and IT leaders in the United Kingdom. The two companies have formal monthly reviews of all of their projects, and every quarter, Aviva's business leaders lay out their operational plans so Wipro's managers know what's coming and can plan hiring and staffing accordingly.

This is no master-servant arrangement. Both sides take responsibility for making the relationship work. In the summer of 2005, for instance, Aviva decided to shift an ongoing software development maintenance project from a local U.K. supplier to Wipro. The switchover had to happen rapidly, by November, or Aviva would be obliged to pay the old supplier for another year, essentially paying twice for the same services. Aviva challenged Wipro to come up to speed quickly. It was no cinch. The business processes and technology involved were quite specialized, so Wipro assembled a team of engineers who had most of the knowledge necessary to do their new jobs. Then Wipro's HR folks arranged to have Aviva provide six weeks of training for engineers in the United Kingdom and India. More typically, a handful of Wipro engineers will spend two to three months at a client site learning the ropes and then return to India to train everybody else on the team. In this case, there wasn't time to do it that way.

Wipro videotaped the lessons presented by Aviva's trainers so it wouldn't have to call on them again. It also hired and trained more people than Aviva had contracted for initially. "We knew they'd want more people eventually, so we trained them in advance," says Rajiv H. K. That foresight paid off. Within a short time, Aviva asked Wipro to begin developing other applications for the same insurance product line. In early 2006, there were 25 Wipro engineers on the case.

What began as a fairly limited engagement has turned into a partnership where Aviva takes full advantage of Wipro's capabilities and appreciates its willingness to do whatever it takes to get the job done. "Wipro is a matured organization and continues to excel in project delivery and building stronger relationships within the organization," says Dinesh Kumar, general manager of Aviva Offshore Services. "Wipro has stepped up to meet some of the business challenges."

This is one of the ways Wipro expands its business rapidly without a lot of marketing hoopla. It gets footholds in clients' businesses and proves itself, and then clients ask it to do more.

Lessons for Outsourcers

Both Wipro and Aviva have learned important lessons from their engagement. They believe their relationship points out success factors for outsourcing companies and their clients. Here are Wipro's takeaways:

- *Align management.* It's vital to choose the right account management team and to map those people to their counterparts in the client's organization. These groups need to be in touch continuously and to conduct regular formal reviews.

- *Teach your customers.* After more than 15 years in this business, Wipro knows it inside and out. So it's well qualified to use its Engagement Maturity Model as a guide and advise clients about how to get the most out of offshoring.

- *Use all of Wipro's resources.* The company does best, for itself and its clients, when it brings all of its capabilities to bear in an engagement. That means tapping the expertise of specialized business units, such as consulting and Centers of Excellence.

Aviva acknowledges making some mistakes early on. For instance, it underestimated how much effort it would take to set up direct communications links between the two companies. But the glitches were minor. Here are the key lessons it took away from its first foray into IT offshoring:

- *Forge a partnership.* If you view information technology as one of your company's core competencies, you can't just hand offshoring work to a supplier and forget about it. You have to integrate the service provider into your organization.

- *Look for a cultural fit.* It's not enough to find a service provider with all the technical skills and staffing capabilities you need. Make sure the two organizations' values and operating styles are in sync.

- *Help your people to adjust.* Explain to employees at all levels the strategy and the advantages of working with an offshoring partner. Show them the places where the work will be done and introduce them to the people with whom they'll be working.

The Next Step for Software Outsourcing

In the outsourcing business, there's no place for complacency. As the Indian companies gain experience and add capabilities, the Western players are rapidly opening programming offices in low-cost countries. IBM, for instance, had 17,000 programmers attached to its Business Consulting Services unit in India in early 2006, up from 4,500 just three years earlier. In addition, Big Blue was rapidly expanding operations in China and Brazil. Those moves were about leveling the playing field with the Indians, costwise.

Even more important for IBM was the way it was creating programs for customers. Its strategy was to build basic software components that it could reuse again and again for different clients, sparing itself the trouble of writing everything from scratch. If half of the software used for a particular job was components, then IBM could cut in half the time it took to complete the project. "This is how we differentiate ourselves from the local Indian companies," says Ambitabh Ray, IBM's vice president for service delivery in India. As of early 2006, IBM had 60 such components and was working rapidly on more. In fact, in March 2006, it established an office in Bangalore as the worldwide hub for creating components.

And Wipro? It has its own component strategy. One example is IBEX, technology for booking orders on Web sites. Wipro created it for one customer and then began including it in projects it does for others. IBM has a lot more technology firepower than Wipro does. Scientists at its fabled Thomas J. Watson Research Center even pitch in to help create some of the software components. So Wipro is under pressure to expand its portfolio of reusable software and keep pace with IBM. This will be the ultimate test of Wipro's software programming abilities, and it will help to determine whether Wipro will one day step up into the top tier of the world's elite technology companies.

18

HOW WIPRO HELPS TEXAS INSTRUMENTS PAVE THE WORLD WITH SILICON

It was a watershed day when Tom Engibous, chairman of Texas Instruments (TI), stood at a podium in Bangalore on August 9, 2005, and spoke to a gathering of TI's Indian employees. The event celebrated the twentieth anniversary of establishing an R&D outpost there. TI had been the first international technology company to recognize the value of tapping engineers in India. Now it had an operation employing more than 1,500 people. At one point during his speech, Engibous held up a disk of silicon loaded with chips designed to be the brains in low-cost cell phones for developing nations. A couple of days earlier, Engibous said, he had made a call to Europe on a mobile phone powered by the chip. "Essentially, what I'm holding in my hand is 2,370 cell phones," he said. "It's incredible to think about, and we could not have done it without the contributions of TI India and our global teams."

Wipro's role in that project was minor, but telling. In the final stages of development, a problem had emerged. TI called on Wipro engineers to quickly investigate and suggest solutions—which they did. "We played a role in making sure that call went through. It was small, but it was crucial for us to respond at that moment," says K. K. Venkatraman, a Wipro engineering manager.

That's the way Wipro's relationship with TI works. A large team of Wipro engineers designs chips and related software to support dozens of TI products and programs, from cell phones to automobile safety systems. As a strategic partner, through efforts large and small, Wipro has played a role in TI's ability to deliver an amazing track record over the past four years. TI's revenues grew by 60 percent, to $13.4 billion, and its profits jumped from a loss of $344 million in 2002 to a gain of $2.32 billion in 2005. According to Bobby Mitra, managing director for TI India, Wipro served as an extension to TI's own global workforce. It provided engineers with valuable technology skills and strong process and quality disciplines. He didn't even mention the obvious: low labor costs.

Wipro as World Leader: R&D for Hire

While Wipro has several claims to fame, such as its achievements in process excellence, there are a few situations where it's literally Number 1 in the world. The one that really matters is its product engineering division. With more than $670 million in revenues in the 2006 fiscal year and 12,000 engineers, it's the largest business of its kind worldwide. It has hundreds of competitors, including HCL Infosystems Ltd. in India and mighty IBM in the United States, but few can match the breadth of skills that it brings to the marketplace. It designs integrated circuits, circuit boards, and devices that range from cell phones and Internet music players to storage devices, communications gear, avionics, and medical equipment. It also writes the core software that makes chips useful, plus applications for consumer devices.

Customers outsource jobs to Wipro because it can typically set up a team twice as fast as they can, and when demand declines, they don't have to fire their own employees. They can use Wipro's engineers as a flexible virtual workforce. "There's a big trend going on here," says Ramesh Emani, president of Product Engineering Solutions. "R&D is following the path of outsourced manufacturing. We think outsourced electronics R&D will move from being about 10 percent of the market today to 35 percent eventually. The big goal is speed to market."

Price counts too. The cost per employee of tapping Wipro is about one-third that of employing people in North America. While the gap has been closing because of wage inflation in India, it's still significant enough to make outsourcing an attractive option.

A lot of Wipro's R&D work is pretty routine. It is often tapped by companies to maintain existing products and provide add-on features for them and to create versions of existing U.S. products for sale in India, China, and other markets. But, increasingly, it is chosen to do original development work, like that so-called physics chip for PC gaming mentioned in Chapter 3.

Wipro has one huge division focusing on product R&D. That division is Product Engineering Solutions, which was the result of the merger of its telecommunications business with its engineering unit in 2005. It was an efficiency move. In product engineering, the company grows not just by expending its practices but by gradually adding new ones. For instance, within the past three years, it added automotive and medical device engineering. It's all part of the company's strategy of targeting specific industries. At the same time, Wipro is adding new capabilities so it can offer customers end-to-end solutions, from consulting on one end to market testing on the other. Its business consultants, for instance, can advise an American consumer electronics maker how to redesign and reprice products for emerging markets.

The goal is to develop deep, long-term relationships with customers that bring in a steady and ever-increasing flow of revenues. For instance, Wipro has been providing services for Nortel, the big Canadian telecommunications equipment maker, since 1991. It now has more than 800 people handling Nortel jobs that span the company's enterprise voice, copper wire, optical, and wireless business units. To enable collaboration, the two companies have direct voice and data communications links, and Wipro labs in Bangalore are set up to mirror Nortel's in Canada.

Wipro stands by its customers through booms and busts. Like other communications equipment providers, Nortel was hit hard by the tech industry downturn that started in 2001. Because of the drop in demand, the company's optical division cut in half its Wipro staffing. At the same time, to help Nortel out of a crisis, Wipro reduced some of its rates. Wipro anticipated that eventually Nortel would see demand recover, so rather than scattering the optical networking specialists to other clients, it parked them in one of its technology Centers of Excellence and put them to work on technology innovations. "When we needed them again, they were there," marvels Gordon Mein, director of strategic development partnerships for Nortel's optical division. "We brought a lot of people back and ramped up more quickly than we would have been able to with anybody else." In fact, Wipro's staffing for that business unit is back close to its peak levels.

It's smart for corporations to have more than one outsourcing partner. Primarily, that's because no single supplier typically can give them everything they need. But, in addition, it makes sense to have at least two suppliers, for added flexibility and to pit one against another for the best pricing. Nortel's Enterprise Voice Business unit, for instance, uses MERA Networks of Russia as a second source in addition to Wipro. Glenn Lidstone, the division's technology strategist, says the two contractors often review each other's work, and when Nortel hands new responsibilities to Wipro, it sometimes transfers more mature projects to MERA. He says MERA's engineers, in general, are somewhat more skilled in engineering itself than Wipro's, but when it comes to English language skills, price, and attention to quality, Wipro has the edge. "On a process basis, MERA is nowhere near where Wipro is," he says.

When Wipro's product engineering group works for a large customer, it typically uses the client's development processes and design tools. That means it has to be adaptable and quickly train engineers in new processes whenever they're assigned to a client's projects. But while the processes and tools belong to the client, Wipro's grounding in quality disciplines comes into play. It follows the rules of CMM and spots and fixes problems using Six Sigma and lean techniques.

Wipro's Engineering Process Excellence

In recent years, the product engineering group began expanding its client base to include smaller outfits, including small chip design companies that don't own their own fabrication plants. Rather than attempting to adopt the development processes of smaller clients (which, often, aren't mature), it instead created its own design methodology: EagleVision. It's both a method for doing things and a software program for managing the process. This is to product design what Wipro's Veloci-Q is to software development. "When you talk to customers, they want to understand what it is that Wipro brings to the table. This gives them confidence that we have a solid methodology and approach, so it's a business enabler," says Vasudevan Moorthy, vice president for Wipro's chip design unit.

By developing a superior set of engineering processes and standardizing on them, Wipro has created a common way of doing things for all of its engineers. Everybody gets EagleVision training and can refer to it simply by logging on to the company's intranet. EagleVision is not just useful when Wipro engineers work for smaller clients either. It's a basic guide for engineers, some of whom may work for large clients, even when they adopt the client's tools and design processes.

Here's how Wipro's chip design team uses EagleVision: First, it's a software program for managing the process of chip design from beginning to end. All the work is coordinated and tracked in the program, beginning with defining the project and continuing with designing the architecture, writing the computer code, completing the physical design, and then sending the completed designs to a database used by the chip fabrication plant. Customers can track the progress of their projects in EagleVision as well. The other major element of the program is knowledge management. Wipro engineers see step-by-step guidelines for completing each phase of product engineering. There's a collection of sample projects that they can use or from which they can learn. And then there are checklists, so they don't miss a single step.

To make sure everything is done correctly and every rule is followed, Wipro has created a set of automated review tools. The tools confirm that an engineer's work complies with the process guide-lines and the checklists. The engineer can run the tests at any time to make sure he or she is on track. When a chunk of work is done, a test is run, the engineer's supervisor reviews it, and the supervisor then signs off on his or her own process checklist.

The goal of all of these processes and tests is to achieve "first-pass" success. That means the first prototype of a chip or circuit board that comes off a production line works the way it is supposed to. If first prototypes fail, it's back to the drawing board. When they succeed, it's off to the marketplace.

How Wipro Teams with Texas Instruments

When TI established a beachhead in India in 1985, it started a rev-olution. Before that, India's smattering of home-grown tech com-panies had been inwardly focused, selling computers and software to the country's businesses and government agencies. TI connected India to the rest of the tech world. At the time, Bobby Mitra was a fresh graduate of the Indian Institute of Technology and was hired by TI to design chips. He remembers that conditions were so prim-itive back then that the company had to use an oxcart to transport its first communications satellite dish to the place it was to be installed. That dish was crucial, as it allowed TI to send software and designs created in India to its development centers in Dallas and Houston. It was the precursor to today's Internet. "It's like a movie unfolding before your eyes," says Mitra, commenting on all the changes that have come to the Indian tech industry. "You not only watch the movie but you make the movie."

Initially, TI didn't outsource work within India. It ran its own development center as a resource to be tapped by all of its business units in the United States. At first, its Indian engineers concentrated on making improvements to mature product lines. Gradually, as they gained expertise, they began designing new chips from scratch. In recent years, those engineers have made a mark for the company, including designing the world's first single-chip modem for broadband Internet access. "It was cost advantage that brought us to India, but that's not why we stayed here," says Sham Banerji, who is now head of TI software operations in India. "We stayed because of the quality of the people we could bring on board."

In the mid-1990s, when Banerji arrived in India to start up TI's telecom chip design operations, Western tech companies had not begun tapping local companies for engineering services. TI was (and is) one of the most innovative chip companies in the world. It had designed the first integrated circuit. And even in the late 1990s, it still handled almost all of its own design work. So why did it pioneer R&D partnerships? The lure was being able to quickly add to its capabilities without having to hire its own people. Banerji was given the assignment of getting things going. Wipro was an obvious choice as an outsourcing partner. TI had just bought Telogy Networks, a U.S. chip software company that already had a relationship with Wipro. Banerji began handing off projects to Wipro in 1999.

He was impressed with Wipro's skills, but the thing that won him over was the commitment of Wipro's leaders to a long marriage. For TI, this relationship was going to be strategic. TI wanted Wipro to be essentially an extension to its India development center capabilities. Vivek Paul, who was then in charge of Wipro's global technology business, pledged to build up his engineering teams so they'd be complementary to TI's. He followed through too. "It's difficult to think of an area where Wipro doesn't have serious competency, or at least dabble. They bring a whole menu of capabilities to the party," says Banerji. Since Paul left, Banerji and the other TI leaders have dealt primarily with Wipro's Emani. But they also meet with Premji. Even in outsourcing, face-to-face relationships matter.

This is not a typical outsourcing deal, however. Both sides say it demonstrates how outsourcing can be raised to the next level of effectiveness. "This has become a model for how we want to handle such partnerships," says TI's Mitra. Wipro now has about 600 people working on TI projects. They're organized primarily in practices that correspond to TI's product groups, including wireless gear, handsets, broadband, automotive, consumer electronics, and audio and video imaging. TI likes to hand off whole projects to Wipro that it can handle independently from start to finish. It has even placed collections of related products in Wipro's hands. "It was a radical thought," says Mitra. "We wanted a company to whom we could give whole families of products, not just stand-alone projects."

The best example of this is how Wipro fits with TI's Advanced Embedded Controls group. That's the business unit that designs chips for use in autos and industrial machinery. Wipro is an extension of the TI design team for products based on the ARM microcontroller for use in automobile brakes, air bags, cruise control, and the like. It does everything from designing chips to preparing designs for production. A Wipro team of one dozen engineers started with a single project in 2000 and now has grown to more than 100 engineers. "Now the Wipro group is just like a TI group for me," says Manny Rao, TI's design manager in Advanced Embedded Controls. "They take entire ownership of a project. They'll even suggest improvements to our processes, and we'll take them up on it."

One of the reasons TI gives Wipro full products is that it wants Wipro's engineers to own the work and feel responsible for the results. There are plenty of things that can go wrong in such arrangements, but the worst of them is attrition. When people leave, continuity is lost. New people have to be trained. But beyond that, there's the motivation factor. Smart engineers want to work on challenging projects. If they don't get them, they tend to move on. In some cases, Wipro managers get together with TI managers and talk over the careers of various Wipro engineers. They'll assign key people they want to keep to do cutting-edge projects.

Wipro's partnership with TI has yielded a significant amount of business. TI is now one of Wipro's top 10 product engineering clients. But that's not all. As a TI strategic partner, Wipro has landed jobs for some of TI's own customers. TI has created core technologies, called OMAP, for use in mobile handsets. It invites technology partners such as Wipro to use them as a foundation for designing mobile phones and wireless applications. The partners not only get to use TI's technology, but they get the TI stamp of approval that certifies their expertise. It's good marketing. Wipro established its own OMAP Technology Center in 2002, and since then it has done work for several telecommunications carriers and handset manufacturers. "TI builds the platform. When their products take off, we have a chance to become the integration partner," says Ganesh Krishnamurthy, Wipro's account manager for TI in India.

Manage the Managers

While TI and Wipro have a true collaboration, one of the keys to their success with each other is that they understand when it makes sense to do things together and when it's better to do things separately. For the most part, Wipro people work in their own buildings, and they work for their own managers, not TI's. "We're more effective when we're in our own facilities," says Ayan Mukerji, a Wipro senior vice president in charge of product engineering solutions in North America. "We have our shared tools, our HR, and our intranet. Most importantly, it's the Wipro culture. You don't get that at a customer's office." Mukerji has sales managers in Dallas and Bangalore who are in charge of the TI account. Delivery managers in India divide up the hardware, software, and wireless pieces of the business.

From TI's point of view, the keys to a good relationship with an engineering partner are defining its goals crisply up front, reviewing progress regularly, and making sure the lines of command and communication are clear to everybody involved. "We have a clean interface. We don't get into the day-to-day management of the project. We take even more care when communicating with a Wipro design team than we do with one of our own design teams. We can handle our own frictions, but we can't handle their internal frictions," says Banerji. TI puts some of its most capable leaders in these cross-company program management roles.

There are three levels of reviews. Project managers from both sides meet or talk formally about once a week (though they speak to each other daily). Division managers meet monthly. And top-level executives, including Mitra from TI and Emani from Wipro, gather quarterly for management revenue meetings, or MRMs.

These are intense two-hour sessions where each of the ongoing projects is put under the microscope. The two companies have adopted a set of metrics that tells them in shorthand if a project is going smoothly, with red, yellow, and green as color keys. If a project is in the yellow or red zone, they take action on the spot. In addition, they compare overall attrition rates for both companies on their joint projects, and they work together to come up with ways to reduce the staff turnover. They also look ahead at the projects TI plans to start over the coming months. This gives Wipro a chance to plan ahead on hiring and training to meet TI's needs.

While Wipro remains TI's largest strategic Indian engineering partner, TI now has a broad program with a dozen significant relationships. In early 2005, Mitra decided to bring a higher order of structure to these interactions. He appointed Sharada Satrasala, who had worked directly with Wipro, to manage all of the strategic partnerships. "We wanted to manage it centrally, and with a process," says Satrasala. "We want to make sure that we are engaged with the right partners on the right projects and have processes in place to get the maximum efficiency out of these engagements." To accomplish that, she worked with TI managers to define performance metrics that TI would use with all of its development partners. In some cases, these are different metrics from those Wipro and TI had previously used— and also different from the key metrics that Wipro tracks internally. Initially, she met resistance from Wipro. But now, she says, "They're very responsive. They have seen the value of what we're doing."

Be on Call at All Hours

One thing that makes this tie-up work so well is that in addition to organization-to-organization relationships, the TI and Wipro people have person-to-person relationships with their counterparts at each level. "We have direct dialing access with Mr. Premji and Emani," says Mitra. "I have the confidence that when we really need something critical done on short notice, all I have to do is ask them. I know I don't have to get into a negotiation to get them to support TI. They'll first say 'yes' and get going."

Down in the trenches, this sort of thing happens routinely. For instance, in November 2005, a TI mobile phone customer decided to accelerate development of a new handset. The customer asked TI to complete its work on a very tight deadline. This matter came up at noon in Dallas on a Friday. Gokul Subramaniam, a manager in TI's wireless systems unit, called his Wipro counterpart, K. K. Venkatraman, on his cell phone, catching him at dinner at 10 p.m. in Bangalore. After two hours of checking with other Wiproites, Venkatraman had his answer: Wipro would help out.

For Venkatraman, this wasn't about getting approval from his bosses. He needed to know that his engineers really would be able to do the job. The first major deadline was in just six weeks. So he had called several engineering managers to make sure they had people available with the right skills. He even checked in with technical experts outside his group with special expertise to see if they would be able to help him out if he needed them. Within five days, he put together a team of four top engineers. In the end, Wipro and TI met their deadlines.

Realize That Bad Stuff Happens, Even in the Nicest Neighborhoods

While Wipro has performed well for TI in general, there have been disappointments. On a couple of occasions, TI handed Wipro assignments that were beyond the skills of its engineers. It was a recipe for trouble. The worse situations were the ones where they ventured into new technology realms and neither TI nor Wipro had a lot of expertise. "It doesn't work when both companies are trying to learn on the job. We won't do that again," says Banerji. Both sides have learned to be wary of situations when Wipro has to ramp up a large number of people quickly. In early 2004, this happened with a wireless hardware project. Wipro committed to assembling 50 engineers in 45 days. But it couldn't do it. At that time, several U.S. multinationals were opening up offices in Bangalore, and they poached some top engineers. "The lesson we learned is that until we're rock-sure about how we'll execute, we won't commit to something," says Wipro's Mukerji.

Learn from Mistakes and Successes

Wipro's relationship with TI has taught it valuable lessons that it applies both to its further dealings with TI and with other clients. Here are some of its rules of engagement:

- *Focus on productivity.* Ultimately, what customers need is partners who can get things done quickly and with high quality. They're less concerned with getting the lowest labor rate.

- *Motivation is the key to success.* Attrition is your worst enemy. Give your best technical people new challenges continuously, so they won't leave to work for competitors.

- *Don't overcommit to your customers.* Set the right expectations. Enthusiasm doesn't count for anything if you can't deliver on your promises.

Likewise, TI has learned lessons from this six-year-old relationship that it applies to other R&D partnerships. Here are its rules:

- *Be strategic.* Set the relationships up as long-term ones. Give your partners independence and ownership.

- *Don't try to manage your partners' employees.* Put some of your own most capable managers in charge of overseeing the relationships.

- *Start slowly.* It takes time for your partners to learn your processes and technologies. Let them learn and prove themselves gradually.

- *Review frequently.* Establish clear goals and metrics to measure whether they are being met. Review weekly on the project level, and quarterly on the executive level.

- *Be prepared for setbacks.* No matter how good the relationships and no matter how capable the partners, problems will arise. Make sure to have people who understand Indian culture on your team.

When people contemplate India's tech industry, they usually

think about software and call centers. But for Wipro, product engi-neering is a big chunk of what it does. This is a good business to be in. The profit margins are in the same ballpark as software services margins. Relationships with customers tend to be deep and long lasting. And, if global demand for product engineering takes off like contract manufacturing has, Wipro should be able to ride the big wave. Over the coming years, this could be the business that distin-guishes Wipro most clearly from its global competitors.

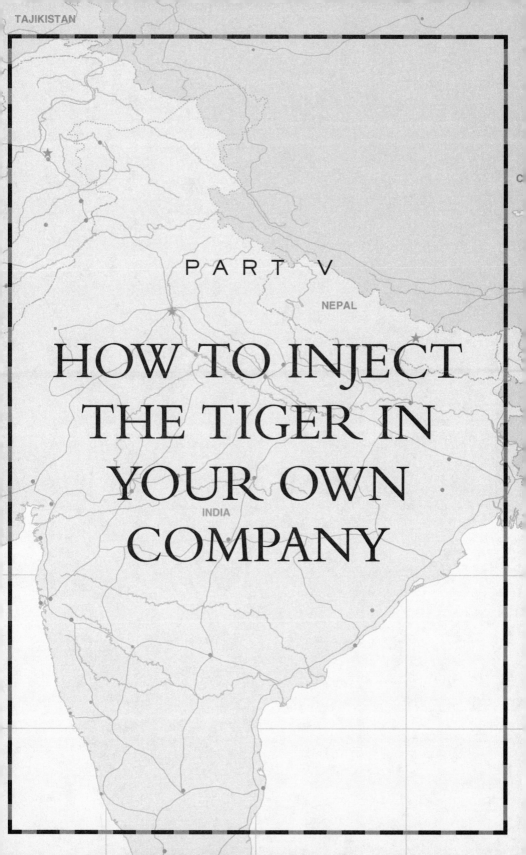

PART V

HOW TO INJECT THE TIGER IN YOUR OWN COMPANY

19

LEARNING FROM WIPRO: HOW TO IMPROVE QUALITY AND CUT COSTS

On first glance, there's a paradox at the core of Wipro's value proposition. The company promises to improve quality *and* cut costs at the same time. How is this possible? Normally, if you cut costs, you have to give up something, such as quality or completeness (maybe both). It's like a financial balance sheet. Yet Wipro escapes this apparent conundrum because it treats quality and cost cutting as two sides of the same coin. The things it does to improve quality also allow it to cut costs and improve its productivity and profits. Because it adopts methods that assure quality throughout its business processes, there will be fewer defects in its services and less waste in its internal doings, and less work that needs to be done over again. Technology is one of Wipro's core competencies, for sure. But much of its competitive advantage comes from its focus on operational excellence. It's world class at organizing processes and people to perform complicated tasks with a high level of quality and efficiency.

The Three Pillars of Strength and the Drive for Excellence

India's tech industry has emerged as a global power based on three pillars of strength: labor arbitrage, abundant technical talent, and global operational excellence. Labor arbitrage and technical talent will continue to be essential elements in the country's success formula, but if they get their acts together, China, Latin America, Eastern Europe, and Russia will eventually match India's capabilities. Operational excellence can be a more durable advantage for the Indians. That's because it's really difficult to organize large numbers of people, who are spread all over the world, to operate efficiently and to improve continuously.

In Premji's case, it's clear where the drive to excel came from. He inherited a collapsing company in a failing economy, so he never had the luxury—like many Americans do—of taking success for granted. He had to tear down a rickety foundation and replace it with a solid one based on a set of fundamental principles, including integrity, openness, and an aspiring culture. He had been trained as an engineer, so the craft of rigorously analyzing problems and painstakingly coming up with solutions came naturally. He studied in America and saw America's leading companies close up, so he modeled his small Indian company on the world's best organizations. And he found that in order to establish a foothold in the global market, his company had to do a lot of things better than the incumbents. Now the competitive playing field is becoming level, so operational excellence is no longer just an equalizer for the Indians. It creates a clear competitive advantage.

This advantage isn't vital just for offshore tech up-and-comers like Wipro. Any company in any industry that masters the craft of achieving operational excellence will greatly improve its chances of thriving in this era of intense global competition. What's happening here is akin to the information technology phenomenon. The early adopters of breakthrough technologies get an advantage over their rivals. As more companies adopt those technologies, there's a bit of a leveling effect. Yet there remains a gap between those who simply use technologies and those who use them really well. Today, the focus by companies on achieving operational excellence is about where their attention to information technology was a decade ago: A lot of companies have discovered how vitally important this discipline is, but not very many have mastered it. Those who do, and stay out in front, will have a sustained advantage.

Wipro and the other Indian tech outfits have no monopoly on this stuff, but because it's so vital to their successes, by and large, they have done a good job at it. They show others how it's done. The following paragraphs lay out a summary of Wipro's approach to achieving operational excellence, which was spelled out in detail in earlier chapters.

A Playbook for Operational Excellence

Live Your Core Values

Operational excellence may sound like a job for a company's chief operating officer and an army of bean counters, but seeing it that way would be a mistake. Wipro shows that this kind of excellence is the result of a tremendous amount of thinking and planning by the chief executive and entire management team. It's a holistic approach that begins with the company's core values and its vision of what it wants to be, cascades into planning and decision making, and then plays out in all of the little things that get the job done every day.

Think about Wipro's original beliefs: respect the individual, be a business leader, accomplish all tasks in a superior manner, maintain the highest ethical standards, serve customers well, and measure performance based on long-term profitability. Those values, established in the mid-1970s, formed the foundation of a performance-based culture. They told the company's new hires what was expected of them. The latest values, adopted in early 2006, retain the focus on integrity and respect for others but add a hard edge: intensity to win. Wiproites are supposed to win through dedication to customers, innovation, and teamwork. Employees know they'll be graded on it. So Wipro's values aren't empty platitudes like the motto on a family coat of arms. They are commands to be heeded on a day-to-day basis.

Plan Like Your Future Depends on It

Wipro's planning regimen has a forceful rhythm. It's designed to make sure that big dreams can be translated into consequential actions. The cycle begins with those visioning exercises that Premji and his lieutenants undertake every half decade. The goal is twofold: to take a fresh look at the marketplace and Wipro's place in it, and to set an audacious goal that gives the entire staff something to shoot for. It's simple, really. You ask yourself what your company should look like in five years. These should be mind-blowing experiences. If not, why bother? But exercises like this wouldn't be much good if Premji and his cohorts treated them like vacations and the effect faded quickly. Setting the grand goal is only the first step. Then comes the serious work of the three-year rolling strategic plan, when new ventures are sketched out and plans are made to upgrade the company's skills and capabilities so it can accomplish what it has set out to do. Finally, the operational plan sets things in motion. Most corporations have fairly elaborate planning processes, but only the best bring to them the rigorous up-front analysis and relentless measurement of results that are Wipro's hallmarks.

There's a role in this visioning and planning process for the company skeptic. Sudip Banerjee, president of Enterprise Solutions, argued forcefully against the "4 in 4" goal ($4 billion in revenues in four years) that Wipro's executives set in their visioning exercise of 2000. The evening the retreat ended, Sumantra Ghoshal, the university professor who led the exercise, invited Banerjee to go on a stroll with him, Banerjee recalls. The professor warned him not to play the role of the holdout, because organizations typically eject people who do that. The two made a bet on whether Banerjee would still be working at Wipro in 2004. Banerjee won. But Premji is the real winner. He gains more from tolerating dissent from his subordinates than he would from shutting it out.

Reduce Risks without Foreclosing Opportunities

Is it possible for a company to be both cautious and entrepreneurial at the same time? Wipro is sure trying. To grow at a healthy rate, it has to constantly place new bets in a combination of new services, new vertical industries, countries where it operates or sells, and acquisitions. Yet because execution is so essential to its effectiveness and its reputation, it can't afford major screwups. So Premji and his team have concentrated on making many smaller bets rather than a few large ones.

The company's activities in early 2006 illustrate this strategy. It began expanding operations in Canada, Germany, France, Eastern Europe, the Middle East, and China. It increased its investments in consulting, infrastructure outsourcing, and data security practices, plus it launched the slew of grassroots projects the staff had cooked up as part of Premji's Growth Accelerator initiative. In addition, it was making one "string-of-pearls" acquisition after another.

When Wipro decides to go forward with a new initiative, it doesn't just plunge in and spend aggressively. Instead, it moves ahead in measured steps. It builds a foundation for the new business, watches for demand, and quickly responds to it. That way, it doesn't spend money unnecessarily on projects that don't pan out.

Think of it this way: Wipro places its market expansion bets like it improves its quality programs. It makes many incremental moves, continuously.

Adopt Zero-Politics Management

Premji has established two core management principles that are instrumental in forging the effectiveness of his company. The first one: The chairman is not a dictator. While Premji owns a controlling stake in the company, he shares visioning and decision-making powers with his staff. They're essentially group activities. The second key principle: Internal politicking is not welcome. There are no secrets. Everything is to be discussed openly. Premji not only permits but demands that his lieutenants debate the merits of ideas and strategies. And he encourages them to openly express themselves when they disagree with him. No yes-men need apply. These two principles create a culture of earnest cooperation.

This may not sound like a big deal, but think again. Many businesses are organized to exploit the overripe egos of their executives. Individual business leaders are pitted against one another, fighting over their slice of the company's assets, maneuvering for favor, undercutting one another for power and promotions. At Wipro, there's plenty of internal competition to see whose business unit performs the best. But because of the way management is set up, executives aren't placed in conflict with one another. In fact, nobody can succeed on his or her own. The people who run the industry verticals need to collaborate with the people who run the service groups, the sales leaders, the HR planners and trainers, and the quality leaders. Teamwork isn't tacked on. It's the essence of the organization.

Make Decisions Quickly, but Don't Be Afraid to Switch

In a company whose strategy is to place many bets continuously, decision making has to be done crisply or the machine breaks down. Back in 1971, when Premji created those weekly management meetings called Quick Management Inputs, his goal was modest: Get managers in touch with the performance of the business so they make rapid adjustments. Over the years, the company has evolved a management rhythm that's organized around the types of decisions managers have to make. The weekly meetings within business units are about spotting and fixing problems and exploiting sales opportunities. The monthly IT management meetings are about introducing or adjusting tactics. And the quarterly Strategy Council meetings are, of course, about strategy. By segmenting this way, the management team avoids mixing purposes and losing focus. The priorities are clear. Decisions can be made quickly.

In each of these settings the spirit of experimentation is pervasive. Managers are inclined to try things and get them going fast—essentially pilot projects. They track the projects closely, so if something doesn't work, they spot it quickly and make adjustments, or even pull the plug.

Spell Out the Rules, Then Follow Them Religiously

At Wipro, services are run with the efficiency of a modern factory. That's largely because every step of managing a client engagement, handling a customer service call, and developing a software program is clearly spelled out. Everything the company does has a formal business process governing it. Each of the approximately 2,000 projects the company is working on at any given time are tracked in its project management systems. It starts with assembling teams. Project leaders select staff members from a huge database that lists employees' skills and availability. Once the projects are started, leaders and team members can log in from any computer equipped with an Internet browser and keep up to date with requirements, progress, and customer feedback. Increasingly, clients gain access to a lot of the same information. Software programming is done with the company's standard process, Veloci-Q, which maps out every step in design, implementation, and testing. Because these core processes are laid out clearly, Wiproites don't have to reinvent the wheel each time they launch a new project. And because everything that happens is documented, if something goes wrong, it's usually relatively easy to spot the cause, using Six Sigma methods, and correct it, using Six Sigma or lean.

Measure Everything

Killer business instincts are a great thing to have, and some companies can be run on a brilliant executive's gut feelings, but they are the exceptions. For everybody else, measurement and analysis are vital. One of the first lessons that Premji learned when he was trying to save his father's company in 1966 was the importance of measurement. His peanut buyers were offering farmers prices based on the feel of nuts in their hands. Under his regime, that imprecise assaying system was soon replaced by simple dryers and scales. Premji has been a great believer in metrics ever since.

At Wipro everything is measured, and a lot of thought is given to coming up with just the right numbers to track and compare. The company sets its goals and tracks its performance using a rigorous scorecarding system. It benchmarks its business practices and performance against those of its competitors and the world's best companies. It uses a 360-degree evaluation system, so managers know exactly where they stand with the people who work above, below, and beside them. And its personal performance evaluation system is as detailed as it is earnest.

These performance measurement systems aren't separate islands of information. Wipro integrates data from one framework into another so efforts to achieve one goal help accomplish others. For instance, an executive's goals and objectives for his or her business unit become the basis for his or her personnel evaluation and pay raise at the end of the year. This integration aligns the goals and efforts of everyone in the company, from Premji all the way down to 20-year-old call center operators.

Wipro's measuring systems wouldn't be nearly so powerful if they weren't transparent. It publishes a tremendous amount of performance data in reports for managers and on its various Web sites for mass internal consumption. That includes everything from details of quarterly earnings reports to the amount of food wasted in the cafeterias. Everybody knows where they stand, and poor performers have no place to hide.

Demand Value for Money

There's a guiding principle that underlies all of Wipro's spending decisions: It demands value for money. The company monitors every kind of expense and looks for ways it can do things less expensively or spend more effectively. Wipro doesn't cut corners when it comes to its employees' health and safety. It gives the staff the latest computing equipment and a pleasant workplace. They're comfortable when they travel. But there are no frills. In a globally competitive landscape where price is so crucial, any company that spends money on frills is asking for trouble.

The philosophy is fundamental to the way Premji lives his life. He expects employees to be just as careful with the company's money as they are with their own. And he sets the example for others. When he travels within India, he flies coach. There are no exceptions. Because everyone plays by the same rules, there's a culture of fairness. So instead of the company relying on managers to spend a lot of time being budget cops, employees police themselves.

Another lesson from the Wipro tightwads: Cost cutting should be an ongoing discipline, not something done in reaction to a crisis. In many companies, when quarterly earnings fall short, there's a rush to trim the staff, freeze the travel budget, and cancel bonuses. While those are quick ways to cut costs, they can have detrimental effects on a company's ability to serve customers and motivate employees. Wipro's approach tends to head off crises and obviate the need for rash and harmful reactions.

Put the Right Skills in the Right Place

A crucial capability for the new transnational-style corporation is the ability to put people with the right skills for a particular task in the right place geographically, whether in a client's office, nearby, in India, or in some other country with just the right mix of skills, proximity, and costs. Wipro and the other Indian tech services outfits call this the "global delivery model." They are adept at hiring and training on a massive scale in low-cost places and coordinating the efforts of those armies of brainworkers with a relatively thin layer of specialists who sit next to or near their clients. Their challenge is to boost the capabilities of their client-facing staffs without significantly raising their costs. For Western companies, the move to the transnational model is much more challenging. Their existing multinational model of maintaining miniversions of their company in each region or country where they operate is too expensive. They have to dismantle parts of those organizations (without infuriating employees and governments), even while they redistribute work around the world in new patterns.

What the Indians and the Westerners have in common is the need to shape and manage an employee supply chain. It's like a manufacturing supply chain, only with people as the components. Wipro is very good at this. The company tracks the status of work on projects and maintains forecasts of upcoming work. Using this data, it does analyses to determine which employees it needs overseas and where it needs them, matching up its supply of available labor with demand. When staff members are called back to India to await another assignment overseas, they are not idle. If there isn't work for them, they are placed in training programs so they can acquire new skills or deepen their expertise. That makes Wipro ever more adept at finding just the right employee with the right skills in the right place for a particular job, exactly when those skills are needed.

Perform Routine Jobs Routinely

A lot of things companies do day to day don't require a lot of creative thinking—once they are set up, that is. Wipro establishes mech-
anistic processes to handle many routine tasks. The best example of
this that I spotted is the BPO organization's remote recruiting program. To deal with the deluge of applicants and massive hiring
needs, the company rents space in about 60 technical and English
language training facilities around the country. Applicants come in,
sit at a computer, and take a series of tests. If they pass, they go into
another room where a PC has been set up to handle videoconfer-
encing. They're interviewed by a Wipro recruiter, who might be
hundreds of miles away. If they are right for the job, they get an offer
on the spot. This technique isn't appropriate for every type of hiring situation, obviously. But it shows how through the use of technology and automation a minimal amount of effort can be
expended to get something very basic done. There are plenty of
tasks that can be handled this way.

Turn Customers into Partners

Wipro's approach to customer relations truly is remarkable. A lot of
companies mouth platitudes about how dedicated they are to customer satisfaction, but Wipro really means it. You can see it in the way
it handles customer satisfaction surveys. The project surveys, done
when a particular contract is completed, gather immediate feedback
from a client's IT, product development, or back-office managers.
The annual surveys of top client executives give Wipro useful critiques of its performance, but they also focus Wipro's people and its
clients on the effect its services are having on the client's performance.
When Wipro is seen as an important contributor to a client's successes, its work is more highly valued. Adopting the Net Promoter
Score benchmark (subtracting the percentage of customers who
would not recommend you from those that would) adds another layer
of rigor to Wipro's self-analysis. In service businesses, it's not enough
to have your customers satisfied with your work. They have to think
you do it substantially better than the competition.

Wipro doesn't wait around for the results of customer satisfaction surveys to make sure it's pleasing customers. If there's any hint that something is amiss, alarms go off up and down the organization, and it makes plans to patch things up. Flexibility is key as well. Wipro has gained a reputation for being willing to set aside the letter of the contract and do whatever it takes to keep a customer happy.

But all of these efforts are just the groundwork for the ultimate goal in customer relationship building: turning your company into a customer's strategic partner, not just a provider of commodity services. These days, Wipro focuses increasingly on using its expertise to help customers transform the way they do business. It's on its way to becoming a trusted advisor. That's the kind of service a client will likely be willing to pay a premium for.

Learn from Others

Wipro is like a submarine with its periscope perpetually up and scanning the horizon. It's on the lookout for techniques established by others that it can apply to its work with the goal of improving quality and achieving operational excellence. Premji never caught the "not invented here" disease so prevalent in the U.S. tech industry. That's the notion that companies should create everything themselves, whether it's technology or a way of doing things. Ever since Premji ventured into the tech realm in 1980, he has believed—and preached—that Wipro needed to spot and adopt the best business practices in the world. GE, IBM, Motorola, Toyota, Unilever, and other global giants have served as Wipro's models and mentors; the Software Engineering Institute and the framers of Six Sigma have been its guides. Adopting best practices helped the company rise above its backwater roots and become a credible player on the world stage.

From the early days, Wipro has seen its quest for operational excellence as a journey that's never finished. So Kaizen, or continuous improvement, isn't something that Wipro stitched on as a result of its adoption of Toyota's lean production techniques. It's a foundation principle. Lean simply gave Wipro new means to accomplish it.

That's true for many of the techniques the company has glommed from others. It already had its own solid platform of values to live by. As a result, adding new things is less risky. There's one caveat, though: The additions have to be truly compatible with the company's own values. Wipro is like a human body that from time to time gets organ transplants; if it chooses well, it doesn't have to worry about its own antibodies rejecting them.

Make Your Own Way

One of the most important things a mature company can do is redefine itself. By being successful over a long period, it earns the right. But because the company is now large and complex, this exercise is a necessity as well. The company needs to tell a clear and comprehensive story—for employees, customers, and investors—that expresses what it believes in, how it operates, and how it adds value. While Wipro is still a continuously changing company in a dynamic business environment, Premji has decided it's time to spell out the Wipro Way.

First, it's a set of clear objectives. Wipro's goal is to have the best operating margin growth in the IT services industry, the best Net Promoter Score, and the highest productivity in a set of key business processes. Second, it's a standard of operational excellence that the company promises to deliver across all of its businesses. That is achieved through constant improvement, focus on customer satisfaction, putting people with the right skills in the right place, and experimentation. In essence, it's distilling everything it has learned over the past 40 years and codifying it. While this exercise is resulting in a set of guidebooks for employees, the ultimate goal is to be able to set the books aside. Once employees truly understand the Wipro Way, living it should come naturally.

For Western managers, it may seem strange—even off-putting—to think they have a lot to learn from these Indian upstarts. After all, in many ways American industries and companies still dominate the world of commerce. But many American businesses grew up in times of plenty, when they had little overseas competition. They weren't built from the ground up, like the Indians, to thrive in harsh conditions and overcome huge barriers. These days, operational excellence is a requirement for success—even survival. Who better to learn lessons from than the companies that have become potent global players against all the odds?

20

MOTIVATING EMPLOYEES
THE WIPRO WAY

To gather material for this book, I interviewed more than 75 current and former Wipro employees, including executives, middle managers, junior managers, and individual contributors. I spoke to Indians primarily, but also to Americans and Britons. Several of them offered up constructive criticism, but overall, they voiced admiration for the organization. For those who had not worked elsewhere, their conversations with friends who worked for other companies assured them that they made a good choice. And those who had multiple stops in their careers made it clear to me that Wipro was one of their favorites. Several people who had worked for GE, often cited as the most admired corporation in the world, said they preferred working for Wipro. They favored Wipro's spirit of collaboration over GE's culture of contention.

Why do employees of all ranks consider Wipro a superior place to work? It boils down to three things: respect for the individual, employee empowerment, and an aspiration for excellence. A lot of companies claim to have these values, but I doubt that a majority of their employees would agree they consistently act on them. Does all of this touchy-feely stuff really make a difference? Wipro's performance record itself makes a strong case that in a hard-edged world, the soft stuff matters.

Whenever I consider Wipro's HR policies, I can't help thinking about Dilbert comic strips. Cartoonist Scott Adams has a field day with corporate politics and peccadilloes. What would he make of

Wipro's penchant for creating an initiative or catchy name for so many of the things it does? I'm sure Dilbert strips elicit plenty of knowing laughs in Wipro offices in Bangalore, Boston, and Silicon Valley. Yet, I'm just as certain that Wipro's people policies aren't cynical feigns. There's a refreshing earnestness there. The place rings true.

Make People Policies a Core Competency

Wipro is in a service business, so naturally people are vitally important to its success, but there's even more pressure on this company than most to give its employees a powerful combination of training, tools, and motivation. The company's chief competitive weapon is operational excellence, and to achieve that, it relies on its tens of thousands of employees not only to cheerfully follow orders but to think creatively and to constantly improve both their own performance and the company's.

This isn't one of those situations where the chief executive can count on a handful of brilliant senior managers to lift the organization to new heights. Wipro's rank-and-file workers have to take it there. Wipro's frontline employees are its early warning system when customers are dissatisfied, its bucket brigade when trouble flares up, and its virtual salesforce, since its best prospects for selling new services are companies for whom it already provides services. For Wipro to stand out from its competitors and escape the fate of a commodity service provider, its employees have to perform noticeably better than those of rivals. And to turn customers into partners, its employees have to become trusted advisors and help clients transform their businesses.

Premji makes it abundantly clear how important rank-and-file employees are to his company's success. Pratik Kumar, the head of human resources, reports directly to Premji rather than to the chief operating officer. And, Kumar asserts, Premji spends even more time on employee development matters than he does on finance. He speaks to new hires about Wipro's values, addresses management trainees, takes young innovators to lunch in groups, and mixes with the staff at social events. Premji is no rah-rah leader. He's more the elder statesman. He speaks quietly and directly, commanding respect and giving it. He sets the standard for an organization that is only as strong as its individual contributors.

To succeed, Wipro and the other top Indian tech services companies must be better at managing and motivating employees than are most other companies, so their HR techniques are valuable benchmarks for others to measure against and learn from. That goes not just for service businesses but for manufacturers, retailers, and distributors too. For all of them, more and more, service is becoming a key competitive differentiator. One of the BPO services that Wipro and some of the other Indian firms provide is HR management, so the most direct way to take advantage of their expertise is to outsource HR to them. But when a corporation hands off pieces of the HR function, or even most of it, that doesn't mean its executives should give up control. Values, strategy, and priorities must come from the client. Nobody should ever outsource those things.

The following paragraphs summarize Wipro's approach to handling employees.

Wipro's Policies for Handling Employees

Act on Your Values

As business increasingly goes global, values are becoming an essential piece of every successful company's suitcase of assets. In emerging markets, where some of the biggest revenue growth opportunities lie, corruption is still routine, workers are often treated poorly, and contracts aren't necessarily considered binding. There's a temptation for companies to play by local rules. Wipro shows it's possible to resist. In fact, by heeding a higher standard, a business can create an aura of righteousness around itself. And good people want to work for good companies.

When a new employee starts his or her job at Wipro, the first priority is values training. But that is hardly the end of it. Values are reinforced on the company's Web sites, in brochures and e-mail, on the backs of business cards, and in performance evaluations. The company signals its values in multiple ways, from conservation of water and food to its many charitable programs. Premji doesn't just do good works through his personal Azim Premji Foundation; he involves the company and its employees. Wipro Cares, the corporate social responsibility initiative, combines company money with employee volunteerism. Its latest project: adopting Pushpavanam village, a town in southern India that was devastated by the tsunami of 2004. Wipro donated fishing boats, built schools and houses, reclaimed land, and planted trees. This kind of thing sends a strong signal to employees: We don't just talk a good game, we live it.

Wipro's ombudsperson program assures that the values it touts are actually practiced internally. Employees who learn of violations or simply have a complaint are encouraged to tell the company about it via e-mail, phone, or fax. Their confidentiality is assured. Ombudspersons investigate and turn their findings over to compliance committees for deliberation and action.

All of these efforts not only buff Wipro's image with customers and partners, but they touch employees deeply. Recall, from Chapter 5, what Rudra Pratap, a 24-year-old support analyst, said: "The values involve each of us. They come into play day in and day out in what we're doing. They make us try to do better."

Train, and Then Train Some More

Most people who go to work for Wipro already have a college degree, so you can consider what happens to them after they get there as a careerlong postgraduate education. They're being taught how to succeed in the global information technology industry. The company has identified 24 competencies that are essential, which it teaches to employees, and upon which they're graded in their annual reviews. Wipro isn't content just to train people in a grab bag of skills. It strives for talent transformation. It's not just technical but professional and behavior, and not just initial but continual. The company's ongoing investments in talent development demonstrate how important it is. How many other companies in the world employ 120 full-time instructors in their own university?

Of necessity, Wipro training starts off like military boot camp. Every few weeks in the summer, a new batch of freshers shows up for the Fundamental Readiness Program that indoctrinates them in the Wipro Way. Then, once orientation is finished, they plunge into weeks of classroom training, which includes technology and business basics, behavioral training, and quality training. While few other companies have to deal with the tremendous volume of inductees (they should be so lucky), the core idea of providing extensive training is useful to them. Wipro reshapes the attitudes and abilities of each of its new employees. Within a few months of joining, they're Wiproites. They know what their employer expects of them, and they are prepared to deliver it.

Working at Wipro isn't just a job, it's a career. Junior employees are presented with the choice of taking a technical or management career path, each with a series of promotional steps and a curriculum of courses to help them take those steps. Using the company's Career Mosaic computer program, they chart their course with advice and encouragement from their supervisors. It's a stretch-goal culture. Wipro believes in giving people the basic technical and social skills they need—then asking them to start doing the next-level job when they're about 70 percent ready.

Training isn't just an opportunity either. It's a requirement. Each promotion carries with it a set of educational prerequisites. Every employee is required to complete a minimum of seven days of training per year. And if there isn't work for them to do at any given time, they're channeled into classes so they can upgrade their skills. Wipro employees can't just tread water. They must swim. Anybody who isn't motivated by this culture will likely not last long there.

Create a True Meritocracy

There's a simple formula for getting ahead at Wipro: work really hard, take training courses, score high on your performance evaluation, and come up with ideas for innovating, growing the business, or improving quality. Not on the list: kissing up to the boss, back-stabbing colleagues, and showboating at meetings. The company is so detailed in its evaluation processes, so thorough in its checks and balances, and so earnest in its intentions that it seems appropriate to call it a true meritocracy. In a country plagued by a caste system, there is none at Wipro.

As usual, Premji sets the tone. Even though he owns the majority of the company, he has shown no favoritism to family members. He discourages Machiavellian intrigues among his lieutenants. He demands that debates and decisions take place out in the open. No backroom deals. His philosophy is to give smart people chances to lead at an early age, give them the tools to succeed, and then watch them grow.

By tying its performance evaluation system directly to compensation, Wipro assures that pay will be based on merit. The same goes with restricted stock. The idea is to identify important contributors and use stock grants to bind them to the company for years. Wipro doesn't pay lavishly, and that policy indubitably costs it some talented managers who go elsewhere to make bigger bucks. But what Wipro loses by saying goodbye to a few leaders it makes up by maintaining a culture of fairness and communalism for a cast of tens of thousands. At Wipro, the bosses aren't the stars; the people and the values are the stars.

Make It about the Job, Not Just the Paycheck

Just as important as compensating employees fairly is creating a truly enriching work environment. Wipro makes employees feel they're respected and they have prospects for rising in the organization. The company also gives them important and challenging work to do and opportunities to shift from one type of work to another. To keep valuable employees happy and retain them, it has three formal programs:

- *Organizational alertness.* Keep an eye out for shifting work-life trends. Try to get out ahead on an issue, so it can be proactive. That tells employees that the company has their best interests in mind and doesn't have to be forced to do good things for them.

- *Supervisory engagement.* Managers are required to spend a significant amount of time helping their subordinates. They are coaches just as much as they are supervisors.

- *Job satisfaction.* HR policies and interactions with employees are crafted to build strong and lasting bonds between the company and employees. Attrition is the enemy. Self-motivated employees are a company's best friends.

Celebrate Employees' Successes

Wipro believes employees will perform better when their efforts are recognized and they are praised publicly. Each business unit has its own rewards and ceremonies for handing them out, but most are based on a standard set of awards designed to encourage behaviors that are vital to the health of the business. Awardees get a diploma-like certificate and, often, gift certificates at local stores, pens, small glass statues, and other trinkets.

These awards may seem quaint, but at Wipro, they make a difference. They're typically handed out at team meetings, so employees' achievements are recognized by their colleagues. Notices are published in newsletters. Customers hear about them, and in some cases, clients even hand out the awards. Proud winners post their certificates on their cubicles. Some even create little shrines to their successes. Employees I spoke to said they were grateful to be recognized, and as a result, they were motivated to do more outstanding work.

Solicit Ideas from the Staff

Chains of command are vital in an organization, but they're not sufficient. At Wipro, information flows freely from bosses to employees, and vice versa. Wipro's executives hold lengthy Q&A sessions with employees when there's news. Employees are surveyed and solicited constantly on everything from new HR policies to the next big innovation. And employees of all ranks are encouraged to approach more senior people with ideas and complaints. This isn't about boosting morale, though that's an effect. Strong internal communications are crucial for an organization that is spread worldwide, growing fast, constantly expanding into new markets, and relies on collaboration to get things done.

While ad hoc communications are crucial, it's important to formalize feedback from employees. That's why the company created Wipro Listens and Responds. The HR department conducts a major employee perception survey every 18 months or so, and then does smaller quarterly and spot surveys. It also conducts open online chats and forums that involve executives. Employees are encouraged to ask questions and make suggestions via e-mail, the Web site, or boxes in offices. It's vital to take action based on feedback. Otherwise, the company loses credibility and misses out on a rich flow of ideas.

Employee participation is most crucial when it comes to quality and efficiency improvements. In a services business, it's the people on the front lines who know when a business process is working well or it's flawed. To encourage the flow of ideas, the company has placed suggestion boxes in many of its offices. Employees are urged to drop notes in the boxes, or to send in ideas via e-mail. They get credit for their ideas when performance evaluation time comes around, but there's even a more important incentive: Employees with smart ideas often get to be on the Six Sigma or lean teams that are set up to act on their ideas. There's no surer way to get noticed at Wipro than to work on a quality improvement team.

Wipro also calls upon its employees to help out with generating big ideas. It has three key growth promotion efforts aimed at getting employees to suggest new business expansion or innovation projects. These are Growth Accelerator, for business ideas; Innovation Initiative, for incremental innovations; and Quantum Innovation, for breakthrough innovations. Through these projects, the company constantly taps its best minds for ideas that might never occur to senior executives who are typically far from the front lines of business. At the same time, the programs help Wipro recruit and hold on to highly talented people. Employees are given the freedom and power to innovate and incubate businesses. They can really make things happen.

Aspire to Excellence

In the end, what makes Wipro so successful is its aspiring culture. There's a collective will to be a leader in everything the company undertakes, and a willingness to do whatever is required to make that happen. This culture emerged as a result of the company's humble beginnings. It was the little cooking oil company that could. Then, when it got into the tech business, Wipro had to become a world-class organization to compete with the giants of the tech industry. Now, to get to the next level—beyond cheap labor—its employees have to be not just less expensive but more effective than those of its Western competitors and emerging rivals in China and Eastern Europe. The spotlight is on them, and Wipro has to give them all the training, tools, and encouragement they need to put on a good show.

Premji is like a bulldog. He keeps everybody's eyes on the company's goals by never losing sight of them himself. Because of his insistence on frequent values reviews, the visioning exercises, and the three-year planning cycle, business unit leaders can't get lost in the weeds of their day-to-day jobs and forget to look up at the sky. And because Premji involves employees in shaping the values and coming up with revenue growth ideas, everybody has a personal investment in making Wipro better. Even if they don't get stock warrants, they feel like they have an ownership stake. They see their potential and Wipro's as being inextricably intertwined.

What makes Wipro a superior place to work? Respect for the individual, employee empowerment, and an aspiration to excellence. It's easy to summarize, and hard to do. Yet in a business environment where global competition is putting new stresses on organizations, every motivated employee counts. Companies that master the art of motivating all of their people greatly increase their chances of being among the winners.

21

INNOVATION: THE KEY TO COMPETITIVENESS

When tech industry observers look at India, they have high praise for the country's thriving tech industry but also a sharp question: What's India's next act? Tech services have become a $23 billion export industry, but still it's low-cost labor that's driving much of the demand. Many people, both in the country and overseas, believe that India's best hope for creating higher-value exports is by focusing more on software product innovations. After all, it is products like Microsoft's Windows computer operating system, SAP's suite of run-the-business applications, and IBM's WebSphere software for integrating applications that set the standards for the corporate tech world and reap some of the richest profit margins. Wipro doesn't plan on shifting to product innovation. It believes that tech services is a dynamic industry where it can thrive by delivering innovations in technology, new service solutions, and improved business processes. Will it be enough? The next few years will tell.

The same goes for every global business. We're coming to a fork in the road that will separate the organizations with energy and creativity from those that have run out of great ideas. In this world, innovation is going to be an ever more vital component of competitiveness.

Make Innovation an Essential Part of Your Strategy

During the go-go 1990s, the tech industry produced a gusher of innovation. There were breakthroughs in everything from networking, high-performance computing, and software to Web sites, consumer electronics, and e-commerce. Much of the nontech world was placid by comparison, but that's changing now. Industry leaders including GE, Procter & Gamble, and 3M have launched new R&D initiatives and are innovating in new ways. The realization has come home: Companies in all industries must innovate aggressively, whether they're young, middle-aged, or have been around for more than 100 years.

A second major revelation is that innovation isn't just about technology, though that's often a key element. Indeed, the very term *innovation* is being redefined and broadened to include all sorts of new ways of doing business. Important innovations can also take place in services (think Amazon) and in business models (think Dell).

A third insight: Innovation has the maximum impact when it doesn't take place in ivory towers disconnected from the marketplace. IBM has the largest research lab network in the world. Its 3,200 scientists are physically removed from the company's factories and software programming offices. But they're connecting ever more closely both with the product teams and with customers, whose problems they sometimes solve directly.

Twenty years from now, we may look back on this period as one of the great flowerings of innovation. But while today's business landscape is a green field for aggressive and creative companies, it's also a time of great peril for others. If innovation doesn't flourish at a company, that outfit risks being left behind.

Wipro has put a great deal of effort into innovation since it entered the tech market in 1980. Its first computers were based on bold concepts and the latest semiconductor technologies. Since then, it has concentrated on bringing the freshest technology to bear on software and hardware development projects on behalf of clients. That's not the kind of innovation that results in many patents (for Wipro, at least), but it provides value for customers. In addition, the company has produced innovative service solutions for customers and business process innovations both for internal use and for customers.

One thing that keeps innovation perking is that it's an essential part of the annual strategic and operational planning exercises. For example, when the company rolled out its new three-year strategic plan in 2006, innovation was one of the key pillars it was counting on to help transform itself from a large Indian player to a large global player. Some specific focus areas: creating packaged solutions for the BPO unit to help promote organic growth, incubating new and potentially game-changing services, and creating breakthroughs to help establish a reputation as an innovation brand.

Wipro's approach to innovation has paid off in a number of important ways, but the company still has a long way to go to turn innovation into a powerful growth engine. Its record of incremental innovation is strong. Its programs for encouraging creativity are intelligently crafted and productive. It has a really healthy attitude. Yet without a track record of breakthrough innovations, it can't stand on the same stage as an Apple, IBM, or Sony. So Wipro can't be held up as the ultimate model for corporate innovation.

Still, Wipro has done many things right. It has come up with a new way of innovating that draws on its entire workforce, not just a few, and that is closely connected to the immediate needs of its business. Think of it as grassroots innovation. These techniques are applicable to other companies. Here's how executives can make their companies more innovative—as a day-to-day discipline—no matter what industry they're in.

Innovation as a Daily Process

Pick the Right Type of Innovation for Your Company

Each company has to decide which kinds of innovation to focus on. At various points in Wipro's history, it has dabbled in product innovation. It revolutionized the Indian tech industry when it came out with its first family of computers in 1980, and it consistently was the first to adopt new computing technologies as they came out. It was the first computer company in India to use Intel's 386 microprocessor for PCs and Sun Microsystems' Sparc processor for servers. Early on, it wrote some software applications to package with its computers, and more recently, it has created a few specialized applications to sell along with services. Yet it has no confusion about where its innovations will come in the future: technology, solutions, and business processes. Not software products.

Some Indian tech industry leaders believe that will turn out to be a big mistake. Rajesh Hukku, chairman of i-flex Solutions, the most successful Indian software products company, insists that the only way Indian tech companies will escape being considered as the digital "hired help" is by doing what his company has done: Create new products from scratch to serve particular industries. i-flex has a suite of banking applications that it sells in more than 100 countries. It was such a tempting target that American software giant Oracle Corporation bought a 41 percent stake in it in 2005. "IT services are rapidly becoming commoditized. If Indian services companies are to stay competitive, they must move away from their low-cost positioning to a value proposition based on domain expertise, intellectual property, and solutions that solve business problems," says Hukku.

Wipro argues that it's very difficult to sell both software services and products; so it's better just to pick one. As a services company, you want to be able to implement applications made by hundreds of product companies. Yet if you're mainly a services company but you make some of your own products, you can get into conflicts with your product company partners. Plus, customers may steer away because they believe you will favor your own software packages rather than picking what's best for them. Wipro is sticking with services and focusing on technology, solutions, and business process innovations because they're totally synergistic with its services business. No conflicts. (The company points out that innovation keeps its services from being commoditized. In fact, it has been able to increase the rates it charges customers as it gains capabilities. Offshore rates rose by 19 percent between 2000 and 2006, and on-site rates rose by 38 percent during the same time span. This was at a time when Western services outfits were lowering their prices.) "The final proof of which model will be dominant is a tough call," says Chief Strategy Officer Sudip Nandy. However, he points to the fact that such software products giants as Oracle, SAP, and Microsoft are experimenting with delivering software as a service. "Why should we switch our model when the world leaders are trying to move to our model?" he asks.

Wipro has an incredibly broad technology skills portfolio. That's both a tremendous asset and a bit of a challenge. Most tech companies focus on a relative few technologies and markets, but Wipro's situation is quite different. To serve 500 customers worldwide, it has gained expertise in a broad range of technologies and is rapidly learning the ins and outs of dozens of industries. It simplifies things by selecting a few dozen key software technologies for special treatment, such as service-oriented architecture (SOA), that can be applied to many applications across the entire spectrum of industries. It does the same thing in the product engineering business—for example, mastering semiconductor technologies that can be put to a wide variety of uses in microchips.

Going forward, the company's biggest opportunity for innovating may be in solutions. These are combinations of services, software components designed by its own programmers, and software products made by others. Wipro wraps them up in a package and sells them over and over again. Because the solutions are prepackaged, Wipro doesn't have to start from scratch with each engagement, and the customers don't have to pay for so much custom programming. Solutions are particularly attractive to Wipro because they elevate the company's importance to it clients. In these engagements, it's not just doing routine coding of applications already mapped out by the customer. It takes large complex problems off its clients' hands.

Process innovations give Wipro a double payoff. First, its own internal process-improvement efforts, which started in the mid-1990s, allow it to deliver ever-higher-quality services at competitive prices. Consider EagleVision, the company's development process for product engineering. It's arguably one of Wipro's most valuable innovations. It has helped the company improve defect rates and win customers. The chip design division alone increased in size from 150 engineers to 1,300 in the past six years. These days, Wipro also brings its process-excellence expertise to bear on behalf of clients, both through process consulting and its BPO division. It used to be content just to take over clients' business processes, often terribly sloppy ones. Now it can offer to help transform them.

Ultimately, the most valuable thing that service companies of all types can do for their customers is become true partners. They offer not just strong backs and nimble minds but wise counsel. The next step for the Indian tech services leaders is to combine their skills for software development, business process redesign, specific industry expertise, and operational excellence into a truly high-end set of service offerings. This is where some of their crucial innovations must come. And it's their big chance to differentiate themselves from the Indian also-rans and to match—or even outdo—some of the top Western services firms.

Strive for Breakthroughs

Incremental innovations are like a steady supply of electricity that keep an organization energized. In Wipro's case, because so much of its value to customers comes from operational excellence, they're crucial to its competitiveness. Yet they're not sufficient, even for a services firm. Wipro needs to start producing breakthrough innovations that, like lightning strikes, have the power to alter the landscape. These disruptive advances create not only a competitive differentiation, which helps a company like Wipro win customers and charge higher prices, but also the aura of desirability, almost a magnetic pull in the marketplace. Think Apple and iPod—only for the corporate IT set rather than the young and hip.

This kind of creativity doesn't come like bolts from the blue, so companies have to create a culture that's conducive to it. This has been a long journey for Wipro. The early years of its tech services business were all about following clients' orders to the letter. Then, as it got larger, it was, well, a big services outfit—hardly the kind of place that risk-taking technologists are normally attracted to. Even now, with "quantum" innovation as a new priority, Wipro won't be the place where radical thinkers congregate. An advantage it has, though, is that for the time being there aren't many opportunities for nonservices start-ups in India. So it has a lot of creative people bottled up and looking for an outlet. If it handles this quantum initiative right, it will get some of these people channeled into exciting and potentially fruitful projects.

There are a couple aspects of the way Wipro is going about this that seem really smart. For starters, it ties the program directly to revenue growth goals. It aims to pick targets that could yield $50 million businesses in a few years, and it wants to boost the contribution to its overall revenues from innovations from 5 percent now to 10 percent in three years. By demanding a relatively quick payoff, the company keeps the heat turned up high. This isn't basic science research that sometimes takes decades to deliver the goods. It's really a matter of targeting smartly, finding the right people to lead the projects, and giving them just enough money and time to create a sharp sense of urgency to go along with the thrill of discovery.

The second thing is: brainstorming works—if it's done boldly enough. Wipro hired an innovation consulting firm, Erehwon, to get this initiative off the launch pad. The consultants are leading various Wipro groups through big-think exercises, both off site and on Wipro campuses. These kinds of events can have a cathartic effect if they shake people out of their comfort zones and encourage them to break the unwritten rules that they normally follow without thinking. The next phase for Erehwon is teaching bright, young Wipro engineers who have been educated largely by rote to be more creative and to take risks. Is this possible? Absolutely, as long their minds are free.

Invest Like a Venture Capitalist

If you want employees to act like they work in a start-up, you have to treat them that way. That means organizing small groups, offering them special financial incentives, and giving them permission to fail. In a sense, Wipro's Innovation Council is an internal venture capital firm. The same is true for the Growth Accelerator and Quantum Innovation initiatives. The company's leaders review entrepreneurial proposals that are brought to them, fund a few, and play an advisory role to help bring the ideas to fruition. The projects have the feel of start-ups. They're usually made up of 5 to 40 people. Those who come up with the ideas get to go along for the ride, and in some cases, the entire team gets a financial stake in the success of the project. After the new services or solutions are launched, they are independent for a couple of years and then are folded into the established business units.

One of the advantages of using internal venture capital to fund innovation is that it takes the investments off of the operational budgets. At places that run leanly, like Wipro does, it's almost an unnatural act for individual business units to set aside money for innovation. Chief executives shouldn't make them do it. Innovation is strategic. It should be funded that way.

This kind of investing stands a very good chance of delivering truly useful innovations. Wipro has representatives from several of its large business units on the Innovation Council. They're plugged in to what their businesses need to serve the clients better. That helps the council choose better and spend its money wisely. Another advantage: The internal start-ups aren't overfunded, like many start-ups in the wild have been. That keeps them focused on doing a few things really well, and it prevents them from spending money needlessly.

Make Everybody Responsible for Innovation

Innovation isn't the province of a few wizards off in a laboratory thinking big thoughts. It must be everybody's responsibility. Wipro considers each employee to be a potential innovator. That's why it has so many mechanisms for spotting, capturing, and developing ideas from its masses. The Innovation Initiative and Quantum Innovation projects both rely on ideas perking up from deep within the ranks, and the Six Sigma and lean disciplines tap employees to be creative and improve operational excellence. Innovation is part of every staff member's performance evaluation, and it is included on every senior manager's business performance scorecard. Unless executives make innovation a requirement, they won't get enough of it.

Give Innovators Room to Think

While innovation has to be everybody's responsibility, a subset of a company's employees have to make it a full-time job. Those people need to be separated from the pressures and influences of day-to-day business. That's the traditional role of the R&D lab, but it's important in Wipro-style grassroots innovation as well. Harvard Business School professor Clayton Christensen explains the reasons for fencing off new initiatives from a company's core businesses in his classic innovation management book, *The Innovator's Dilemma*. Organizations by nature focus their attention and their resources on the things that have made them successful in the past. They strangle new ideas, says Christensen. So new ideas must be set free.

Wipro has begun separating off some of its innovators into R&D lab-type facilities. This physical separation removes them from the daily buzz of business activities that might distract inventors from longer-term projects. Having special labs set aside for innovation also elevates the work to an exalted status within the company. People assigned to these projects understand that great work is expected of them, and it signals to every employee just how vital innovation is to the company's future.

Spread the (Innovation) Wealth

Some innovation, by necessity, needs to be done in a lab, but it must not be bottled up there. A number of high-profile corporate technology research centers have failed to deliver full value for their corporate masters, most notably Xerox's famed Palo Alto Research Center (PARC). Scientists at PARC came up with some of the key inventions of the PC era, yet Xerox didn't capitalize on most of them. On the other hand, IBM Research produced breakthrough after breakthrough all across the tech spectrum that fed not only its products but gave birth to whole industries. One example: The relational database, used for easy storage and quick retrieval of all sorts of information.

Wipro follows the IBM model. It doesn't do basic scientific research like IBM does, but the philosophy is similar. Innovation feeds directly its core businesses and gives rise to new ones. The expertise that Wipro's Centers of Excellence develop isn't confined to the practices that spin out of them. Ditto the technologies and practices that emerge from the Innovation Initiative and that will come in the future from the Quantum Innovation project. Even while these projects are in the labs, the ideas and technologies that they are working on are distributed throughout the organization. Engineers write white papers for everybody in the company to read, and they train people in the established service practices to use with their technologies and for their solutions. After a short period of incubation, these innovation projects grow up and are attached to the business units. There's a natural flow back and forth between invention and application that is both efficient and productive.

Augment R&D with P&D

Inventions used to be businesses' most closely guarded secrets, never to be discussed, much less shared, with outsiders. That idea is breaking down. Because of increased competition, companies are under intense pressure to bring new products to market faster and more efficiently than ever before. To do so, they are increasingly relying on others to help them. In the tech industry, the main ways that this is done are through open source software, industry-standard technologies, and outsourced product development. In addition to R&D, companies are engaging in P&D—partnering and development.

Wipro handles partnerships in several ways. It adopts technologies specified by industry standards groups whenever possible, so its services and solutions can be easily integrated with other software and services based on the same standards. It uses open source software, which is developed collectively by thousands of people, when its clients ask for it, which spares them the cost of creating the software themselves or licensing it from companies such as Microsoft, Oracle, and IBM. It's also a major player in product development partnerships.

As the world's largest provider of engineering for hire, Wipro each year helps more than 100 clients take products from concept to the marketplace. Traditionally, this has been a pay-for-labor type of business. But Wipro is now experimenting with new business models. It's yet another type of innovation. In certain cases, it's willing to share the risk with clients by taking lower fees up front in exchange for a share of the profits once a product enters the market. "Our clients are under a lot of pressure to get new products faster into the market. They're looking for partners who can do it successfully for them and who are willing to take some risks and put some skin in the game," says Premji. This is a way for Wipro to be a strategic partner with its clients, rather than simply a servant organization.

Transform Your Company, and Your Customers

Clearly, this is not Thomas Edison's type of innovation. A big change is underway. The old narrow definition has outlived its usefulness and is being replaced, in fits and starts, by something much more expansive. Innovative companies today aren't just pioneering new technologies; they are experimenting with new ways of creating value and delivering it to customers. What used to be products are becoming services, or combinations of the two. Secrets and capabilities are being shared, not hoarded and held back. The very idea of what a company is and how it operates is changing. Companies are being challenged to reinvent themselves and then help their customers do the same.

Wipro is in the thick of all of this. It's perpetually in motion, searching to discover new things to do for its clients and new ways of doing things. This is the quest that Premji has been on for better than three decades. Think about that fateful phone call from his mother back in 1966 to tell him that his father was dead and he was needed back in India. He knew nothing of business and was studying engineering only because it was his passport to America. What made him such a striver? It certainly wasn't the lure of money.

Though he's one of the richest people in India, he doesn't even know how to spend his wealth. Perhaps what motivated Premji was that jarring contrast of crowded, suffering India with golden, thriving California. Ultimately, Premji helped erect a bridge between those two worlds over which people, money, electronic bits, and creativity flow freely. He built a world-class company, and now he's helping to shape a new India. That's his ultimate innovation project.

India's Future

What will India's future be? There's a temptation when a company or a country is on the rise to imagine it will soar indefinitely. But one only has to tour a slum in an Indian city or drive 10 miles on a potholed road to be reminded of how far this nation has to go to truly become a citizen of the First World. Something I saw outside of Bangalore in the summer of 2005 gives me hope for the Indians. I was traveling on a government tour bus between Bangalore and Mysore, an ancient city 90 miles away. The road was being expanded from two to four lanes. On sections that weren't yet open for traffic, the Indian farmers were using the fresh asphalt to dry their rice harvest. In the distance, I could see farmers down in the fields scything their crops. They forked the sheaves onto oxcarts and hauled them up onto the new highway and spread them out to dry. Then they gathered the sheaves in bunches and beat them against primitive wooden benches to separate the rice from the chaff. What a country! Part Silicon Valley; part Stone Age.

Those rice harvesters told me something: The Indian people have the ingenuity to overcome huge obstacles. And from ingenuity comes innovation. You'd better get ready to make room for them.

INDEX

ABOUT THE AUTHOR

Steve Hamm is a senior editor and the software editor for *Business Week*. He contributed to *Business Week*'s special August 2005 double issue on the emergence of India and China as global economic powers, which was awarded the Fund for American Studies/Institute on Political Journalism Award for Excellence in Economic Writing. A business journalist since 1985, Hamm has chronicled the tech industry since 1989 and has tracked the progress of India's tech services industry since 2001.